Horse Health & Nutrition FOR DUMMIES®

by Audrey Pavia with Kate Gentry-Running, DVM, CVA

WILEY

John Wiley & Sons, Inc.

Horse Health & Nutrition For Dummies®
Published by
Wiley Publishing, Inc.
111 River St.
Hoboken, NJ 07030-5774
www.wiley.com

WILEY

About the Authors

Audrey Pavia is the former editor of *Horse Illustrated* magazine and an award-winning freelance writer specializing in equine subjects. She has authored articles on various equine topics in a number of horse publications, including *Western Horseman, Horses USA, Thoroughbred Times, Appaloosa Journal, Paint Horse Journal, Veterinary Product News,* and *USDF Connection* magazines. She has written five horse books besides *Horse Health & Nutrition For Dummies,* including *Horses For Dummies,* 2nd Edition (Wiley), *Horseback Riding For Dummies* (Wiley), and *Trail Riding: A Complete Guide* (Howell Book House).

In addition to her experience as an equine writer, she's also a former Managing Editor of *Dog Fancy* magazine and a former Senior Editor of the *American Kennel Club Gazette.* She has authored more than 100 articles on the subject of animals and has written several books on various kinds of pets.

Audrey has been involved with horses since the age of 9. She has owned and cared for horses throughout her life, and has trained in both Western and English disciplines. She currently participates in competitive trail riding. Audrey resides in Norco, California.

Kate Gentry-Running, DVM, CVA, is a practicing veterinarian with 27 years of experience and an emphasis in equine integrative medicine. She has a particular passion for educating horse owners.

Dr. Running received her veterinary degree in 1980 from the University of Missouri College of Veterinary Medicine. She was certified by the International Veterinary Acupuncture Society in 2001 and is currently pursuing a Master's degree in Traditional Chinese Veterinary Medicine at the Chi Institute in Gainesville, Florida.

Dr. Running breeds and trains cutting horses at her ranch in Tolar, Texas.

Dedication

Audrey: For my sister, Heidi Pavia-Watkins, DVM. I'm so proud of you.

Authors' Acknowledgments

Audrey: Thank you to my editors Georgette Beatty and Tracy Boggier; my coauthor Dr. Kate; copy editor Sarah Faulkner; technical reviewer Carol Habig, DVM; brilliant writer and friend Gina Spadafori; my husband Randy Mastronicola; my sister Heidi Pavia-Watkins, DVM; my colleagues Sharon Fibelkorn and Moira C. Harris; and my dear friend, Kelly Mount (I'm never going to stop thanking you).

I must also thank my very patient horses, Milagro and Red, who didn't get ridden as much as they should have while I was writing this book.

Dr. Kate: Thank you, God, for creating this marvelous wonder, the horse.

Thank you, Audrey, for your patience in teaching me the fundamentals of writing a book. Your passion for horses and educating their owners is second to none. I'm very proud to have assisted you in this endeavor!

Thank you, Wiley Publishing, for creating the *For Dummies* books (the best in instructive guides), and for understanding the need for this book.

Thank you, Dr. Huisheng Xie, for your teachings that have allowed me to help horses and their owners in ways I never dreamed possible as a veterinarian.

A special thank you to Dr. Leea Arnold for being a veterinarian's veterinarian and a highly respected colleague and dear friend, and for giving me the opportunity to apply acupuncture in your practice as an important healing tool. Your support and encouragement to excel as a practitioner are gratefully acknowledged.

Finally, a heartfelt thank you to my husband Curt. Your knowledge and understanding of the equine psyche is amazing.

And a special thank you to all the horses in my life who have taught me and given so much of themselves to help me to be a better horsewoman and veterinarian: Glo, Tuffy, Careta, Plano, Birdie, GT, KT. Space won't permit me to list them all, but my heart will never forget them.

Publisher's Acknowledgments

We're proud of this book; please send us your comments through our Dummies online registration form located at www.dummies.com/register/.

Some of the people who helped bring this book to market include the following:

Acquisitions, Editorial, and Media Development

Project Editor: Georgette Beatty

Acquisitions Editor: Tracy Boggier

Senior Copy Editor: Sarah Faulkner

Editorial Program Coordinator: Erin Calligan Mooney

Technical Editor: Carol Habig, DVM

Editorial Manager: Michelle Hacker

Editorial Assistants: Joe Niesen, Leeann Harney

Cover Photo: © Sharon Fibelkorn for HorseStock.biz

Cartoons: Rich Tennant (www.the5thwave.com)

Composition Services

Project Coordinator: Erin Smith

Layout and Graphics: Joyce Haughey, Melissa K. Jester, Christine Williams

Special Art: Illustrations by Kathryn Born, MA

Proofreaders: Caitie Kelly, Jessica Kramer, Nancy L. Reinhardt

Indexer: Glassman Indexing Services

Special Help Victoria M. Adang, Megan Knoll, Alicia B. South

Publishing and Editorial for Consumer Dummies

Diane Graves Steele, Vice President and Publisher, Consumer Dummies

Joyce Pepple, Acquisitions Director, Consumer Dummies

Kristin A. Cocks, Product Development Director, Consumer Dummies

Michael Spring, Vice President and Publisher, Travel

Kelly Regan, Editorial Director, Travel

Publishing for Technology Dummies

Andy Cummings, Vice President and Publisher, Dummies Technology/General User

Composition Services

Gerry Fahey, Vice President of Production Services

Debbie Stailey, Director of Composition Services

Contents at a Glance

Table of Contents

Introduction

Welcome to *Horse Health & Nutrition For Dummies.* If you want to know the best ways to take care of your horse, this is the book for you.

Horses are delicate and complicated creatures, despite their massive size and strength. Horse owners, more so than owners of cats and dogs, tend to be much more knowledgeable and vigilant about their animal's health. And with good reason. When a horse gets sick, it's not only upsetting, but expensive too.

A good working knowledge of equine nutrition and healthcare is absolutely vital if you plan to take adequate care of your horse. You need to know exactly what, and how much, to feed your four-legged "hayburner." You need to know what kind of preventative care is vital to keeping your horse in good physical shape. And you need to be able to recognize the signs of illness when things go wrong.

In this book, we give you all the advice that you need to comprehend the sometimes complicated subject of equine nutrition and healthcare. In clear, precise language, we explain everything that you need to know about how the horse's body functions and what you need to provide to keep that body in good working order. We also give you details on the illnesses and conditions most likely to plague the domestic horse.

Whether you're a complete novice to horses, or have been involved with these amazing creatures for decades, this book has something for you. It will serve as a reference guide as you care for your horse on a daily basis, and it will help you prepare for the day you decide to breed or retire your horse.

We hope that you enjoy reading this book. We enjoyed writing it and hope it helps you give your horse a happy and healthy life.

About This Book

Horse Health & Nutrition For Dummies was designed to be a useful reference for horse owners of novice and intermediate knowledge levels. Turn to any section of the book that interests you and begin reading at that point — you won't feel lost. You don't have to remember what you read yesterday, and you don't have to read chapters or sections in order. Just find an area that you want to know more about, read it, put it into practice, and put the book back on your shelf. We don't expect you to read this book from cover to cover (but we won't complain if you do!).

If *Horse Health & Nutrition For Dummies* were a building, it would be a department store that you could enter on whatever floor you like. You don't have to walk past that smelly perfume counter to get to the housewares section on the third floor. You just walk into the housewares section.

We worked hard to create a book that serves as a primer on equine health and nutrition. We hope that you find it as rewarding to read as we found it to write. We also hope that you take all our advice — that would make us feel really important.

Seriously, we find great joy, comfort, and fulfillment in caring for our horses, and we hope for you the same kind of experience. Whatever you give to your horse in the way of love and care, you'll get back tenfold.

Conventions Used in This Book

In this book, we refer to horses with the male pronoun (he, his, and him) in some sections and the female pronoun (she, hers, and her) in others. We do this so that both genders get equal coverage!

Here are a few additional conventions that we include to help you navigate this book:

- ✔ *Italics* indicate definitions and emphasize certain words.
- ✔ **Boldfaced** text highlights key words in bulleted lists and actions to take in numbered lists.
- ✔ Monofont points out Web addresses.

When this book was printed, some Web addresses may have needed to break across two lines of text. If that happened, rest assured that we haven't put in any extra characters (such as hyphens) to indicate the break. So, when using one of these Web addresses, just type in exactly what you see in this book, pretending as though the line break doesn't exist.

What You're Not to Read

Throughout this book, we share some information that may be interesting to you but isn't crucial to your understanding of a given topic. This information is either in a sidebar (a shaded gray box) or marked with a Technical Stuff icon. We won't be offended if you skip any of this text — we promise!

Foolish Assumptions

In this book, we assume that you have a basic knowledge of horses (maybe you already read *Horses For Dummies*!), and you probably own one or more horses. We also assume that you care a lot about your horse or horses and want to give them the best care possible. You want to know what kind of care you can provide safely at home and when you should seek professional help.

We also assume that you're no dummy. You may not be a horse vet, but you're not one to go around pretending that you are. You know that the best way to find out about things is to read up and ask questions of those who've been around the block. You also know to call a vet when you're concerned about your horse's health.

How This Book Is Organized

Horse Health & Nutrition For Dummies is made up of five parts. Each part covers a particular topic.

Part 1: Honing Basic Horse Care Skills

In order to provide your horse with good healthcare and nutrition, you need to know the basics first. In Part I, we give you detailed information on how to tell whether your horse is healthy, the connection between behavior and health, and our views on good routine horse care. You find out how to groom your horse, care for his feet, get rid of parasites, and locate a good vet. To wrap up the part, we also explain how to exercise your horse for his optimum health.

Part II: Good Eats: Nutrition and Feeding

Part II gets into the meat of the matter (even though horses are vegetarians!). Here we start your exploration of the art and science of feeding your horse. We go into detail on the basics of equine nutrition and the types of food that are available to horses. You also get the skinny on dietary supplements, and you even find out how to grow your own horse food if you're lucky enough to have a lot of land out in the country.

Part III: Recognizing and Treating Illnesses

Part III gets to the nitty-gritty of equine health conditions and disease. You first get a look at the inside of your horse with an overview on equine anatomy. Then you get a close-up look at the most common conditions and illnesses plaguing horses today. So that you can care for your horse right away in an emergency, we cover first-aid in depth. And finally, if you're curious about alternative therapies, such as acupuncture, chiropractic, and the like, you get a primer on all the different alternative treatments that are available to horses today.

Part IV: Horse Care for All Stages of Life

Horses have different healthcare needs at different stages of their lives, and in Part IV, you discover them in detail. We start by providing you with information on breeding your horse, followed by how to care for a pregnant mare and a newborn foal. Next, we leap to old age, and give you advice on making your senior horse's twilight years the best and most productive they can be.

Part V: The Part of Tens

In the Part of Tens, we give you a rundown of signs that you can look for to see whether your horse is feeling under the weather and what you should do about it if she is. We also present you with a list of ways to help ensure that your horse stays healthy and sound throughout her life.

Icons Used in This Book

As with all the other books in the *For Dummies* series, this book has little icons in the margins to call your attention to specific types of information. Here's an explanation of what each of those icons means:

This icon appears frequently throughout this book. It shows up next to information that we think is very important and shouldn't be missed or forgotten.

This icon highlights information that's pretty interesting (at least to us!) but isn't necessary for understanding the topic at hand.

This icon alerts you to helpful hints regarding caring for your horse's health. The information so marked in this book helps you take better care of your equine companion.

When you see this symbol, beware! It indicates something serious to watch out for.

Where to Go from Here

Okay, it's almost time to really start reading. If you have something specific that you're dying to know, flip to that chapter first and check it out. No need to remain in suspense! Or, if you want an overview of everything that this book covers, start with Chapter 1.

No matter where you begin in this book, you can't go wrong. Anything you learn about equine health and nutrition will go a long way toward helping you take better care of your horse.

Part I
Honing Basic Horse Care Skills

The 5th Wave   By Rich Tennant

"Quiet and listless, huh? Let me ask you a question. When's the last time you groomed the coin return slot?"

In this part . . .

In the chapters of Part I, you find fundamental information on equine healthcare. We show you how to tell whether a horse is healthy and explain the connection between behavior and health. We also give you the lowdown on routine horse care and detail the importance of exercise for health.

Chapter 1

Taking on Your Horse's Health

In This Chapter

▶ Recognizing a healthy horse

▶ Knowing the horse's mind and its connection to health

▶ Doing horse care and exercising every day

▶ Exploring equine nutrition and disease

▶ Taking care of your horse through all stages of life

*I*f you're a horse owner, or a horse caretaker, you want your equine companion to be healthy. Nothing is sadder than seeing a magnificent creature like a horse feeling sick and uncomfortable. (If you've ever had a sick horse on your hands, you know what we mean.) In order to keep your horse healthy — both mentally and physically — you need to understand what makes him tick.

Horses need good preventative care and good nutrition. These two aspects of horse husbandry are more important than any other. If you can get these two right, chances are you won't have to deal with too many problems. Should illness strike, however, recognizing the signs of a problem early on can make all the difference.

In this chapter, we introduce you to the basics of horse health and nutrition. We show you the signs of health to look for in your horse, explain how to feed your horse and take care of him when he's sick, and walk you through all the stages of equine life.

Knowing the Traits of a Healthy Horse

You want your horse to be healthy. But knowing exactly what that means is important. Healthy horses have the following characteristics:

✔ **Normal temperature.** It should range from 99.5 to 101.4 degrees Fahrenheit.

✔ **Pink gums.** Look to see that your horse has moist, pink gums — not white, bluish, or dark red.

✔ **Gut sounds.** Your horse should have gurgling sounds coming from his rear abdominal area when you listen with a stethoscope or with your ear close to him.

✔ **Healthy manure.** Your horse's manure should be round and firm, not loose and runny, or dry.

✔ **Good appetite.** Your horse should be an enthusiastic eater.

✔ **Normal pulse.** When at rest, your horse's pulse rate should be 26 to 44 beats per minute. You can feel his pulse by placing your fingertips under his jaw.

✔ **Normal respiration.** When you count your horse's breaths, you should see 8 to 16 in one minute.

✔ **Relaxed attitude.** Under normal circumstances, your horse should be calm and relaxed, and not worried or agitated.

✔ **Bright eyes.** Your horse's eyes should be clear, bright, and open, without redness, swelling, or excessive tearing.

✔ **Shiny coat.** In the spring and summer months, your horse's coat should be glossy.

✔ **Right weight.** Your horse shouldn't be too thin or too fat.

You can find more details on how to determine your horse's health in Chapter 2.

Understanding the Equine Mind's Link to Health

In order for your horse to be truly healthy, she needs to be happy too. Science has discovered that the human mind is closely tied to the health of the body, and this appears to be true of horses as well.

How do you know whether your horse is happy? If you know equine body language, you don't need to have a conversation with your horse to get a sense of her frame of mind. In Chapter 3, we give you a description of equine facial expressions to help you determine your horse's attitude with a single glance. You also discover the special language of the horse and how to translate it.

The way horses see the world is an important key to providing them with an environment that will make them happy. As social creatures who become stressed and lonely when kept on their own, horses thrive on companionship. They also frighten easily because of their long evolution as prey animals.

Grazing is an intrinsic part of the equine repertoire and is another aspect of their intrinsic design. Nature intended horses to eat for nearly 18 hours a day to allow them to take in enough nutrients to survive. Their digestive tracts need almost constant work to stay healthy. Providing horses with plenty of forage, served to them at least three times a day, is so important for this reason.

Movement is another requirement of the horse, and is also left over from the days when all horses were wild. Horses fending for themselves on the open range travel for many miles a day looking for food. As a result, the equine body developed to need plenty of exercise.

Thwart some of these natural urges in the horse and you can end up with behavioral problems in the form of stall vices. Cribbing, weaving, and pacing are just some of the few neurotic behaviors common in horses who can't handle not having what nature intended them in the way of diet, movement, and stimulation. (See Chapter 3 for a detailed description of these behaviors.)

Other less neurotic but no less troublesome behaviors can also result when horses aren't happy. Bucking, rearing, and excessive spooking are just a few. Finding out what's plaguing your horse and causing her misbehavior is key to solving the problem.

The Details of Routine Horse Care

Probably the most important component of horse health is routine care. Without the right care every day, your horse won't stay healthy. It's as simple as that.

Good horse care starts with choosing the right veterinarian. Picking a vet for your horse should be just as important as choosing a doctor for yourself. Ask other horse owners for referrals, interview the vet to get a sense of his or her bedside manner, and find out what kinds of services he or she offers.

Consider taking out insurance on your horse as well. Medical insurance for horses can go a long way toward helping you pay for an illness if it strikes.

Your horse should get an annual checkup, just like you do. During this exam, your vet checks your horse's teeth, gives him necessary inoculations, and checks his vital signs. He or she also asks you questions about your horse's diet, behavior, and general attitude, and assists you in figuring out whether your horse could benefit from a change in daily care.

The way you house your horse is another vital part of how you care for him:

- ✔ If you're boarding, choose a stable that's well-maintained, requires equine boarders to show proof of vaccination, and has a professional staff.

- ✔ If you plan to keep your horse at home, develop a daily routine for your horse to ensure his proper care. This routine should include feeding several times a day, watering, stall cleaning, grooming, hoof cleaning, and exercise.

Your horse's hoof care is tremendously important — "no hoof, no horse," as the old saying goes. Find a qualified farrier through referrals from fellow horse owners or your veterinarian, and stick to a regular trimming and/or shoeing schedule.

Keep parasites at bay on a regular basis by practicing fly control, making your horse's environment inhospitable to mosquitoes, and deworming regularly.

Tooth care is important to your horse's health and well-being, too. Make sure that a veterinarian examines your horse's teeth at least once a year.

Flip to Chapter 4 for the full scoop on all these horse care tasks.

Exercising for the Best Health Possible

Exercise is incredibly important for your horse's health, and is something that many horse owners overlook. Horses who are stabled are in dire need of daily exercise to keep their joints, tendons, and muscles in good shape. Exercise is also a must for a horse's mental well-being.

Horses who aren't regularly exercised need to start out slowly as they build up their bodies. Warm-ups and cool-downs are exceptionally important, and should consist of at least 20 minutes of the horse's total exercise time each day.

Horse owners can exercise their horses in any number of different ways, including the following:

- ✔ **Turnouts:** These exercises allow the horse to roam at liberty in a large area and are important to every stabled horse's mental health.

- ✔ **Hand-walking:** This is another option and helps improve a horse's ground manners — as well as the owner's fitness!

- ✔ **Longeing:** This is another way to exercise your horse, and it can be used as part of a training program. It requires that you stand in the center of an imaginary circle while your horse moves around you at the various gaits. Warm-ups and cool-downs are especially important with this form of exercise, which shouldn't be overdone because it can be hard on a horse's legs.

> ✔ **Riding:** If you like to ride (and you probably do if you're reading this book), getting on your horse and exercising her this way is most likely your best option. Make sure that you have a saddle that fits your horse properly, and slowly work your horse up to a good fitness level if you haven't been riding her regularly.

Horses who work sometimes become injured and need time to rest so that they can heal. Laying up your horse doesn't have to be hard on you and the horse if you take the time to provide some mental stimulation for your recovering equine. Stall toys, companionship, and even light exercise can do wonders to keep your horse happy while she's healing.

See Chapter 5 for full details on exercising your horse for good health.

Feeding Your Hungry Horse

Probably the single-most important way to keep your horse healthy is to feed him right. Horses definitely are what they eat, and the expression "garbage in, garbage out" most certainly applies to horses.

Although it's often overlooked, water is the single most important part of your horse's daily diet. Without water, your horse would die in a very short time. Providing plenty of clean, fresh, palatable water is essential to keeping your horse healthy.

Horses also need plenty of forage to keep their digestive systems working efficiently. Most often in the form of hay or pasture, forage provides different types of nutrients and protein and carbohydrate levels, depending on the type.

Fats are also important in the horse's diet, and should be provided on a daily basis. The easiest way to provide fat to horses is to give them oil on their feed each day. Corn oil is the best choice because it's the least expensive and easy to find (your grocery store!).

Horses must have vitamins and minerals to stay healthy, of course, but that doesn't mean that you need to give them a vitamin and mineral tablet every day. The right feed should provide your horse with all the vitamins and minerals he needs if it's fresh and of the right type.

Chapter 6 provides full details on all these building blocks of equine nutrition. Chapter 7 covers feeding fundamentals; we describe different types of hay and pasture, talk about other types of feeds that you may want to consider, and walk you through the steps of feeding your horse properly.

Do you have an equine friend with special diet needs? Chapter 8 is the chapter for you! We discuss using dietary supplements and helping horses with weight and allergy problems. And if you're a do-it-yourself kind of person, Chapter 9 provides an introduction to growing food for your horse.

Tackling Disease

If the worst happens and your horse comes down with something, the best way to handle it is to stay calm and educate yourself. Call your vet out as soon as you sense that something is wrong, and learn as much as you can about your horse's diagnosis. Knowledge is power when it comes to veterinary issues, and you'll feel better with a thorough understanding of whatever is ailing your horse.

In the following sections, we discuss common equine ailments and infectious diseases, give you the basics of first aid, and introduce you to complementary therapies available for horses.

Common ailments

Issues that most often plague horses can be grouped in the following categories:

- **Soundness issues.** These problems affect the joints, tendons, ligaments, and/or muscles of the horse's legs.
- **Digestive woes.** Manifesting themselves as colic or diarrhea, these problems relate to either the upper or lower digestive tracts.
- **Skin disorders.** Anything from allergies to bacterial and fungal infections falls into this category.
- **Eye problems.** Horses are prone to some of the same eye problems as humans, plus a few of their own.
- **Respiratory issues.** Breathing problems aren't common in horses, but when they occur, they can be very troublesome.
- **Systemic problems.** Metabolic and immune system disorders make up this category.

Chapter 11 gives a detailed rundown of common conditions in each of these categories, and provides information on how each is treated.

Infectious diseases

A whole slew of infectious diseases regularly sweep through equine populations, and every horse owner needs to know how to recognize the symptoms of these ailments.

Some of these ailments are similar to infectious diseases that affect humans as well. These include equine influenza (the horse version of the flu), equine herpes virus (similar to the herpes virus that affects people), rabies, and tetanus.

Other infectious diseases that are unique to horses include strangles, a bacterium that affects the lymph nodes; equine protozoal myeloencephalitis (EPM), a protozoan parasite that attacks the nervous system; and equine infectious anemia, a virus that causes an anemic reaction.

Chapter 12 details all these diseases, as well as a few others that affect horses. The good news is that many of these diseases have vaccines (we talk about vaccinating your horse in detail in Chapter 4).

First aid

For some reason, horses seem prone to injury, which is why it's important for all horse owners to know basic first aid. Keeping a first-aid kit around is a must if you want to be ready to handle whatever injury your horse may incur.

Your first-aid kits should include the following items:

- ✔ Antibiotic ointment
- ✔ Antiseptic cleanser
- ✔ Bandages
- ✔ Cotton sheets or quilted wraps
- ✔ Duct tape
- ✔ Flexible bandages
- ✔ Gauze pads
- ✔ Hand sanitizer
- ✔ Latex gloves
- ✔ Lubricant
- ✔ Pocket knife
- ✔ Rectal thermometer

> ✔ Rubbing alcohol
>
> ✔ Scissors
>
> ✔ Tweezers
>
> ✔ Wound medication

Chapter 13 provides information on how and when to use each of these items. It also covers details on how to know when to call the vet, and when to handle an emergency yourself.

Alternative therapies

More and more horse owners today are becoming interested in alternative and complementary therapies. These types of therapies, which include acupuncture, Traditional Chinese Veterinary Medicine, and chiropractic, have been demonstrated to help horses in ways unprecedented in conventional veterinary medicine.

Veterinarians and other specialists working in these modalities are now practicing throughout the United States, making these types of therapies more accessible to the average horse owner. Chapter 14 covers a number of alternative and complementary therapies used on horses, detailing how they work and for what types of conditions.

Caring for Mare and Foal

If you have a mare you plan to breed so that you can have your own foal, you're embarking on a very special adventure in horse ownership. Breeding and birthing a foal, which we cover in Chapter 15, is an exciting experience that you'll never forget.

Before you breed, though, you need to research this aspect of horse husbandry carefully. Pregnant mares need special attention in order to deliver a healthy baby, and you as the mare owner must provide this care.

The birth of a foal is a crucial moment for both mother and baby, and it must be handled expertly if both horses are to survive. Your veterinarian will educate you about what to expect the day your mare delivers her foal, and coach you about when you need to call him or her to help.

After your baby hits the ground, your job as caretaker doesn't stop. Young foals need special monitoring during their first 24 hours to have a chance at survival. Training of the foal begins right away, and you're the one who needs to start teaching your youngster from the get-go. Chapter 16 provides information on how to start teaching your baby how to grow up to be a good horse.

Easing into the Senior Years

Aged horses are those who are more than 15 years old. Although these are considered your horse's golden years, they're likely to be the best ones of his life. Older horses are wise in the ways of the world, and they rarely waste their time worrying about the kinds of stuff that upsets younger horses — like plastic shopping bags blowing down the trail. Boo!

Senior horses also tend to be more patient and forgiving than their younger counterparts, so they make the best teachers for children and new adult riders.

The trade-off for all that your senior horse gives you is that you need to take special care of his needs as he gets older. Older horses are more prone to lameness, vision problems, and tooth problems. They sometimes need special consideration when it comes to feeding and exercise.

Senior horses do best when they have a job to do, and although many horse owners think that their older horses would rather be retired, these horses often become depressed and feel neglected when their work stops. Chapter 17 tells you how to keep your senior horse active for as long as possible, and how to ease him into retirement when he can no longer work.

In Chapter 18, we take a look at the end of your horse's life. Euthanasia is a humane option for horses who are incurably ill or suffering, and it's often the best gift an owner can give his or her horse. Loss of a horse is often followed by intense grief. In this chapter, we let you know that you aren't alone, and we help you find ways to remember and celebrate your horse's life.

Chapter 2

Sizing Up a Healthy Horse

. . . .

In This Chapter

▶ Recognizing a horse in good health

▶ Examining your horse each day

▶ Judging a new horse's condition

. . . .

*H*orses are big, strong animals, but they're surprisingly fragile. They can easily and quickly become ill. Add their ability to hide their illnesses (sick animals attract attention from predators) and it can be challenging for horse owners to know when their horse is ill.

In this chapter, you discover the telltale signs of a horse who's at the peak of health. If you plan on adding another horse to your family, you also find out how to make sure that horse is in good health. After you can recognize the signs of health in a horse, you'll be quick to tell when your horse *isn't* feeling well.

A great way of keeping track of whether all is well is to groom and go over your horse's body every day. Check out Chapter 4 for details on grooming tasks such as brushing your horse and cleaning her hooves.

Gauging the Signs of a Healthy Horse

Whether you own a foal or a senior, a draft horse or a miniature, you can tell whether your horse is feeling ill by looking at a number of different factors. Each of the following factors alone or combined with other elements can tell you whether your horse is fighting an illness. If you suspect that your horse is sick, either based on the results of checking the following different aspects of her health or for any other reason, call a veterinarian right away.

One of the greatest benefits of being able to recognize the signs of a healthy horse (versus an unhealthy one) is that you can share important information with your veterinarian. Should you need to call the vet to report a problem with your horse, being able to pass along specific details on the horse's condition will help the vet determine whether or not your horse needs to be seen right away. Knowing what's normal for your horse when she's feeling her best enables both you and your veterinarian to determine whether your horse needs veterinary care when she's under the weather.

A normal temperature

If your horse is off her feed or just doesn't seem right, check her temperature. You probably know that 98.6 degrees Fahrenheit is considered a normal temperature for a human being. Horses have a normal temperature too, which is slightly higher than that of their human companions. A healthy adult horse has a body temperature of 99.5 to 101.4 degrees Fahrenheit. Healthy young horses, specifically foals and yearlings, can have slightly higher temperatures.

Environmental factors can affect a horse's temperature. A horse may have a higher temperature if the weather is particularly hot (or a lower-than-normal temperature if the weather is cold), or if the horse has just finished exercising or eating. Time of day can also be a factor: body temperatures of both horses and humans tend to be higher in the afternoon than in the earlier or later times of the day. Nerves can also affect a horse's body temperature, causing it to rise slightly.

If a horse's temperature is lower than 97 degrees Fahrenheit, something isn't right with her body, and she may be suffering from shock, chill, or a serious illness. If her temperature is higher than 102, she's likely battling an infection of some kind, is dangerously overheated, or is colicky. Body temperatures below 97 or above 102 warrant an immediate call to the vet.

Taking your horse's temperature isn't as easy as taking your own. Unlike humans, horses don't have the ability to hold a thermometer under their tongue, and you can't insert it in their ear. Instead, you have to go the old-fashioned route, the one that your mother probably used to take your temperature when you were a baby. The job must be done rectally.

Before you can take your horse's temperature, you need to purchase a veterinary thermometer from a pet supply or tack store. Veterinary thermometers have a loop at the end, and you can tie some string or yarn onto the device, making it easier to hold onto while taking the horse's temperature.

You need lubricant, too. K-Y Jelly or another human-grade lubricant is sufficient. Stay away from petroleum jelly because it can irritate the sensitive lining of the rectum. In a pinch, you can use your own saliva as a lubricant.

Follow this procedure to find out your horse's temperature (be sure to halter and tie her first):

1. Prepare the thermometer.

Make sure that the thermometer reads 96 degrees or below by shaking it down first.

2. **Lubricate the thermometer.**

   Apply a good amount (about an inch) of lubricant to the thermometer's tip so that it slides in easily.

3. **Prepare your horse.**

   Some horses are very calm when you take their temperature; others freak out. If you have the kind of horse who doesn't appreciate the procedure, untie her and ask someone to hold the lead rope while you insert the thermometer. Position the horse against a wall so that she can't move away from you. Be patient and try to reassure the horse that nothing terrible is about to happen to her.

4. **Insert the thermometer.**

   Stand to the side of the horse and not directly behind her so that you don't get kicked if the horse reacts violently to insertion of the thermometer. (Figure 2-1 shows you how to stand before inserting the thermometer.) Hold the thermometer at an angle parallel to the horse's back, lift the tail, and slowly insert the thermometer about 3 inches into the horse's rectum. The thermometer should slide in gently.

   If the thermometer stops part way in and won't move forward, don't force it. Instead, pull it out and reinsert, angling it slightly up or down until it gently slides in.

5. **Wait three minutes.**

   Keep the thermometer inside the horse's rectum for three minutes, holding onto the end or the string the entire time.

6. **Read the thermometer.**

   After three minutes, you can remove the thermometer and read it. Be sure to wash your thermometer in soap and lukewarm water and dip it in rubbing alcohol after every reading. Don't forget to wash your hands, too.

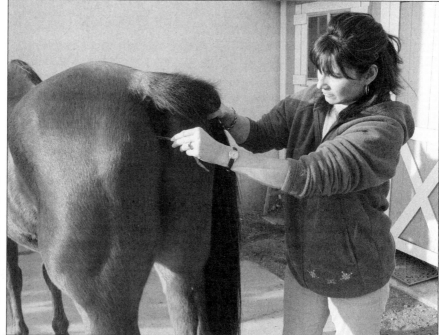

Figure 2-1:
When you take a horse's temperature, stand to the side and not directly behind her.

Pink gums

It may not have occurred to you that you can tell the state of your horse's health by looking at her gums, but in fact, you can. The gums can be a good indicator of digestive health and blood flow. Different colors mean different things:

- ✔ A healthy horse has gums that are a pinkish color. This color indicates, via the horse's mucous membranes, that she has good blood flow in her body.
- ✔ Horses who are suffering from colic, shock, or illness may have pale gums that are almost white.
- ✔ Horses who have an illness or fever may have bright red gums.
- ✔ Horses suffering from poor circulation may have bluish gums.

Check your horse's gums when she's feeling fine so that you get a sense of what her normal gum color looks like. That way, if you suspect that she's ill, you have something to compare the color to.

Gum color alone isn't usually the sole indicator of trouble for a horse, but combined with signs of colic or other types of distress, it can indicate a severe condition that requires a phone call to the vet. See Chapter 11 for more about colic.

If you've never looked at your horse's gums before, halter your horse and follow this procedure to get it done. Having a helper is best, but if you can't find anyone to assist you, you can do it alone.

1. **Secure the horse.**

   Have your helper hold the lead rope for you. If no helper is available, hold the lead rope in your left hand.

2. **Prepare the horse for your approach.**

   Stand at the left side of the horse near her muzzle. Talk to your horse and reassure her, and stroke her on the cheek a few times.

3. **Lift her lip.**

   With your palm facing the horse's face, gently lift the side of your horse's lip until you can see her gums.

4. **Finish up.**

   When you're able to get a good look at the color, you can drop her lip.

If your horse struggles when you try to lift her lip, continue a few more times. If she absolutely won't allow you to touch her mouth, a vet will have to check it for you.

Gut sounds

The digestive system is one of the most delicate and crucial systems in a horse's body (as you find out in Chapter 10). Because horses are unable to vomit, whatever they consume must be passed, regardless of what it is or how it may affect the digestive system.

Horses who are suffering from colic, which is another term for abdominal pain, may be experiencing a problem in their digestive system. In most cases, colic causes the digestive system to shut down. The result is that gut sounds — the noises the stomach and intestines make as they're working normally — aren't present.

If a horse appears to be showing signs of colic, such as pacing and sweating, straining to urinate or defecate, pawing at the ground, rolling repeatedly, standing in a stretched-out position, or kicking and biting at her sides, you may be able to get a sense of how serious her condition may be by listening for gut sounds. A horse with no gut sounds is a horse in trouble — and in need of a vet. However, the presence of gut sounds doesn't always indicate normal gut motility or health.

You can listen for gut sounds in one of two ways, either with a stethoscope (the best way) or your naked ear. Whichever you use, halter your horse and follow this procedure:

1. **Secure the horse.**

   Tie your horse, or have someone hold the lead rope for you.

2. **Find gut sounds.**

   Place your ear or stethoscope on your horse's barrel, just behind her last rib. Listen for several seconds for gurgling sounds. (See Figure 2-2 to get an idea of where to listen.)

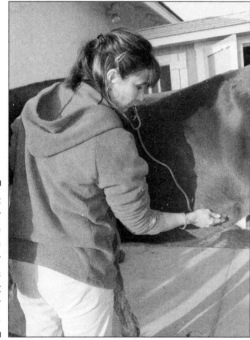

Figure 2-2: Place your ear or the stethoscope on your horse's barrel, just behind her last rib.

3. **Check the other side.**

   If you don't hear sounds on the side that you're checking, move to the other side of the horse and listen again.

4. **Assess the results.**

   If you hear gurgling sounds, your horse's digestive system may still be functioning. If you don't hear gurgling sounds, your horse is in trouble.

Either way, if your horse is showing symptoms of colic, with or without gut sounds, you need to call the vet. Your assessment of the presence or absence of gut sounds is important information to convey to your veterinarian.

Good manure

A sure sign of a healthy equine digestive system is good manure. Although examining your horse's poop every day may seem silly, keeping an eye on it can really help you stay in touch with your horse's well-being.

Good manure indicates that a horse is properly processing her food. It shows that she's drinking enough water and that her system is passing feces in a productive manner.

If you break apart horse manure, you see that it's made up of digested plant material. Healthy horse manure comes out in moist, firm, round balls. It shouldn't be runny or unformed. Nor should it be hard and dry. (See Figure 2-3 for a picture of healthy manure.)

Figure 2-3: Healthy manure should look like firm, round, moist balls of digested hay.

Horses defecate several times a day, depending on how much and how often they eat. A horse who eats three meals of hay per day eliminates anywhere from five to eight piles of manure. These piles translate to about 31 pounds of poop per day. This number varies from horse to horse, so take note of how much manure your horse produces when she's healthy to help you determine whether something isn't right on the day she doesn't seem to be feeling well. If you see that her manure output is lower than normal, even though she's eating as much as usual, keep a close eye on her. Her intestines may be slowing down due to a problem.

Horses who produce no manure at all throughout the day even though they have eaten are in trouble. Something is preventing the manure from passing through the intestine, and a blockage is sure to occur. This blockage could be the result of anything from lack of water intake to an abundance of sand in the intestine. Only a vet can determine the actual cause behind the lack of manure production.

A healthy appetite

Horses are big eaters by nature — they're designed to consume food 18 hours per day. That's why they never turn down a meal or a snack — unless they're under the weather.

Horses eat anywhere from 1.5 to 3 percent of their body weight every day. If you're around your horse at mealtime, you no doubt notice her eating habits. Most horses who are kept stabled eagerly await their meals and dive right into them when they're served. Horses kept on pasture graze almost all day and into the night if grass is available.

Horses who are sick turn their nose up at foods that they normally enjoy. They may sample a little and then walk away. Or they may show no interest at all. A horse who won't eat is a very sick horse and needs veterinary care right away.

On the other hand, just because a horse is eating doesn't mean that she's healthy. Many horses with serious illnesses maintain their normal appetite through much of their sickness. They may start turning down food only at the most acute stage of the disease or condition.

If your horse won't eat, or isn't eating as much as is normal for her, she's not feeling well. If she shows other signs of illness but is still eating, don't assume that she's okay; contact your vet immediately.

A normal pulse

Just like people, horses have a normal, resting pulse rate. The pulse rate indicates how many beats per minute your horse's heart is pumping. When horses are exercising, their pulse rate increases normally. When they're ill, under extreme stress, or in pain, their pulse rate quickens.

For most adult horses, a normal resting pulse rate is 28 to 40 beats per minute. This number can vary substantially based on breed and age, however. Knowing your horse's normal pulse rate when she's feeling well gives you something to compare it with if she seems to be under the weather.

Taking your horse's pulse takes a little bit of practice. Locating the pulse can be hard at first, but if you keep trying, you'll get the hang of it. After you halter and tie your horse, follow these steps to take her pulse:

1. **Find the pulse.**

   Put the tips of your index, ring, and middle fingers behind the horse's girth on the left side; on the inside of the foreleg; or under the jawbone, below the jowls. You can detect the pulse in all these areas. Figure 2-4 shows you one spot where you can look for the pulse. (See Chapter 10 for a diagram showing the parts of the horse.)

2. **Count the beats.**

   When you find the pulse, start counting the beats for 15 seconds, using a watch or a clock with a second hand.

3. **Calculate the rate.**

   Multiply the number you get by four — that's your horse's heart rate per minute.

Take your horse's pulse when she's healthy so that you know her normal pulse rate. Having this information will be valuable to your veterinarian if your horse becomes ill. It gives the vet a baseline reading for comparison.

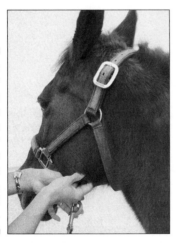

Figure 2-4:
Find your horse's pulse by placing the tips of your fingers under the jawbone, below the jowls.

Normal respiration

The way a horse breathes can be a good indicator of her health. Horses at rest with abnormal respiration, or breathing rate, are likely not feeling well. They may have a fever, they may be experiencing pain, or they may be having trouble taking in air.

Respiration is the inhalation and exhalation of air into and out of the lungs. Normal respiration rate for a horse from weanling to adult age — and who hasn't been active for at least 20 minutes — is 8 to 16 complete breaths in one minute.

Determining how many breaths per minute your horse is taking is easy. All you need to do is watch her breathing while you count. Halter and tie your horse, wait until she's quiet, and then follow these steps (and take a look at Figure 2-5) to check your horse's breathing:

1. **Count breaths.**

   Using a watch or clock with a second hand, count the times her flanks (or area between her barrel and thigh) expand outward in 15 seconds. (See Chapter 10 for parts of the horse.)

2. **Calculate the number.**

   Multiply the number of breaths by four. The resulting amount is the number of breaths per minute.

Take your horse's respiration rate when she's healthy so that you have a baseline reading to compare with when your horse is under the weather.

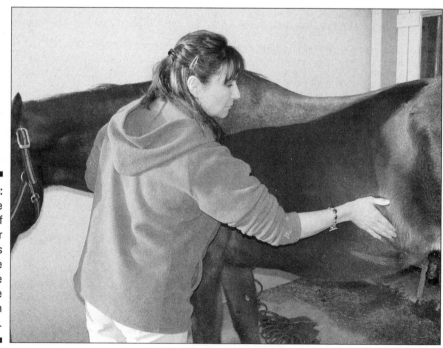

Figure 2-5:
Count the number of times your horse's flanks move to determine the respiration rate.

A relaxed attitude

When a horse is feeling well, she tends to have a relaxed attitude when she's at rest. Her muscles are void of tension, she has a calm expression, and she seems to be enjoying life. (See Figure 2-6 for a picture of a horse with a relaxed attitude.) Horses who are sick, on the other hand, tend to be tense or depressed. They may have taut muscles, or they may stand with their heads hanging down.

Familiarity with your horse and horses in general can help you determine whether a horse's demeanor is relaxed or distraught. Relaxed horses tend to doze, eat, and interact with other horses with a quiet manner. Sick horses, however, become either aggressive or submissive with other horses, sleep too much or not enough, and eat in an anxious manner or not at all. If you notice these behaviors in your horse and see some of the other symptoms covered in this chapter as well, call your veterinarian.

Figure 2-6:
Horses with a relaxed attitude have a calm, peaceful expression.

Bright eyes

The expression says, "The eyes are the window to the soul," and this is most certainly true of horses. You can tell a lot about a horse's health by looking at her eyes. A horse with healthy eyes is most likely a horse with a healthy body. Look for the following signs:

✔ Healthy equine eyes are bright and alert. They're clear and lacking in discharge. The horse holds them wide open when you approach her, and you see no swelling or redness.

✔ Horses who are in moderate pain or who are seriously ill have a dull look in their eyes. They may keep one or both eyes half-closed or completely shut. Their eyes may be runny, swollen, and/or a reddish color where white *sclera* (the part of the eye that surrounds the iris) should be.

✔ When a horse is in acute pain, her eyes are wide open, and white sclera will show. Horses in this much pain often behave in an anxious manner as well.

Check your horse's eyes daily. Stand to the side of your horse, and concentrate on her eye. Make sure that it's open, bright, clear, and not runny. Peek into the corners and edges without touching the eye, and look for warts or growths. Do the same thing on the other side with the other eye.

If your horse's eyes appear irritated, swollen, runny, or cloudy, call your vet. Mild irritation may be the result of dust or wind, but any dramatic change in your horse's eyes should be evaluated by a vet. Horses with a cloudy or milky looking eye(s) may have an eye disease or injury and should be evaluated by a veterinarian immediately.

A shiny coat

A shiny coat is a sign of good health in a horse. In the summertime, after a horse sheds her coat, the hair should be glossy and slick. Horses who are seriously ill or infested with internal parasites develop a dull, unattractive coat. Horses who are malnourished also have a coat that's lacking in shine.

In the wintertime, many horses grow thick, wooly coats to help them ward off the cold. These bushy coats are often too dense to have any real sheen to them. The best time of year to judge a horse's coat is in late spring or summer when the winter coat has shed out and been replaced with a shorter coat.

If your horse doesn't shed her winter coat, or is slower to do it than other horses who live near her, she may be overburdened with intestinal parasites, or she may be developing Cushing's syndrome (see Chapter 11 for more information on Cushing's syndrome). Call your veterinarian for a checkup.

The right weight

Horses who are either underweight or overweight are inherently unhealthy. Figures 2-7, 2-8, and 2-9 give you an idea of what underweight, just-right, and overweight horses look like.

- An underweight horse has a sunken rump, a cavity under the tail, easily visible ribs, and a prominent backbone. Horses who are underweight often suffer from a lack of energy. They have trouble staying warm in cold weather, and they're more susceptible to illness than a horse at normal weight.

- A horse at a good weight has a rounded rump, ribs that are covered but easily felt, and no crest to the neck.

- An overweight horse has a well-rounded rump, a gutter along the back, ribs and a pelvis that are hard to feel, and a slight crest to the neck. Overweight horses are at great risk for leg problems, particularly laminitis (see Chapter 11 for more about this condition). They also become winded sooner than fit horses do, and they may develop other health problems as a result of their weight.

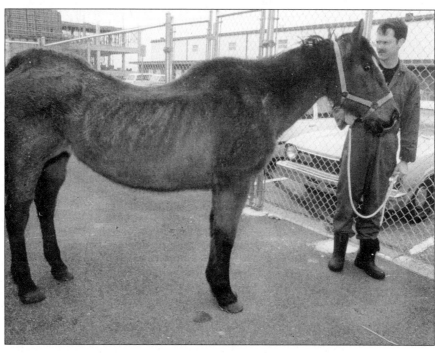

Figure 2-7: An underweight horse.

Dr. Janice Sojka, Purdue University

Dr. Janice Sojka, Purdue University

Figure 2-8:
A horse at a
good
weight.

Bob Langrish

Figure 2-9:
An
overweight
horse.

One way to judge your horse's weight is to eyeball her. Using Figures 2-7, 2-8, and 2-9 as a guide, you can determine whether your horse is underweight or overweight. To get the approximate weight of your horse — which is helpful when determining whether your horse has lost or gained weight — halter and tie your horse securely on level ground, and then follow these steps (see Figure 2-10 for help):

1. **Measure the girth.**

   Use a measuring tape to measure your horse's girth, about 4 inches behind the front legs. Start at the withers and wrap the tape all the way around until it meets the end of the tape. It should be tight enough that it puts a slight depression on the flesh. (See Chapter 10 for an illustration showing the parts of the horse.)

2. **Measure the length.**

   Next, measure the length of your horse, starting at the point of the shoulder, near the chest, to the point of the buttock.

3. **Do it again.**

   Repeat these measurements several times to ensure accuracy.

4. **Do some math.**

   Take the girth measurement and multiply it by itself (square it, in other words). Then multiply this number by the length measurement. Divide this number by 330. The answer is your horse's weight.

   The formula is:

   $$(\text{Girth}^2 \times \text{Length}) \div 330 = \text{Weight}$$

   So if your horse measures 68 inches around the girth, and 74 inches in length, she weighs approximately 1,036 pounds:

   $$(68^2 \times 74) \div 330 = 1,036$$

   Many horses fall in this weight range, but your horse's height and breed may cause this number to vary by several hundred pounds in either direction. Have your veterinarian evaluate your horse's weight and advise you on whether your horse needs to lose or gain weight — or is just right.

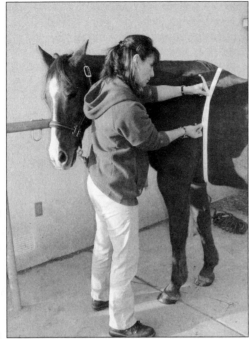

Figure 2-10:
Measure your horse's girth and length to determine her weight.

Keeping a horse at the right weight can be a challenge. Each horse's metabolism is different, and too much food for one horse isn't enough for another. Getting to know your horse and what type of feed and amounts have the most positive effect on her body is your task as a horse owner. Chapter 7 can help you determine the best diet for your equine companion. Your veterinarian should be able to help you come up with a feeding plan that's right for your horse.

Adding Another Healthy Horse to the Family

Horses are like potato chips, and if you don't already have more than one, you'll probably get another one soon enough. But before you add another horse to the family, make sure that the animal you're considering is healthy. This step helps ensure the health of your existing horse, and prevents you from taking on an animal with conditions that need to be treated.

You can determine the new horse's health in two ways. The first is just to give him the once-over. The second is to call in a professional and have him examined thoroughly. The latter is the more effective of the two and the one we most recommend.

Recognizing general signs of health before you buy

When looking at a horse that you're thinking of buying or adopting, ask yourself the following questions:

✔ Does the horse have an alert attitude?

✔ Does the horse have an appetite?

✔ Can he walk, trot, and canter without limping or stumbling?

✔ Are his eyes clear and bright?

✔ Is his coat shiny?

✔ Does he have healthy-looking manure?

✔ Is his nose free from thick, white, yellow, or green discharge?

If you can say yes to all these questions, the horse has passed the first, most cursory health test. If you say no to even one of these questions, call your vet right away (see the next section for details).

Getting a vet check

The best way to determine whether a horse you're planning to add to the family is healthy is to hire a veterinarian to do a thorough pre-purchase exam. During a pre-purchase exam, or vet check, an equine veterinarian takes a close look at the horse to determine whether the animal is healthy.

The veterinarian examines the horse in the following manner:

✔ The vet looks in the horse's eyes, listens to his heart and lungs, and checks his gut sounds to make sure that the digestive system is in good working order.

✔ The vet looks for signs of lameness. He or she watches the horse trot on hard ground, and performs a flexion test, which involves bending each of the horse's legs and holding the hoof tight against the elbow or stifle and then watching the horse's trot immediately afterward. This test helps determine whether the horse has issues with one or more legs. The horse may limp on any of the legs that may have problems.

The vet will also evaluate the hooves with the hoof testers. This evaluation involves taking a tool called a hoof tester and squeezing the top and bottom of the horse's foot. If the horse pulls away or twitches, it indicates pain, which in turn may indicate a problem.

If the veterinarian finds issues with any of the horse's legs during the lameness exam, you may want to take X-rays to help determine exactly what may be causing the problem.

✓ You may want the veterinarian to do blood work. Blood work can consist of a basic blood panel, where the vet checks the horse's red and white blood count and other areas of the blood that indicate overall health.

After the exam is completed, the vet discusses the results with you. The veterinarian can help you determine whether the horse is the right choice for you, depending on what you plan to do with the horse after you buy it. Whether you buy the horse is ultimately up to you.

Chapter 3

Connecting Your Horse's Behavior to Health

In This Chapter

▶ Recognizing typical equine behavior

▶ Coping with misbehaviors

*B*ehavior and health are closely related in the world of horses. Happy, healthy horses are generally more cooperative than unhappy, unhealthy horses. Your goal as a horse owner is to keep your horse not just physically healthy, but mentally well too. The two go hand in hand.

The way your horse behaves is closely related to how he feels. Horses can't talk, so the only way they can let you know how they're feeling is through their behavior. When horses are feeling physically well, they often behave well too. Of course perfect health doesn't give you a perfectly well-behaved horse, but you can be sure that if your horse is feeling sick, he's going to communicate that to you somehow. And those feelings may be cloaked in bad behavior.

In this chapter, we take a look at normal horse behavior and how it manifests itself in a horse's daily life. We also investigate horse *mis*behaviors and how they can communicate the way a horse is feeling on the inside.

Horse Behavior 101

In order to use behavior observation to understand how your horse is feeling, you must know the difference between typical equine behavior, which we discuss in the following sections, and bad behavior with a message of poor health, which we discuss later in this chapter.

Seeing the world from a horse's perspective

If you want to keep your horse happy and healthy, you have to know what life is like from her perspective — and you have to understand her basic needs. Not just her needs from a physical perspective, but from a psychological viewpoint as well.

Keep the following points in mind when you're handling your horse, determining how to provide her with daily care and housing. Knowing what's best for her mind leads you to what's best for her body.

- **Horses are prey.** Horses evolved over the millennia as prey animals, dinner on the hoof for all kinds of large predators. Consequently, horses tend to be nervous creatures who are programmed to always be on the lookout for danger. Be patient and understanding with your horse when she acts scared of something that seems silly to you.

- **Horses are social creatures.** An integral aspect to the horse's survival as a species has been its evolution as a herd animal. There's safety in numbers, and horses feel safest and the least stressed when they live and work around members of their own kind. (Watch a group of horses in a field and you see how much they genuinely enjoy each other's company. Horses in a herd express strong bonds by grooming each other with their teeth, taking turns tail-swishing flies from each other's faces, and playing silly horses games like tag and "let's bite each other.") Those horses who are kept alone are living an unnatural life and simply don't do as well. Try to stable your horse near at least one other horse so that she has someone to keep her company.

- **Horses recognize hierarchy.** Part of living in a social structure is recognizing the hierarchy that inevitably forms when creatures of the same species live closely together. Horses follow a precise pecking order, with a leader at the top of the heap who lords over the group. The individual personalities of various herd members, along with factors such as age and physical ability, determine which horses take on which roles within the herd.

Every horse looks for a leader (whether human or equine) to guide her. In the absence of one, she either takes over the role herself or becomes stressed out. Horses do what humans ask them to do because they see humans as their leaders. You have to earn this role — another reason the proper training of young horses is so important. (See Chapter 16 on training baby horses for more on humans as herd leaders. If you're looking for more help on developing the leadership skills to handle your horse, see *Horses For Dummies,* 2nd Edition, written by coauthor Audrey with Janice Posnikoff, DVM, and published by Wiley.)

✔ **Horses need stimulation.** In the wild, horses spend their days interacting with one another, picking through different kinds of plants to see which ones they want to eat, and traveling through unfamiliar territory. They get bored living alone in stalls with little to eat, no one to visit with, and nothing to do. Feed your horse frequent small meals, and take her out to exercise daily.

Tuning in to equine communication

Horses are social creatures. And like all social creatures, they have a refined way of communicating with one another. While humans use verbal language to get messages across, horses use facial expressions and body language to say what they mean.

Typical facial expressions

Just by looking at your horse's face, you should be able to judge whether she's relaxed, alert, frightened, or aggressive. After you understand what the different equine expressions mean and what's behind them, you're in a position to know your horse's state of mind — and body.

Here's a list of the most common equine facial expressions and what they mean (see Figure 3-1 for illustrations of these expressions):

✔ **Relaxation:** Happy, healthy horses are often relaxed, especially when eating, being groomed, or even when being ridden. You know that your horse is relaxed when her ears aren't pointed too far forward, and in fact are often pointing backward. She has a calm look in her eye, and her head is at medium height.

✔ **Alertness:** Healthy horses abound in this expression, which indicates that they're content and curious about their surroundings. If your horse is alert, her ears are pricked forward, and her eyes are focused on whatever has piqued her interest. She holds her head at medium height.

✔ **Anxiety:** Because they're prey animals by nature, horses are often fearful, waiting and wondering where the next predator will come from. A horse who's scared points her ears toward her source of fear. She holds her head high and the whites of the eye are showing. You can sometimes actually see the muscles in the neck tense up. In cases of severe pain, horses may show this same expression, although their concern isn't focused on an outside source — instead, it seems to be generated from within. Horses who are afraid of the vet or of your approach with medication show the same expression.

✔ **Aggression:** If your horse lays her ears back flat against her head, her nostrils take on an oblong shape, and her teeth are bared, look out. She's in aggression mode. Some horses are basically ill-tempered and don't like anyone, or only like certain people and other horses. Others behave with aggression only if they're in pain or afraid (see the later section "A bad attitude" for more details). Whatever the reason, take heed if your horse shows you an aggressive face. Horses are dangerous when they're in an aggressive mood. Gauge what's making the horse aggressive if you can (some horses get this way when they're eating, for example), and talk to a professional trainer about how to fix the problem. It's not okay for your horse to behave aggressively toward you.

Spend time with your horse and get to know her expressions when she's feeling well. You'll be better able to gauge when she's showing you something other than health and well-being.

Figure 3-1:
Horses use four distinct facial expressions to help get their message across.

Common body language

Facial expressions are only one way that horses get their message across to each other and to their human companions. Body language is an important tool in communication, and something every horse relies on.

- **Biting:** Horses like to bite each other. Sometimes they do it in play; other times they do it out of aggression. Sometimes they bite humans for the same reason, which is, of course, unacceptable.

  When horses are in pain or very unhappy, they may bite. The bite may be directed toward another horse or toward a human handler.

- **Kicking:** When horses kick, they do it to play, to be aggressive, or in self-defense. Kicks can be directed at each other or at humans. Sick horses or horses being handled by a veterinarian are more likely to kick, usually out of self-defense because they don't understand that humans are trying to help them.

- **Pawing:** Horses paw the ground with a front hoof when they're anxious, excited, or bored. They also do it if they're in pain. Colicky horses sometimes paw at the ground as an expression of their discomfort. (See Chapter 11 for more about colic.)

- **Pacing:** Horses who are bored or anxious may pace back and forth across their stall or pasture. This reaction is common when horses are separated from other herd members. It can also be a sign of abdominal pain. If your horse is pawing and showing other signs of colic, call your veterinarian. (See Chapter 13 for other signs of colic.)

- **Pushing:** Horses use their bodies to send messages to other horses, and one of these maneuvers is pushing. Horses use "shoulder blocks" to shove other horses out of the way. A dominant horse shoves a more subordinate horse away from food, or uses her body to move the horse in a certain direction. Horses who haven't been properly trained may also use their bodies to push or crowd humans. A sick horse may use this maneuver to keep a veterinarian or other handler away.

- **Vocalizing:** Horses use a wide assortment of vocalizations to communicate with each other. Some horses also use these vocalizations to communicate with their favorite humans. Whinnying (a high-pitched call similar to a neigh), neighing (the loud call that most people associate with horses), nickering (a low throaty sound like a chuckle), and squealing (a short, shrill sound) are all common equine vocalizations. Depending on the situation, they may be a way of expressing excitement or anxiety. Horses who are sick rarely vocalize.

Taking note of daily equine activity

If you live with your horses, you have the opportunity to observe their daily routines. If a horse is in a pasture with grass and other horses, she spends her time in the following ways:

- ✔ **Eating:** Horses graze up to 18 hours a day, if food is available. Horses who are forced to live in small quarters with limited amounts of food spend much of their time just standing around staring off into space. Some of them become neurotic and develop stable vices, such as cribbing and weaving (which we cover later in this chapter). A sick horse often won't eat at all.

- ✔ **Sleeping:** A horse who feels safe in her environment may lie down and get about 15 minutes of REM sleep per day. She also spends a few hours a day dozing on her feet.

- ✔ **Interacting:** A horse spends a small amount of time grooming another horse, arguing, or playing.

We cover the basics of sleeping in the following section, and we explain everything you need to know about feeding your horse in Part II.

Sleeping habits

Yes, horses do sleep standing up. But not always. To get good REM sleep — a necessity for all mammals — they usually need to lie down. When horses lie down to sleep, they often recline in a sternal recumbent position, which means that their legs are tucked underneath them and their chins are resting on the ground. During this REM period of sleep, their breathing is shallow and their period of rest is much deeper. (See Figure 3-2 for a horse in the recumbent position.)

The rest of the horse's sleep time is actually spent lightly dozing. Using something called a "stay apparatus," the horse can remain on her feet while sleeping. The stay apparatus is an adaptation of the horse's musculoskeletal system, and it allows the animal's limbs to lock in position. Very little muscle function is required to remain standing. (Chapter 10 has full details on a horse's musculoskeletal system.)

A sick horse may sleep more or less than a healthy horse, depending on what kind of health problem the horse is experiencing.

Figure 3-2:
In REM sleep, horses are in a sternal recumbent position (lying down with legs tucked under).

Bob Langrish

Regular exercise

Mother Nature built the horse for nearly constant movement. If you watch horses grazing in a pasture, you see that with just about every bite of grass, horses take a step. In a short amount of time, the horses move quite a few feet from where they were originally nibbling.

For horses to stay healthy, regular movement is mandatory. Your horse releases energy when she moves around the pasture, even if it's slowly. Prevent a horse from moving and you have a horse with pent-up energy. You also have the potential for leg issues because joints, tendons, and ligaments aren't moving as they should. Gut motility is also dependent on movement, so horses who move more are less prone to colic.

For the horse who must live in small quarters without the freedom to move around and graze, daily exercise is of vital importance. Confined equines need to be taken out of their stalls and allowed as much time as possible to move around freely. They also need to be ridden. Confined horses are much more likely to become colicky than horses who are allowed ample turnout. The amount of turnout time that a horse needs varies from one individual horse to another. If horses don't have the opportunity to release energy, they often express their anxiousness through misbehavior or neurotic vices. Flip to Chapter 5 for more info about different types of equine exercise.

Sick horses are often depressed and lethargic and may not want to exercise or interact. Some horses become anxious when they're in pain, however, and may be more hyper than usual.

Detecting and Fixing Behavior Problems

Horses bring incredible joy to the people around them, but they can also cause problems. Like young toddlers who can't speak, sometimes horses can express themselves only by "acting out." The result is that horses can present a whole variety of behavior problems, each with its own cause.

Finding out what's causing your horse's behavior problem is the first step in fixing it. In many cases, horses misbehave because they don't feel well, either mentally or physically.

Understanding why horses misbehave

Imagine having a job that requires you to work no matter how badly you feel. Even if you have a headache, a backache, or the flu, you have to go into work and put in time doing physical work, regardless of your comfort level. At some point, you'd rebel and start protesting your situation.

Now imagine living in a tiny apartment all day with your only stimulation and exercise coming once a day, or less, when you're allowed to leave the apartment and do something besides look at four walls. Before too long, you'd develop a bad attitude about life, and maybe even became neurotic.

Both of these situations reflect the reality of life for many horses. Because they can't protest uncomfortable situations verbally the way humans can, horses take to expressing their emotions in more demonstrative (and possibly destructive) ways. Your task as an equine caretaker is to figure out what's going with your horse's body or mental state and rectify it the best you can, on your own, or with a trainer or veterinarian.

Checking out common misbehaviors

Misbehaviors in the horse world can come in one of two forms: acting out behavior and neurotic behavior. Either type of behavior can be the result of emotional angst, while acting out is sometimes the result of physical pain. Neurotic behavior has health implications as well as the capability to drive horse owners crazy.

A bad attitude

A sour attitude is the most common expression of unhappiness in a horse who's suffering either physically or mentally. Here's a list of some things horses typically do to express their pain or anxiety:

- **Aggression:** If your horse becomes nasty toward you, whether it's when you're feeding him, when you're tacking him up, when you're leading him, or when you're riding him, suspect some kind of physical discomfort. Coauthor Audrey once met a horse who started lunging aggressively at her young owner shortly after being moved to a new training stable. When the horse was removed from the facility and brought somewhere else, the behavior stopped. The new trainer determined that the horse wasn't being fed enough at the old facility and was literally starving all the time. This made her incredibly aggressive over her food.

  Horses can also become aggressive if you tack them up with ill-fitting saddles or ride them when they have a sore back. Horses who are uncomfortable when being ridden produce specific misbehaviors (like the ones we mention here), or may just have an aggressive expression.

- **Bucking:** Some horses buck because they're lazy and don't want to be ridden. Others buck because they have excess energy or just poor training. Still others buck because they're experiencing pain somewhere in their body, and being ridden hurts. The pain is often in the back, legs, or neck.

- **Evading capture:** If your horse turns tail and runs when you try to catch him, he may be unhappy about what happens to him after you take him out of his pasture or paddock. He may experience pain when being ridden, and evading capture is his way of protesting. The pain may be in the back, legs, or neck.

- **Rearing:** In most cases, rearing is a bad habit that develops when a horse is poorly trained or has learned that this behavior can intimidate the rider. But sometimes horses rear because they're in pain, either due to a poorly fitted saddle or to problems in their mouths due to poor dental care.

- **Refusing to move:** Horses can refuse to move if they're in pain — although some do it simply because they're lazy and poorly trained. Coauthor Audrey once knew a horse whose feet were so sore from a bad trim that he refused to move when a rider got on his back. He knew that he was going to be uncomfortable after the trotting and cantering started, and he wouldn't budge as a result. A horse who won't move may feel pain in his legs, hooves, back, neck, or another area of the body.

✔ **Spooking:** All horses spook. It's a fact of life. But some horses spook a lot more than others, at different times of their lives. Spooking may indicate pain in the back. Coauthor Audrey's horse Milagro, who's normally a very calm boy, started spooking a lot all of a sudden. She had him seen by a veterinarian, who referred him to an equine physical therapist. The physical therapist said that he had a lot of tension — and probably pain — in his back muscles as a result of a fall he'd had in the round pen. After a series of therapeutic massages, his calm personality returned.

Neurotic Nellies

On the scale of neurosis, horses can develop the following stable vices. A tendency to form one of these unpleasant habits is sometimes hereditary or just inherent in a particular horse's nature when the animal is under stress:

✔ **Bolting feed:** Horses who bolt their feed eat too quickly. They do this when they're overly hungry, anxious about another horse taking their food away, or simply anxious in general. When a horse bolts his feed, he doesn't chew it thoroughly. This may result in an esophageal or intestinal blockage.

✔ **Cribbing:** A bizarre but all-too-common habit, cribbing seems to be the equine version of obsessive-compulsive disorder. The cribbing horse grabs a fence post or barn door between his teeth, arches his neck, tenses up his neck and facial muscles, retracts his larynx, and sucks air into his stomach. This air sucking creates an endorphin release that becomes addictive. Cribbing is a sign of extreme boredom, and it can also damage the horse's front teeth.

✔ **Pacing:** Pacing horses walk endlessly around in their stalls. Most horses who pace live in box stalls, although some horses in paddocks pace, too, especially if they're anxious. This can eventually cause damage to the horse's legs.

✔ **Weaving:** When a horse weaves, he stands in one place and shifts weight from one foot to the other in a rhythmic motion, back and forth, his head swaying from side to side. Weaving is a sign of extreme boredom or anxiety. This habit can be hard on the horse's front legs.

✔ **Wind sucking:** This vice is similar to cribbing. The horse takes hold of a horizontal surface between his teeth, flexes his neck, and gulps air in as he emits a grunting sound. Or, he may suck air into his windpipe without taking hold of something with his teeth. Horses who learn to wind suck seem to be very bored and probably don't have enough roughage to eat throughout the day. A lack of roughage can lead to colic, as well as wind sucking.

Handling a naughty horse

You must handle horses with bad behaviors carefully. Your first priority is to keep yourself safe. Your horse may seriously injure you, even without meaning to, regardless of what's causing the behavior. Stay on guard when you're around a badly behaving horse, and consider getting help from a professional trainer.

If your horse exhibits a bad attitude on a regular basis — especially if the behavior has suddenly developed — have him checked out by an equine veterinarian. If he gets a clean bill of health, he may have a training issue, which requires assistance from a professional horse trainer. Even better, find a board-certified veterinary behaviorist to help you with your horse's problem. You can find one of these experts by contacting the Animal Behavior Society. (See the appendix for contact information.)

Horses with neurotic behaviors are a lot tougher to deal with. Their behaviors may not be dangerous to you (except for the fact that it drives you nuts to watch), but they're harmful to the horse. Your best bet is to provide your horse with the most natural environment possible to help relieve the boredom and frustration that undoubtedly led to the vice in the first place. In the cases of weaving, bolting feed, and pacing, a natural environment can do wonders. Unfortunately, neurotic behaviors such as cribbing and wind sucking are a lot harder to cure after they've taken hold. In fact, in most horses, they're impossible to fix.

Chapter 4

Getting Up to Speed on Routine Care

An ounce of prevention is worth a pound of cure. It's a cliché, but one that bears repeating, especially when it comes to horses. When these large animals get sick, it's no fun for them or their owners. Taking good care of your horse to keep her healthy is your most important task as an owner.

In this chapter, we tell you how to help your veterinarian work to keep your horse in good health. You also discover the best living situations for your horse, as well as how to groom, care for hooves, and keep parasites at bay.

Working with Your Vet to Ensure Good Care

Next to you, your horse's greatest ally is her veterinarian. He or she is the one to monitor your horse's condition if a problem arises, and is there to administer treatment if your horse needs it.

More so than cat or dog owners, horse owners work very closely with their equine companions' veterinarians. Your horse's vet relies on you to keep a close watch over your horse's health, make appointments when necessary for evaluation and diagnosis, and comply with treatment after it's prescribed.

In the following sections, we explain how to select a great vet for your horse, pay for the vet's care without breaking the bank, and get an all-important annual exam for your horse.

Decisions, decisions: Choosing a vet

Finding a good horse vet — or a new vet, if you're looking to make a change — isn't hard if you know how to look. And finding a *good* horse vet is important. Just like human doctors, veterinarians come in different packages. Some have great bedside manner, some are great diagnosticians. Some are simply better doctors than others. It's up to you to find the professional you most want to work with. The steps in the following sections can help you find a good vet for your horse.

Although your horse may be healthy right now, don't wait until something goes wrong before you go looking for a vet. An emergency isn't the time to start interviewing potential doctors — especially if the problem strikes in the middle of the night. Having a vet lined up before your horse officially needs one is good pre-planning, and will pay off most when you need help.

Ask for referrals

If at all possible, work only with a veterinarian who has a special interest in equine care. Equine veterinarians have chosen to work exclusively with horses (and sometimes with donkeys and mules too), and are specially trained to diagnose and treat equine illnesses. They have much more knowledge of horse issues than their small animal counterparts. At the very least, if you can't find a veterinarian in your area who deals only with equines, make sure that the vet you choose has at least moderate experience with horses.

In order to locate a good horse vet, you need to do a little research. Don't pick your horse's vet from the phone book — use referrals as your best source for names.

The most important way to find out who the best horse vets are in your area is through other horse owners. Ask people who have horses which vets they prefer and why. Ask questions about why they like these particular doctors. Do they have good bedside manner? Do they have an area of special interest, such as lameness or dentistry? Find out the doctors' strong points and narrow your search down to one or two who appeal to you.

In addition to asking other horse owners for opinions, talk to trainers, breeders, and farriers. Anyone in the horse business in your area should have opinions about the best vets in town. You can also contact the American Association of Equine Practitioners (AAEP), which can provide a list of member horse veterinarians in your area. (See the appendix for AAEP contact information.)

Interview the vet

After you have a veterinarian's name or two, get on the phone and start asking questions. In most cases, you get a receptionist or answering service when you call. Tell the person you speak to that you're thinking of becoming a new client, and find out whether you can talk to the veterinarian. Find out how long he or she has been practicing; whether he or she has any areas of special interest — and what they are; and what he or she charges for routine procedures, farm visits, and emergency calls. Find out where the vet will refer your horse in the event the animal needs hospitalization or major surgery.

After you make contact with the vet over the phone or in person, don't be afraid to ask about training and credentials, especially if you're seeking a vet trained in acupuncture and chiropractic, or any other type of alternative medicine. (See Chapter 14 for more information about alternative medicine.)

If it's time for your horse to get vaccinations or have other preventative care performed, make an appointment with the vet to have those things done so that you can see how he or she handles your horse — and you — while also getting in your interview. If your horse is up-to-date on shots and doesn't need any particular care right now, schedule a wellness exam so that you can meet the vet while also getting your horse a professional once-over. (We discuss checkups and vaccinations in more detail later in this chapter.)

When talking to the veterinarian, be sure to ask what he or she does for emergencies. Some vets are on call 24/7 and you can always reach them, even in the middle of the night. Other vets refer emergencies to another veterinarian, or to an equine hospital. Make sure that the vet's emergency policies are to your liking.

Make a decision

Ultimately, the vet you choose to be your horse's medical care professional should be someone you're comfortable with. This person should have good bedside manner and should be able and willing to explain complex situations to you in easy-to-understand terms. The vet should also show a strong interest in your horse's well-being, as well as your horse's behavior and training, and your personal goals with the horse. The vet should also be accessible day and night, either directly or through an answering or referral service.

No matter how impressive a vet's credentials, it's more important that the person really cares about you and your horse. A vet who truly cares refers your horse to a specialist when necessary, goes the distance to find answers to difficult problems, and constantly seeks knowledge and further training to improve his or her services to you and your horse. Your vet should provide you with information on the risks and benefits of any and all treatments and procedures, and should explain costs as well. A good vet is willing to recommend the best course of treatment for your horse given your financial and lifestyle circumstances.

If you make a decision and ultimately decide that you don't like the services you're given, don't hesitate to switch veterinarians. Just make sure that you're being fair to your vet and discuss any problems or issues with him or her before you seek out a different professional.

Covering healthcare costs right off the bat

One of the most difficult areas of horse ownership is paying for healthcare costs when your horse gets sick. Horses are big animals, and their veterinary bills are often large in stature as well.

Many unfortunate horse owners have had to make painful decisions to euthanize a sick horse because they couldn't afford the treatment. You can avoid this heartbreaking dilemma if you plan ahead by using some or all of the info in the following sections.

Setting up a savings plan

One way that smart horse owners deal with the potential for high veterinary costs is to create a savings plan for their equines. By putting money aside for a rainy day (or, in this case, a serious horse ailment), they wisely provide themselves with peace of mind.

To know how much money to put aside for an illness — or even for routine care — talk to your vet. Find out how much colic surgery costs in your area, because that's often the greatest expense a horse owner faces. Then, get a schedule of associated costs for the yearly routine care that your horse will need. This care includes vaccinations, deworming, dentistry, and a Coggins test (which checks for equine infectious anemia), as well as health certificates if you plan to travel with your horse. After you have this information, figure out how much you need to put away each week or each month. Set the money aside in an interest-bearing, easy-access account, and add an extra 25 percent buffer just in case.

Having a credit card as a back-up plan, dedicated only to costly emergencies like a colic surgery, isn't a bad idea. Coauthor Dr. Kate knows a number of horse owners who use this tactic, and it's made the difference between life and death for their horse when an expensive, unexpected crisis has occurred.

Buying horse insurance

Another good way to be prepared for an equine health issue is to purchase horse insurance. Believe it or not, a number of insurance companies offer major medical insurance for horses. A policy like this can be a literal lifesaver in the event of a catastrophic illness. You can find equine insurance companies by checking the advertising in local and national horse publications, or ask your veterinarian for a suggestion.

Where horses are concerned, major medical policies — which require a single premium paid once a year, determined by the declared monetary value of the horse — typically cover costs such as diagnostic procedures, surgery, medication, and visits by a veterinarian associated with an illness or injury. Each incident has a deductible, which is usually determined by the insurance company. (It's unlikely that you'll get to choose this amount the way you can with a human health insurance policy.) In many cases, you must supply a veterinary health certificate to the insurance company to prove that your horse has no preexisting conditions.

Major medical insurance for horses does have a drawback. Age restrictions almost always apply, and it's rare if not impossible to find a policy that will cover a horse who's 15 or older. Because most serious illnesses happen to horses in the senior category, discovering that your horse is too old to be covered can be frustrating.

A slightly less expensive alternative to major medical insurance for horses is a surgical-only policy. Surgical-only policies cover your horse's expenses only as they relate to surgical care. Because equine surgeries tend to be expensive (anesthetizing and operating on an animal this big isn't easy), many owners opt for this type of insurance because of the lower premium.

If you take out a major medical policy or a surgical-only policy, you're also required to have full mortality coverage on the horse. This type of insurance pays out if the horse dies due to illness or accident, and usually pays the estimated or declared value of the horse. Technically, major medical and surgical-only policies are considered riders to a full mortality policy. You can't purchase them separately.

Joining a clinic-based HMO

Many veterinary clinics are creating their own healthcare plans as a service to their clients, and as a way to make sure that horses get the routine and preventative care that they need. These plans also provide a savings to the owner. Veterinary HMOs work by having the client pay, in advance, a fee that covers all routine veterinary care for the coming year. These services usually include vaccinations, deworming, and dentistry. The fee is less than it would be if you had the services administered one at a time.

Not all veterinarians offer this service, but it's a good idea to ask whether your vet has such a plan. If your vet does offer an HMO, ask him or her to give you details of the plan in writing so that you know the specifics of the coverage.

Getting an annual checkup for your horse

Most people realize the value of going to the doctor for a wellness exam every year. It's a good time to touch base with your doctor and make sure that everything is in working order.

Horses need annual physical exams too, especially if they're on the younger or older side. (But unlike humans, who have to go to the doctor's office for an exam, the vet usually makes a house call to see your horse.) Making an appointment once a year to have your horse checked out is a good idea. As with humans, most horse health problems are much easier to fix if they're caught early. In the following sections, we walk you through the phases of a typical exam.

Your horse's health history

The first thing your vet does when he examines your horse is ask about her health over the past year. Has the horse shown any signs of illness or injury? Have you seen any lameness, weight gain, or weight loss? What about performance? Is your horse behaving as well under saddle as she has in the past?

The answers that you provide to these questions help your veterinarian determine whether trouble may be brewing somewhere in your horse's health. For this reason, it's important to pay close attention to your horse's behavior so that you have useful information to pass along to your vet. Flip to Chapter 3 for information on observing your horse's behavior and linking it to her health.

The physical exam

Next, your vet gives your horse the once-over. He performs the following steps during the physical exam:

- ✔ **Eye exam:** Your vet looks into your horse's eyes, using a light source. He's looking for corneal scarring, cataracts, inflammation, and other signs of disease.

- ✔ **Gut sounds:** Your vet checks to see whether your horse's digestive system is working well. Using a stethoscope, he listens to the sounds coming from the horse's gastrointestinal system.

- ✔ **Heart and lungs:** The vet listens to your horse's heart and lungs with a stethoscope.

- ✔ **Tooth check:** Your vet examines your horse's mouth for missing teeth, overgrown molars, and poor alignment.

- ✔ **Vital signs:** The vet checks out basic life functions, including temperature, respiration, and pulse while at rest (see Chapter 2 for details on these functions). After some light exercise, your vet may check these again. Abnormal readings are sometimes a way to detect illness.

After this exam, your vet will have a good sense of how well your horse is feeling overall and how her body is functioning.

Blood work

If you want your vet to get an even more complete picture of what's going on with your horse, you can have him run a complete blood panel; this way, you get an idea of the general internal health of your horse. This test requires taking blood from the horse's jugular vein and sending it out to a lab for analysis.

With a blood test, your vet can get an overview on how well some of your horse's organs are working. He can get a picture of your horse's liver and kidney function, as well an accurate count of how your horse's immune system is working at that time. You can also request a thyroid evaluation and other tests. Discuss the options with your veterinarian and see what he suggests.

Vaccinations

A host of infectious diseases (like the ones described in Chapter 12) are lurking in the environment, ready to compromise your horse's health at any moment. Vaccines are the best way to protect your horse from some of the most deadly of these infections. Regular vaccination is particularly important if your horse is exposed to other horses by going to shows or living in a boarding stable (we talk about stables later in this chapter).

Here are basic vaccines that are needed in most parts of the country:

- ✔ **Equine encephalomyelitis:** Western equine encephalomyelitis (WEE), Eastern equine encephalomyelitis (EEE), and Venezuelan equine encephalomyelitis (VEE) are three strains of the same encephalomyelitis illness. They're known to infect horses through the bite of a mosquito. This disease attacks the central nervous system and can cause severe neurological symptoms and even death. This vaccine is given at least once a year (more often to pregnant mares and foals).

- ✔ **Influenza/rhinopneumonitis:** These two respiratory illnesses have similar symptoms. Influenza can sometimes cause neurological disease, and abortions in pregnant mares. Some veterinarians recommend that horses be inoculated with flu/rhino vaccine as frequently as every three months to avoid respiratory conditions. (No vaccines are currently approved to prevent the neurological form of the virus.) Some vets may recommend it only once or twice a year if the horse is at low risk of exposure.

- ✔ **Tetanus:** Tetanus is contracted through open wounds. This bacterial disease can cause serious symptoms and even death. Horses are particularly susceptible to tetanus, so veterinarians recommend an inoculation of tetanus toxoid at least once a year.

✔ **West Nile virus:** This virus has been in the news a lot over the last few years. Humans, birds, and horses are most susceptible to it. Spread by mosquitoes, it attacks the nervous system. Horses who contract this disease can become permanently damaged, and death often results. Some vets inoculate twice a year for this illness, others just once a year.

The series of vaccinations that your horse needs each year depends largely on where in the country you live, the horse's age, her environment, your travel plans with her, and her health history. Many vaccines require several boosters to be given periodically after the initial vaccine, and then annual or semiannual boosters. The horse's vaccination history can help your equine veterinarian advise you correctly on this aspect of your horse's routine healthcare. Certain illnesses are more common in different places in the country, and vets are more vigilant about giving particular vaccines in those areas.

The frequency with which your veterinarian recommends vaccination depends on the vaccine, your region of the country, and your veterinarian's attitude toward vaccines in general. See the nearby sidebar "Vaccinate with care" for more details.

Vaccinate with care

Although vaccinations are necessary to keep your horse healthy, a trend has developed away from over-vaccination. Veterinarians are now much more interested in providing individualized vaccine programs versus "flock-shooting" all horses and vaccinating for everything several times each year. Many veterinarians have become concerned in recent years that over-vaccinating causes immune-related problems in the long term.

If you're concerned about over-vaccinating, ask your veterinarian to check vaccine titers (a measurement of specific antibodies in the blood) to see whether an adequate level of protection already exists. (Keep in mind that checking titers may prove to be more costly than giving the vaccine again.) If the titers show that the horse has adequate protection, discuss with your vet the possibility of skipping the vaccine this time around, and possibly using it next time instead.

Another issue of concern is giving too many vaccines at once. If possible, try to spread out your horse's vaccines so that you're not giving too many antigens (the element in vaccines that prompt the body to produce protective antibodies) at one time. Remember, all a vaccination does is ask the horse's body to start producing immunity to that particular disease. A horse who's stressed at the time of vaccine administration, or soon thereafter, may not respond by producing a sufficient amount of immunity to ward off that particular disease. Though one scientific study has shown otherwise, too many vaccines administered at one time may be too much of a stress on the horse to achieve adequate immunity to all the diseases. Ask your vet to devise a schedule that spreads out your horse's yearly vaccination program over several visits.

Housing Your Horse Safely and Comfortably

If your horse lived in the wild, all the world would be his home. Wild horses roam far and wide every day, searching for the best plants to eat. They can cover as many as 20 miles a day, rarely staying in the same area for very long.

Domestic horses are in a completely different situation. Unlike their feral brethren, they're forced to live in confinement. Their physical and mental health can suffer under these conditions if their owners don't manage things right. It's your job as a horse owner to do what you can to make their living arrangements as natural and pleasant as can be, using the guidelines in the following sections. (For even more details on housing your horse, see *Horses For Dummies,* 2nd Edition, written by coauthor Audrey with Janice Posnikoff, DVM, and published by Wiley.)

Telling the difference between different types of enclosures

Whether you board your horse at a stable or keep your horse at home (see the following section), three basic types of enclosures are available:

- **Pasture:** The most natural setting for a horse is in a pasture, because it mimics conditions in the wild. The horse can walk around and eat all day, the way he would in nature. If you have the option of boarding your horse in such a setting, you're more likely to have a happy horse. Your horse is less likely to develop stable vices (see Chapter 3 for details on these), digestive problems, and lameness if he has access to a pasture. Just be sure that the pasture is able to maintain the number of horses being kept on it, and that your horse is able to get along with the other horses. (See Chapter 7 for more details on pastures.)

- **Paddock:** The next best thing to a pasture is a paddock, and the bigger the better. A paddock is a large enclosure that doesn't include pasture grass. Horses love to be outside, because it feels most natural to them. They enjoy being around other horses and seeing the comings and going of everyone at the stable. Horses kept in large paddocks are healthier of mind and less prone to digestive and lameness issues than horses who are kept in stalls.

✔ **Box stalls:** Box stalls are the least natural enclosure choice for a horse. The horse is kept indoors (except in cases where the box stall has an outdoor run attached), and doesn't have direct contact with other horses. Many people think that they're doing their horse a favor by keeping him in a plush box stall filled with shavings and out of the weather, but in truth horses like to be outdoors in the dirt. Humans are the ones who prefer to live indoors!

Horses need a box stall only if you need to confine them for some reason, or if the weather is inclement and they have no other option for shelter. You may need to confine your horses when they recoup from a health problem or give birth (although some people, like coauthor Dr. Kate, prefer their mares to foal outside).

The big question: Boarding stables versus home accommodations

Whether to keep your horse at a boarding stable or at home is often a decision that's determined by where you live. If you can't keep a horse at your home, you're pretty much restricted to keeping him at a boarding stable (unless you have a friend or neighbor with private horse property). If you have your own horse property, you may want to keep your horse at home, and with good reason. Having your horse with you is rewarding, and it gives you more control over your horse's feeding and general care.

Boarding stables

Horse owners who aren't fortunate enough to own their own horse property — or who don't want the day-to-day tasks of caring for a horse — rely on the services of boarding stables. Boarding stables are commercial facilities that provide housing and limited care for clients' horses. They earn their income from the fees paid by horse owners every month.

Accommodations at boarding stables vary greatly by facility and region. Some provide large pastures where you can keep your horse in the most natural setting possible. Others have paddocks that are either fairly large or rather small. Many provide *box stalls,* small enclosures that keep your horse constantly indoors (see the earlier section, "Telling the difference between different types of enclosures," for details).

You can find boarding stables advertised in your local equine publication, in the newspaper, or on the Internet. You can also ask other horse owners in your area where they board.

When choosing a boarding stable, keep the following points in mind to ensure that your horse stays happy and healthy:

- ✔ **Clean, safe accommodations:** Make sure that enclosures are clean, well constructed, and well maintained; if you see days' worth of manure piled up and/or you get a strong smell of urine, find a different place to board. Gate latches must be secure and horse-proof. Avoid stables that use barbed wire, and make sure that pasture boarding provides shelter.

- ✔ **Clean, safe surroundings:** Avoid boarding at a run-down facility with junk lying around. This environment isn't safe, healthy for your horse, or pleasant for you. Also, if management doesn't take care of the property, they probably won't take good care of your horse either.

- ✔ **Clean, fresh water:** Inspect the facility and make sure that each horse at the stable has a generous supply of water at all times. If you live in a cold climate, find out what method the facility uses for keeping water from freezing in the winter.

- ✔ **Good security:** Your horse is safest at a stable with 24-hour security. Not all boarding stables provide this kind of protection, but it's a definite bonus if you can find one.

- ✔ **Quality feed:** If you're pasture boarding, make sure that the grass is of good quality, and that it's not overgrazed. (See Chapter 9 for more information on growing quality pastures.) If your horse will be eating hay, make certain that it's of good quality. Inspect it, using Chapter 7 as a guide.

  If grain is stored on the property, be sure that it's kept securely locked up so that the horses can't get to it. Any escaped horse who gets into the grain is in danger of becoming colicky or developing laminitis. (See Chapter 11 for more information on these problems.)

  Use caution with stables that feed only commercial pelleted feed with no other options. A diet consisting solely of pellets and no, or minimal, roughage (in other words, no hay or pasture) is unhealthy for your horse. If a stable that you like feeds only pelleted feed as part of your regular boarding agreement, make sure that it agrees to feed your horse hay if you provide it.

- ✔ **Good care:** Get details on what kind of daily care your horse will receive. Your horse's stall should be cleaned at least once a day, every day. Your horse should be fed at least twice daily. Find out what kinds of pest control management is in place. You want to be sure that flies and rodents are being kept under control. (We discuss pest control in more detail later in this chapter.)

- ✔ **Health requirements:** Horses being boarded at the facility should be required to be up-to-date on inoculations. The particular inoculations may be different from what your vet recommends. If this is the case, discuss the situation with your veterinarian to find out whether she thinks that you should have your horse vaccinated for these illnesses. If not, discuss your vet's opinion with the stable management.

✔ **Professional behavior:** Be prepared to sign injury liability waivers and a boarding agreement, and to fill out other official papers stating the name of your veterinarian and a person to contact in case of an emergency. Management should also provide you with written rules of the stable. Be wary of any boarding stable that has an overly casual attitude about your boarding agreement. They may also have an overly casual attitude about caring for your horse.

After your horse is moved to a boarding stable, contact your veterinarian and make arrangements that your horse be cared for in case of an emergency when you can't be reached. Notify the boarding stable of your vet's emergency number. Provide a backup vet's phone number just in case your regular vet is unavailable.

Accommodations at home

Having your horse at home can be a wonderful experience — as well as a lot of work. To keep your horse happy and healthy, you need to provide the right care and accommodations to your equine companion.

Before you can bring your horse home (if you're a brand-new owner or if you're moving your horse from a boarding stable), make sure that your accommodations are ready:

✔ Your horse should have a pasture or paddock with shelter or a stall. (We describe these enclosures earlier in this chapter.)

✔ Water should be available at all times, either through an automatic waterer or from a minimum 30-gallon (per horse) large pail or trough that's refilled daily. (See Chapter 6 for more information.)

✔ Find a good supplier where you can get your hay. (If your horse is on quality pasture, you may not need to feed hay, or you may need to feed hay only during the times of the year when the pasture is inadequate. See Chapter 9 for details on growing good pasture.) Order as much hay as you can store or afford to buy at once. Be sure to keep your hay in a covered shelter, protected from rain and snow. Chapter 7 has all the info you need to keep your horse well fed.

Develop a daily routine for your horse to ensure his proper care. This routine should include the following:

✔ **Feeding:** If your horse is in a pasture, he can eat to his heart's content, and if your pasture is good quality, you don't have to worry about feeding him unless you're giving him supplements to his grass diet. (See Chapter 7 for information on how to judge whether your pasture is good quality, and Chapter 8 for details on dietary supplements.) If your horse is in a paddock or stall, feed him at least twice a day or more. (The quantity of food can remain the same, but the greater the frequency, the better.)

- ✔ **Watering:** Your horse needs fresh water every day. Horses drink as much as 20 gallons of water a day. If you don't have an automatic waterer, you need to fill your horse's water bucket or trough daily.

- ✔ **Cleaning:** Clean your horse's stall or paddock of manure at least once a day, more often if you can in warm weather. The less manure in the environment, the fewer flies you have.

- ✔ **Grooming:** Take your horse out of his stall, paddock, or pasture at least once a day to give him a daily grooming and hoof cleaning (we explain how to do these tasks later in this chapter).

- ✔ **Exercise:** If your horse is in a paddock or stall, provide him with exercise every day. Even a 20-minute hand-walk is better than no exercise at all. See Chapter 5 for the basics of exercising your horse.

Grooming Your Horse

Part of your routine should be to groom your horse. The benefits of grooming, including daily brushing, regular bathing, and occasional clipping (if you choose), are plentiful:

- ✔ Grooming not only keeps your horse looking pretty, but it also provides your horse with much needed attention and strengthens the bond between you; you help your horse feel loved and cared for, which goes a long way toward keeping her healthy.

- ✔ Grooming gives you a chance to examine your horse's body for abnormalities; if you groom daily, you're more likely to notice changes or problems as they arise.

- ✔ Grooming works to remove sweat and dirt from your horse's coat, helping keep her skin clean and healthy. A well-groomed coat is less prone to chafing and skin irritation.

Brushing your horse

Brushing your horse can be a therapeutic activity for both you and your equine companion. Use the following steps to create a routine for your grooming sessions:

1. **Bring dirt to the surface of your horse's coat by rubbing it with a rubber currycomb, using a circular motion.**

2. **Dissipate the dirt you brought to the surface by brushing in short strokes with a stiff brush in the direction of the coat (see Figure 4-1).**

3. **Remove the remaining dust from the coat by using a soft brush, moving along the lay of the coat with short strokes.**

4. **Wipe down the horse's body with a cloth (a clean rag will do).**

5. **Clean out the insides of your horse's nostrils with the cloth.**

   Dirt and mucus tends to accumulate there.

6. **Gently groom your horse's face and head with long strokes of the soft brush.**

7. **Pick out shavings, burrs, or other foreign material lodged in the mane, tail, or forelock with your fingers.**

8. **Use your fingers to separate tangles in the mane and tail.**

   You may need to add mane and tail detangler, available at tack stores, for this step.

9. **Groom the base of the horse's tail with a soft brush.**

10. **Groom the base of the mane with the soft brush.**

11. **Brush out the hair of the mane and tail with a soft brush, gently removing any tangles with your fingers.**

While you're brushing your horse, keep a lookout for areas that may be swollen or abraded. This is the best time to spot a problem on your horse's body before it becomes more serious.

Figure 4-1:
Brushing the hair in the direction it grows helps remove accumulated dust and dirt.

Bathing your horse

Horses need baths on a regular basis, and it's not surprising when you think about it. After all, they spend most of their lives in the dirt!

Dust and mud are only two elements that need to be washed off during a periodic bath. Horses sweat a lot too, especially when ridden. A buildup of sweat and dirt can cause itchy, irritated skin.

The frequency of your horse's bathing needs depends on your climate, how dirty your horse is, and what you use her for. Don't worry; it's easy to tell when a horse is dirty! If you have a show horse, wash her often — and especially the day before a show — to keep her looking good for competition. Keep in mind, however, that bathing a horse too often isn't good because the shampoo can strip the natural oils from the horse's skin and coat.

Here are some tips when bathing your horse:

- **Wait for warm weather.** Don't wash your horse if the weather is below 60 degrees, or if it's late in the day and your horse won't have time to dry before the temperature drops. If your horse's skin is wet when the air gets cold, she'll become chilled.

- **Be sure that your horse is okay with being washed.** If you don't know whether your horse has ever been bathed before, have someone hold her and run a garden hose on her legs and shoulder. Gauge her reaction before you start giving her a full-fledged bath. If she's nervous about it, give her a bath anyway but be patient and tell her that she's a good girl when she cooperates.

- **Choose a good place to bathe your horse.** Use a wash rack or area with a concrete floor for safety, and to keep mud from gathering under your wet horse.

- **Have access to lukewarm water.** Washing your horse with ice-cold water isn't nice, especially if the weather is on the cooler side. Use a bucket warmer to heat up cold water before you splash it on your horse.

- **Wash your horse's body.** Give your horse a good rubbing all over her body with a wet, shampoo-laden sponge or cloth. Start on either side at the neck, and work your way back. After you scrub that entire side of the horse, rinse thoroughly. When all the soap and dirt are gone, the water from the hose should run clear. Repeat on the other side of the horse.

- **Use shampoo made especially for horses.** Shampoo for horses is designed with the equine coat and skin in mind. Avoid using other types of shampoo because they can dry out your horse's skin.

✔ **Don't forget to condition and rinse the horse's mane and tail.** Wash the mane and tail with horse shampoo, and rinse thoroughly before applying conditioner. Your horse's hair will look wonderful, and keeping these areas clean prevents itching and rubbing.

✔ **Remember to wash the horse's head.** Dirt and sweat gather behind your horse's ears and along the sides of her face, where her halter and bridle go. Use warm water to clean these areas and keep your horse free from itching and chafing (see Figure 4-2).

After you wash your horse, she's probably going to want to roll in the dirt. To keep her from turning your hard work into mud, hand-walk her until she's dry (see Chapter 5 for more about hand-walking).

Considering clips

Most horses can stand to have some clipping done now and then, just to neaten them up. Controversy rages over whether clipping a horse is a good idea, however. Consider the following issues when deciding whether you want to clip your horse (keep in mind you'll be doing this yourself, or paying your trainer to do it):

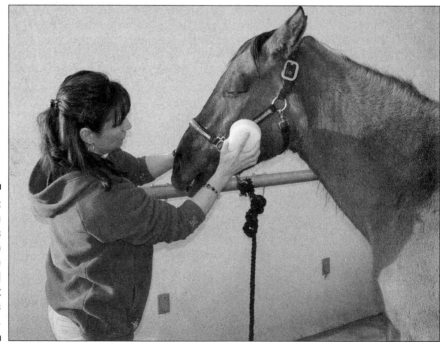

Figure 4-2: Gently wash your horse's face to remove sweat and dirt that gathers under tack.

✔ **Whisker shaves:** Many people like to clip a horse's whiskers and trim the long hair above the eyes. People who show their horses find this practice to be mandatory. It gives the horse a neat appearance, but some experts say that it robs her of tools that nature gave her to help her sense objects near her head and protect her eyes and muzzle from injury. We prefer that you don't clip these if you don't have to.

✔ **Fetlock trims:** Trimming the hair on your horse's fetlocks helps produce a cleaner, neater look to the legs. Some people believe this hair should be left in place, however, because it helps water run off the back of the leg and away from the hoof.

✔ **Body clips:** Many horses become wild and wooly in the coat department come winter. Horses who work hard and have these kinds of coats — especially in warm climates — end up hotter than they should be and soaking wet. And they take forever to cool down. The answer is to clip most of the horse's hair down so that it's very short, and then keep her blanketed in cold weather to make up for the missing coat. Some people don't think this is a good idea, however, because it robs the horse of her natural winter protection.

✔ **Ear buzz:** Trimming the long hair out of a horse's ears gives her a neat, trim appearance. It also removes her protection against biting insects, which prey upon the delicate insides of the horse's ears.

Cleaning your horse's privates

Part of a thorough bathing is cleaning your horse's most delicate of areas. On mares, this area is between the udders. On geldings, it's the penis. If these areas become overly dirty, they can become itchy and start causing your horse to rub and itch.

If you have a mare, the good news is that udders are fairly easy to clean. Just don a latex glove, and use a mild soap or gel to remove the waxy substance that has gathered between the teats. If you've never done this cleaning on your mare before, stand safely to the side when you first attempt it. Most mares don't object to being cleaned in this area, but some kick out when they feel you touch them in that delicate spot. If your mare proves difficult, have your veterinarian clean her when he or she comes out for the next visit. Some mares need cleaning as often as every couple of weeks, others every couple of months.

Geldings are much harder to clean than mares, mostly because they don't usually cooperate. The good news is that you don't have to do this "sheath cleaning" every time you bathe your horse. Every six months to a year is usually enough.

Cleaning this area on your gelding is important because of something called "the bean," which is a pellet of gunk that forms in the pocket at the end of the penis. This bean comes from a buildup of secretions, and can cause irritation and swelling. It needs to be removed either by you or your vet.

If you've never cleaned your gelding's sheath, have a veterinarian do it the first time. Your horse may not appreciate your attempts at cleaning this very private area and could kick you. Chances are your vet will give your horse a shot of sedative before he or she even attempts to do this cleaning, just to make sure that no one gets hurt.

Whether you ultimately decide to clip your horse — and how much you choose to clip — is your decision. If you show your horse, you're expected to clip her to some degree. (Some breeds are heavily clipped, while others need just a light trim.) Be aware of any potential health issues that may arise for your horse as a result of a clip and work with your vet to minimize these problems.

Taking Care of Your Horse's Hooves

Caring for your horse's hooves is one of your most important tasks as a horse owner. Without good hoof care from you and a trustworthy farrier, your horse won't be able to stay sound and healthy.

Cleaning the hooves yourself

It's vital that you keep your horse's feet clear of manure and packed debris to avoid a fungal infection called thrush. Follow these steps to properly clean your horse's hooves:

1. **Start at the left side of the horse, with the front leg.**

2. **Put a hoof pick in your dominant hand with the handle in your fist and the point of the pick facing away from you.**

3. **Ask your horse for his hoof; when he gives it to you, hold it so that the bottom of the hoof is facing upward, and begin to clean the underside with the hoof pick.**

4. **Clean out the areas around the triangular frog of the hoof.**

   Look for rocks, nails, and other items that may be lodged around the frog (see Figure 4-3).

5. **Use a hoof brush to wipe away excess dirt on the sole of the foot.**

   This step allows you a good view of the foot, enabling you to see stones or other objects that may be lodged inside.

6. **Repeat this procedure with the rest of the hooves, going to the back left leg, the front right leg, and then the back right leg.**

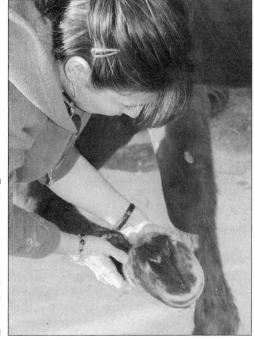

Figure 4-3:
Remove packed manure and other debris from around the sides of the frog of the hoof.

Working with a farrier

In the wild, horses wear their feet down naturally as they travel many miles each day searching for food. (Because they spend so much time on their feet, horses have hooves that constantly grow.) Horses who live with humans don't have the opportunity to trim down their own feet with wear and tear, so they must rely on farriers to keep their hooves from overgrowing. In the following sections, we explain how to find a farrier and discuss the work of a farrier: trimming and shoeing.

What happens at the ground level affects every step your horse takes. Pain or imbalance in the foot travels up the leg and eventually to the horse's back. One bad foot can spoil the entire horse, so don't skimp on your horse's hoof care. Allowing a horse's hooves to become overgrown, whether he's shod or not, is a dangerous game to play. Lameness can easily result, and over time, may become permanent.

Finding a farrier

Next to you and your vet, the most important person in your horse's world is your farrier. To find a good one, ask your vet, trusted colleagues, and others involved in your particular sport for recommendations.

The farrier you choose should be knowledgeable and willing to talk to you in easy-to-understand language. He or she should also be willing to confer with your vet about your horse's particular problems.

If the farrier you choose wants to see X-rays of your horse, it's a good sign. If your horse has a problem, the farrier may want to see films of your horse's feet to better determine the best shoeing procedure. Also, high level performance horses are often X-rayed on a regular basis for just this purpose.

A good farrier is worth his or her weight in gold. Coauthor Dr. Kate has occasionally recommended a particular shoe or shoeing procedure for a horse only to have the farrier explain to her why it's not the best option in that case. She loves working with real professionals who have her patient's best interests at heart.

Trimming and shoeing (if you choose)

The average horse needs to have his feet trimmed once every four to eight weeks. Horses who wear shoes may need their shoes replaced in the same amount of time. Have your farrier help you determine the best trimming and/or shoeing schedule for your horse, and budget that cost. Put that money into your horse's savings account if you have one (we discuss setting up a health savings account for your horse earlier in this chapter).

You may be wondering whether shoes are even necessary for your horse. Over the last several years, a revolution has taken place in the horse world. Horses have started kicking off their shoes for good, thanks to a movement known as "barefoot." (Check out a barefoot hoof in Figure 4-4.)

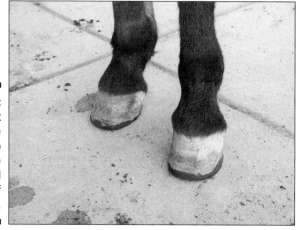

Figure 4-4: Barefoot trims are designed to mimic the natural hooves of wild horses.

The barefoot movement is based on the notion that horses are meant to go without shoes. Debate rages over whether or not this is true — after all, horses have been wearing iron shoes for centuries. Proponents of barefoot believe that shoes simply aren't natural and shouldn't be there. Traditionalists believe that shoes protect a horse's hoof from the unnatural activities that humans ask them to do. The two sides rage on, and horse owners are left wondering which camp they should be in.

We believe that barefoot is best, whenever possible. Neither one of your humble authors has ever met a good farrier who recommended shoes unless it was absolutely necessary. That said, it's important not to just jump onto the no-shoes bandwagon without discussing the issue with your veterinarian and doing research on your own. (You can find resources for barefoot and other hoof care information in the appendix.)

Ridding Your Horse of Pests and Parasites

An important aspect of horse care is keeping small critters from bugging your horse. Insects and parasites make your horse feel bad, and they can also seriously affect your horse's health.

Horse-pestering pests come in a variety of shapes and types, and keeping them in check will keep you on your toes.

Flies and gnats

Flies and gnats are dirty bugs that transmit disease and filth on their feet. Some also have painful bites that can drive horses completely out of their minds. Many horses are allergic to fly bites and become very itchy during fly season, rubbing their manes and tails nearly off their bodies as they frantically scratch against everything in their environment.

Flies come in an annoying array of species, several of which live to make horses' lives miserable. Here are the top culprits when it comes to flies that like to bother horses:

- **Face fly:** This disgusting insect feeds on secretions from the horse's eyes and nostrils.
- **Stable fly:** This flying pest draws blood from the horse's legs with painful bites.

- ✔ **Horsefly:** This large fly sucks blood from the horse's upper body, usually the withers.

- ✔ **Black fly:** Considered by most to be a gnat, this tiny bug feeds on blood from the inside of the horse's ears.

- ✔ **Botfly:** This fly lays its eggs on the horse's front legs, belly, or hind legs and waits for the horse to accidentally ingest them when grooming himself. When that happens, the horse swallows the eggs, the eggs hatch inside the digestive tract, and new botflies pass out through the manure. These parasites are harmful to your horse and can cause stomach ulcers, as well as other digestive issues.

- ✔ **Housefly:** This common pest lays its eggs directly in the horse's manure. The eggs hatch, and the larvae feed and turn into annoying adult flies.

Your job as a horse owner is to keep these bugs at bay the best you can. Here are options for keeping your horse and stable fly-free:

- ✔ **Clean manure often.** Many flies thrive in dirty environments, and some lay their eggs in horse manure. By cleaning manure frequently during fly season, you can do a lot to control the fly population in your horse's environment.

- ✔ **Hang fly traps.** Place traps or strips near your horse's living quarters. Flies are attracted to these objects and become trapped in or on them.

- ✔ **Use biological controls.** You can find companies that specialize in biological fly control. These businesses provide regular shipments of a predatory wasp in the Chalcididae family. This wasp is so tiny that you won't even know it's there. Yet these insects do wonders to keep fly populations down by feeding on the larvae of flies in the environment.

- ✔ **Apply fly sprays and wipes.** Applying these products to your horse daily during fly season helps keep your horse relatively pest free. Fly control wipes and sprays are available in a variety of formulas, and include everything from all-natural sprays to oil-based chemical wipes.

- ✔ **Install stall fans.** Some horse owners install large fans near the ceilings of their horse's stall to keep flies (and mosquitoes) from being able to land on the horse.

- ✔ **Utilize fly coverups.** You can place fly masks, ear covers, fly sheets, and leg wraps on horses during fly season to minimize bites.

  Be aware that some horses won't tolerate these coverups and will tear them off themselves or other horses not long after you put them on.

You'll never completely rid your horse's environment of flies and gnats, but by waging war on these pests, you can keep them to a manageable level.

Mosquitoes

No one likes mosquitoes, least of all horse owners. Not only do these insects leave itchy bites behind, but they're also capable of spreading a number of potentially fatal diseases to horses, including West Nile virus and encephalitis (see Chapter 12 for more about these diseases).

The best ways to protect your horse from mosquitoes include the following:

- ✔ **Use repellant.** Mosquito repellant for horses is readily available at tack and feed stores, and it discourages mosquitoes from biting.

- ✔ **Cover your horse.** Sheets designed to keep mosquitoes from biting are available in different designs and colors.

- ✔ **Vaccinate your horse.** Stay current on vaccines for mosquito-borne diseases to make sure that your horse stays healthy. We discuss vaccinations in detail earlier in this chapter.

- ✔ **Debug your property.** Eliminate standing water anywhere on your property where mosquitoes might breed. Put mosquitofish in ponds or large water troughs. Keep high weeds cut down to discourage mosquitoes from gathering.

- ✔ **Hang traps.** Mosquito traps are available at hardware and garden stores. Hang them near your horse's stall.

- ✔ **Install fans.** Stall fans keep mosquitoes from landing on your horse and biting.

By being vigilant against mosquitoes, you'll keep your horse healthy. As a bonus, you may have fewer itchy bites, too!

Ticks

If you're a dog owner, you're probably familiar with ticks, those nasty arachnids that latch onto an animal's (or a human's) skin and suck the blood for nourishment. Ticks go after horses, too, and can easily spread disease. Tick-borne illnesses that can make your horse very sick include Lyme disease and encephalitis. (See Chapter 12 for details on these diseases.) That's why keeping ticks at bay — and off your horse — is important.

The tick most likely to latch onto your equine companion is the deer tick, a tiny black bug that lurks in high brush during warm seasons. Although these ticks especially like horses, and are the ones most likely to carry Lyme disease, any type of tick can latch onto your horse.

A nasty creature called the ear tick likes to attach to the horse's ears. These pests can cause head and/or ear shyness, as well as bleeding from the ear. Horses with ear ticks may also hold their ears down, or off to the side. Sometimes, they rub their ears on anything they can find.

It's important to keep ticks off your horse to prevent disease. A large infestation of ticks can also cause anemia, so be vigilant about these pests. To deal with ticks, follow these guidelines:

- ✔ **Apply tick repellant.** Before riding your horse through wilderness areas, or if he lives in an area that has tall plants, apply tick repellant to keep these bugs from latching onto him.

- ✔ **Groom carefully.** When you groom your horse, keep an eye out for ticks that may have grabbed onto your horse.

  Check the ears carefully because it's a favorite spot for ticks.

- ✔ **Remove body ticks.** Using tweezers, grasp the tick at the base of the head and use slow, steady upward pressure to pull the creature from your horse's body.

  Be careful not to squeeze the tick's body with the tweezers, because it will re-inject possibly contaminated blood back into the horse. If you fail to get the tick's entire head out of the skin, call a veterinarian.

- ✔ **Clear out ear ticks.** If you think that your horse has ear ticks, and the ear isn't especially sore, you can take a tissue-wrapped finger and very gently probe the ear canal in a sweeping motion. If you're lucky, you'll retrieve the nasty little culprits. Be careful not to rigorously dig into your horse's ears with your fingers because you'll drive the ticks deeper into the canal. (If this tactic doesn't immediately alleviate the problem, call your vet.)

Worms

Internal parasites in the form of worms are a huge scourge to horses if they aren't properly controlled. A variety of worms prey on horses, and can do serious and permanent damage to their internal organs if left unchecked.

A worm-infested horse is a sorry sight to see. A dull, ratty looking coat and an underweight appearance are sure signs of worm infestation. Although 150 species of internal parasites can cause harm to horses, the most common ones include:

- ✔ **Bots:** An egg-laying fly (see the earlier section "Flies" in this chapter), the bot begins as larvae that attaches itself to a horse's stomach after being swallowed. The result can be colic.

- ✓ **Pinworms:** These worms reside in the horse's rectum and cause irritation and discharge. They can prompt a horse to rub the dock of her tail obsessively.

- ✓ **Roundworms:** Foot-long roundworms are truly disgusting to see. They live in the digestive tracts and cause horses to become colicky and lose condition.

- ✓ **Stongyles:** This intestinal parasite uses the horse's circulatory system to spread its larvae through the bloodstream. This parasite can cause serious and permanent damage to the horse's organs. Recurrent colic can also be a result of a lack of good blood supply to the intestines. Also, certain stages of strongyles can encyst in the horse's intestinal tract and remain there for long periods of time. This may cause unthriftiness, diarrhea, and colic.

Keeping worms from infecting your horse to some degree is nearly impossible, but you can control how many worms your horse has with regular deworming. Several chemical agents are available over the counter, allowing horse owners to regularly deworm their horses. Or, your vet can deworm your horse for you.

 Because worms can develop a resistance to some dewormers, it's important to discuss a deworming program with your veterinarian. Your vet can tell you how to best rotate different types of deworming drugs to avoid resistance, and how often to deworm your horse, depending on where you live and your horse's environment.

Smile Pretty! Caring for Your Horse's Teeth

Your horse needs healthy teeth to chew up all that roughage you're feeding him — and that roughage is so important for his digestive health. In order to keep your horse's teeth healthy, you need help from your veterinarian.

Wild horses wear their teeth down naturally as they graze on a variety of different plants in their environment. Domestic horses need help keeping their teeth in good shape, though, because their diet is different from that of wild horses.

Uneven wear on a horse's teeth results in sharp points that can cut into the horse's cheeks. These sharp points can hurt the horse when he chews and when he wears a bit in his mouth. For this reason, horses need to have their teeth filed down, or *floated,* on a regular basis.

Your equine veterinarian performs this task for you. In most cases, your vet gives your horse a sedative (to ensure cooperation) and uses a handheld or power-driven file to grind the points off your horse's teeth.

Most horses need to have this procedure done about once a year, but your horse may need it more often depending on his age and particular circumstances. Coauthor Dr. Kate recommends a dental exam every six to nine month in horses who are 2 to 5 years old, because horses' teeth change the most during this time and around the time a bit is first placed in the mouth.

Your veterinarian should check your horse's teeth when he or she comes to inoculate your horse, and can advise you as to your horse's dental needs.

Chapter 5

Exercising for Health

In This Chapter
▶ Working your way into exercise
▶ Exploring ways to exercise your horse
▶ Helping your horse during lay-up

*O*ne of the most crucial elements to your horse's health is exercise. Nature designed horses to walk almost constantly as they graze, so your horse's joints, tendons, and ligaments need movement to keep them in good working order. Exercise is also good for your horse's digestive system, and for his metabolism. Even your horse's mental health benefits from regular exercise.

In this chapter, we show you the safest ways to exercise your horse. You discover how to begin and end your horse's exercise regimen, and how to make the most of your time spent getting him to move. For horses recovering from injuries, we provide details on how to help them recuperate with movement.

Starting Safely with Exercise

When it comes to exercise, horses are a lot like people. If you exercise only occasionally, you wouldn't start jogging 5 miles a day without building up to this distance first. Or at least you shouldn't! The same goes for horses. If your horse isn't doing much right now, you need to slowly get him into an exercise regimen. In addition, each time you exercise your horse, it's important to warm him up and cool him down, just as human athletes do. In the following sections, we take a look at how to safely handle exercising your horse.

Easing into a routine

Horses need to work up to their full exercise potential. If your horse has been a stall potato for too long and you've decided to get serious with his exercise, don't go hog wild and start working him for long periods at a time right off the bat. Or, if you've been riding only a day or two a week and want to start doing more, don't ask your horse to suddenly hit the trail every day.

Instead, condition your horse for whatever his ultimate exercise goal will be. If you plan to ride on the trail for hours at a time, work up to it. If you plan to ride him in jumping sessions for 45 minutes a day, this is his exercise goal. Make sure that your horse is sound and healthy first by having your veterinarian examine him (if it's been a while since he's seen the doc), and then start to add 15 minutes more to each of your ride times. If you currently ride your horse for 30 minutes twice a week, increase your rides to 45 minutes twice a week. After a couple of weeks, add another day of exercise so that you're riding him for 45 minutes three times a week. After two weeks, you can add another day of riding.

The goal is to add exercise slowly so that you don't make your horse sore or lame. Increasing his exercise gradually rather than suddenly helps keep your horse in a positive frame of mind for work. Nothing sours a horse more than feeling sore and uncomfortable after being asked to do more than he's physically capable of doing.

Warming up

Whether you plan to ride your horse, longe him, or work him in the round pen (we discuss these options later in this chapter), it's vital that you warm him up before you start his workout. A proper warm-up helps get his joints, tendons, and ligaments ready for the job ahead. Horses who are properly warmed up are less likely to injure themselves during exercise.

Start by asking your horse to stretch before you get on him. You can do this by holding the reins and bending down, holding a carrot between his front legs. This forces him to stretch his neck and back. Then, hold a carrot at the left side of his abdomen and let him stretch his head around to reach it. Do the same on the other side.

After you get on, you can begin the next phase of warm-up. Before you start trotting your horse, have him walk for five to ten minutes to warm him up. Ask him to do circles and figure-eights to get his mind warmed up too. Then trot for a good five minutes or more before you ask for a canter or gallop.

Cooling down

Just as important as warming up is cooling down after a hard workout. Among horse people, the expression "ridden hard and put away wet" is used to describe someone who has received poor care. Giving a horse a hard workout and then sticking him back in his stall dripping with sweat and breathing hard is not a good thing. (Doing so can lead to muscle and respiratory disorders; see Chapter 11 for more information.)

If you work your horse hard, take at least 10 minutes to cool him down before putting him away. Remember these tips when cooling down your horse:

- **Relax the girth.** When you get off your horse after riding him hard, loosen the girth a notch to give him some relief from the pressure of the saddle as he tries to catch his breath.

- **Walk him.** Whether you're still in the saddle or on the ground, walk your horse for at least 10 minutes or until his breathing returns to normal.

- **Avoid food and water.** Don't allow your horse to eat or drink until he stops breathing hard. If you aren't sure whether he's cooled down enough, check his respiration and compare it with his normal rate. (See Chapter 2 for details on taking your horse's respiration.)

- **Let him dry.** Your horse should stop sweating after he's sufficiently cooled down. If the weather is cold and his coat is soaked with sweat, it may take quite a while for it to dry. Cover him with a cooler or sweat sheet while you walk him to keep him from catching a chill until he dries off.

- **Rub him down.** Horses enjoy a good rubdown after a hard workout. Use a rubber currycomb to give him a good grooming, followed by a brushing and maybe a short massage. (See Chapter 4 for details on grooming.)

- **Let him roll.** If your horse wants to roll after you ride him, go ahead an allow it. Rolling works as a self-administered chiropractic maneuver, and is good for your horse's back.

Cooling your horse down properly helps keep his attitude about exercise positive. He'll feel good after his workout instead of feeling fatigue and discomfort.

Surveying Workout Options for Your Horse

As you probably know, you have a few options when you're exercising your horse. What's important is that you get her feet moving and stimulate her mind at the same time. In the following sections, we give you the lowdown on a few activities, ranging from gentle to vigorous.

Mixing up your horse's exercise routine is a good idea. Horses get bored with the same activities every day, just like people do. Although they appreciate having a regular routine, the actual activities can be varied from day to day to keep them from becoming dull.

Turning out

One way to get your stabled horse some exercise is to turn her out, which means letting her run loose in a large paddock or pasture. If your horse lives in a pasture, she already has all the free room she needs to run, roll, buck, and just be a horse. But if she lives in a stall or small paddock, she'll appreciate some time in a larger enclosure where she can let loose.

Horses who receive regular turnout tend to have less pent-up energy. Even if your horse just stands around in the turnout and stares at you, getting her out of her stall and providing a change in scenery does her good.

Turnout is great in theory, but you must handle it with caution. Horses who have been standing in a stall for hours on end can seriously hurt themselves if they're suddenly let loose to go crazy. Bowed tendons and even irreparable fractures can occur during turnouts.

If you want to turn your horse out (as in Figure 5-1), follow these precautions:

- ✔ **Work out first.** Consider turning your horse out after you ride or work her in a round pen or on the longe line. She'll be less likely to go berserk and hurt herself.

- ✔ **Warm up.** If you can't turn her out after riding or exercising (some horses feel so cooped up that they need a turnout before you can get on them), loosen up her muscles, ligaments, and tendons with a 10-minute walk first.

- ✔ **Cover the legs.** If your horse wears shoes, put protective leg wear on her. This protective wear helps to keep her from nicking herself with a shoe when running around.

- ✔ **Turn out alone.** Don't turn your horse out with another horse if the horses don't know each other, don't get along, or are wearing shoes.

- ✔ **Check for safety.** Make sure that the turnout area has a fence at least 5 feet high so that your horse won't jump it.

- ✔ **Teach your horse.** Don't let your horse bolt away from you the minute you take off her halter, because this is a dangerous habit. Instead, put the lead rope around her neck before you undo the halter and make her stand for 20 to 30 seconds before you release her.

- ✔ **Reduce space.** Try to use an arena that's on the smaller side. This prevents your horse from galloping wildly.

- ✔ **Stay close.** Keep a close watch on your horse while she's in the turnout.

- ✔ **Stay calm.** Kissing to your horse to let her know that this is her time to cavort if she wants to is okay, but don't get carried away and start chasing her with a whip or other object.

- ✔ **Watch for riders.** If you can only turn a horse out in a riding arena, make sure that the arena is clear of riders before you let your horse go.

- ✔ **Turn out often.** Turn your horse out frequently to minimize her urge to behave in a crazy manner that may get her hurt. Most horses need to be turned out at least once a week.

Figure 5-1:
To avoid injury, horses who live in stalls should be warmed up properly before being turned out.

Hand-walking

For days when you can't ride — the weather is bad or your horse is recovering from an injury or illness (we discuss recuperation from injury later in this chapter) — hand-walking is a good alternative. You can hand-walk your horse for 10 minutes or an hour, depending on how much time you have. The longer you walk her the better, especially if your horse lives in a stall or small paddock.

Hand-walking your horse is easy if you have a well-behaved horse. Simply dress her in her halter and lead rope, and go for a stroll. Hand-walking loosens her joints, tendons, and ligaments; gets her circulation going; and provides her with mental stimulation.

You can also use your hand-walking times as training sessions. If you want to get your horse used to an unfamiliar trail before you climb on her back, hand-walking is a good way to get started. Horses are braver when being led as opposed to being ridden, and are more likely to get used to a strange place without incident if you're on the ground and in the lead.

Hand-walking also gives you a chance to bond with your horse and school her on her ground manners. She should walk nicely alongside you, and stop and turn when you ask her to. Ask her to back up on a loose lead rope, back up in a circle, and do anything else that you can think of to challenge her mind. You can work on all these things while you're hand-walking your horse. You'll discover that she's better behaved in the saddle after you spend time walking her from the ground. (To brush up on the basics of leading your horse, see *Horses For Dummies,* 2nd Edition, co-written by your coauthor Audrey with Janice Posnikoff, DVM, and published by Wiley.)

Longeing

Yet another way to exercise your horse is by longeing her. *Longeing* requires that you stand in the center of an imaginary circle while your horse moves around you at the various gaits. You can do this at the end of a *longe line* (a rope that attaches to the horse's halter or bridle), or in a round pen.

Longeing is a good way to exercise your horse for several reasons, including the following:

- ✔ You can provide controlled exercise on days you can't ride.
- ✔ You can use longeing to help your horse get rid of excess energy before you get on her.
- ✔ Longeing helps teach your horse to respect you and to respond to voice commands.

If you've never longed a horse, you should get an experienced person to help you. (You can also read about longeing in *Horses For Dummies,* 2nd Edition.) Horses have to be trained to longe, so if your horse has never done it, she needs to be taught. You'll have to get help for that too.

Follow these guidelines for longeing (and check out Figure 5-2 to see what it looks like):

- ✔ **Longe smart.** Be sure to warm up and cool down your horse before and after longeing (we discuss warming up and cooling down earlier in this chapter).
- ✔ **Work both sides.** Longe your horse in both directions so that you don't build up muscles more on one side of the body than the other.

✔ **Build up.** Slowly work your horse up to longeing with a 15-minute session, gradually getting to your ultimate goal. A half an hour to 45 minutes is the maximum time that you should spend longeing your horse at a time.

✔ **Don't overdo it.** Avoid longeing more than a couple of times a week because traveling in tight circles can cause stress on your horse's legs.

✔ **Protect the legs.** If your horse wears shoes, put protective leg wear and bell boots on her to avoid possible injury.

✔ **Cover your hands.** Wear gloves when you longe to protect your hands.

Figure 5-2: When you longe your horse, warm her up and cool her down just as you would when riding.

Riding

Of course the most fun you'll have exercising your horse is by riding her. Whether you work hard in the arena or simply stroll down the trail, riding provides great exercise for your horse while also stimulating her mind. Plus, the more you ride your horse, the better she'll become under saddle.

In order for your horse to enjoy being ridden by you — and for riding to be good, healthy exercise for her — pay attention to these guidelines:

✔ **Fit tack.** Make certain the saddle, bridle, and other tack you use on your horse is in good working order and fits properly. Poorly fitting tack can make your horse sore and uncomfortable. It can also make your horse appear lame when she's really just trying to compensate for the pain of poorly fitting tack.

✔ **Groom well.** Be sure to groom your horse thoroughly before riding her. Dirt and debris can get caught between your horse's coat and her tack, causing irritation and soreness.

✔ **Warm up.** Don't jump on your horse and just take off. Always warm your horse up first for about 10 minutes with mostly walking and some trotting to get her muscles, ligaments, and tendons warmed up.

✔ **Cool down.** Don't stick your horse back in her stall or pasture sweating and breathing hard. Cool her down with a 10- (or more-) minute walk so that her respiration goes back to normal before you put her away. (We discuss both warming up and cooling down earlier in this chapter.)

✔ **Take lessons.** Even the best rider still has more to learn. Continue your education as a rider by taking lessons now and then. The better you ride, the easier it is on your horse.

✔ **Vary your riding.** Don't do the same activities over and over again with your horse because it'll make her bored. Mix up your riding with arena work, trail rides, and group activities.

✔ **Be considerate.** Work your horse only at the level she's comfortable with. If you ride only once a week, don't expect her to go on a four-hour ride in one day. Be considerate of your horse and condition her for long rides, as we explain in the earlier section "Easing into a routine."

For more details on how to ride, see coauthor Audrey's book *Horseback Riding For Dummies,* co-written with Shannon Sand and published by Wiley.

Helping Your Horse Recover from Injuries or Illness

Horses are athletes and, like all athletes, run the risk of injury. When a human athlete gets hurt, he or she has to go on the disabled list. Same goes for horses. When a horse has to be "laid up" because of an injury or an illness, he has to stop his normal exercise routine and go into recuperation mode. In the following sections, we explain the importance of full recuperation and show you how to ease your horse back into exercise.

Knowing the importance of rest

Horses have amazing recuperative powers. Their bodies can do self-repair on some of the scariest of injuries, especially injuries to muscles and tendons. But in order for a horse's body to work on repairing itself, the injured area needs to rest. Putting further strain on damaged muscles, ligaments, or bones only worsens the problem, possibly to the point of no return. For this reason, it's vital that injured horses receive proper lay-up so that they can heal.

Lay-up can be extremely frustrating for horse owners. You spend a lot of money and time on your horse every month, and you want to enjoy him. If he's laid up, you can't do much of anything with him except pay the feed and vet bills. So, the tendency of many owners is to rush horses through lay-up. As soon as they see that the horse is feeling better, they want to get the horse back into work. The truth of the matter is that getting a horse back into work too soon can cause the injury to reoccur, and the lay-up to start all over again.

The amount of time and the type of recuperation depend on the injury; your veterinarian will tell you how long your horse needs to be laid up. In some cases, laid-up horses can be hand-walked or even ridden at a walk, depending on the injury. Other horses are given "stall rest," which means that they aren't even supposed to leave their enclosures. Whatever type of lay-up is required, it's vital that you follow your vet's instructions in order to give your horse the best chance at recovery. Your horse will thank you for it, and you'll reap the rewards after your equine companion is back in fighting shape.

Keeping your horse sane during lay-up

Humans aren't the only ones who get frustrated during lay-up. Horses — especially active, high-strung horses — can literally go crazy during a long lay-up. A horse who's been working hard, particularly at a competitive activity, and has to suddenly stop all activity and become sedentary often has a difficult time adjusting. This is especially true of horses put on stall rest. These poor creatures aren't even allowed to leave their immediate confines.

As a compassionate horse owner, you can do a few things to help your horse keep his sanity while being cooped up during lay-up. Here are some suggestions:

- ✔ **Walk him.** If your horse is allowed hand-walking but nothing else, take advantage of it and get him out every day. A 20-minute walk for a normally active horse isn't much, but it's better than nothing and can do wonders to keep a horse from feeling like he's gone into no man's land.

- ✔ **Find companionship.** If your horse is stuck in lay-up, get him a buddy. This can mean moving him to a stall or paddock with a horse next door to interact with. You may not want to put another horse in the same pasture with your horse because the two of them may decide to play and run around. But a next-door neighbor can relieve the boredom and loneliness of lay-up.

- ✔ **Add stall toys.** Some horses like to play with toys in their stall or paddock. You can find balls, hanging treats, and all kinds of other goodies designed for horseplay at a tack store or online. Having something like this in your horse's stall can help him keep from going stir crazy.

✔ **Groom him.** Even if your horse is on stall rest, you can still shower him with attention by grooming him every day. Clean his feet to keep them healthy, and brush and massage him to keep him from feeling neglected. (See Chapter 4 for grooming information.)

✔ **Cut his feed.** If your horse has been on grain, alfalfa, or any kind of high-performance diet or supplement, you need to change his diet during lay-up. Giving him high-energy feed during his recuperation will make him put on weight and leave him feeling even more pent up. Your vet can recommend a feeding program for lay-up. (Part II has the full scoop on nutrition and feeding for your horse.)

✔ **Alter his feed.** Give your horse grass hay to munch on during the day and at night to give him something to do. If your horse puts on weight easily, give him smaller portions more frequently instead. Giving him something to chew on will help keep him mentally and physically stimulated.

Be patient with your laid-up horse. He may start to get cranky, mouthy, or spooky as time goes on — all signs of a bored horse with pent-up energy. Reassure him — and yourself — that the lay-up is just temporary and life will eventually get back to normal.

Returning your horse to his exercise routine

When it's time to get your laid-up horse back into an exercise routine, things can get tricky. Your horse doesn't know that he needs to take it easy so that he doesn't reinjure himself. Instead, he's going to be anxious to run, buck, and get out all that energy that's he's had pent up for so long.

Your veterinarian can be a huge help during this part of the process. He or she can give you instructions on exactly how to start your horse back on his journey to normal exercise. These instructions depend on your horse's injury as well as his age and personality.

Keep these pointers in mind when getting your horse back into the swing of things:

✔ **Go slowly.** Whatever you do, make his reintroduction to exercise slow and methodical.

✔ **Short but frequent.** Making a slow reintroduction to exercise is a challenge because your horse wants to go hog wild at first. You can help combat this tendency by making his exercise sessions short but regular. After getting a 10- or 20-minute workout daily for a few days, your horse should start to calm down and allow you to slowly get him back into shape.

✔ **Keep control.** Avoid any kind of exercise in the beginning that limits your control of your horse's behavior. If he's been living in a stall or small paddock, don't turn him out for at least a couple of weeks after regular exercise. Otherwise, he'll run, buck, and go crazy — and possibly reinjure himself. Instead, longe him (if your vet says it's okay), or make him canter around loose inside a small round pen (50 feet in diameter or less).

✔ **Stay safe.** Remember that your horse has been cooped up for a long time and may not have the same attitude he does when he's being exercised on a regular basis. Don't get on your horse until you know that he's over his initial burst of energy at being "free" again. This means that you may need to exercise him from the ground by longeing him or working him in a round pen for a couple of weeks before you get on.

After your horse is back to his normal routine, and is sound and healthy again, you'll discover that the long lay-up was well worth the effort.

Part II

Good Eats: Nutrition and Feeding

In this part . . .

Chapters in Part II get you started on the art and science of feeding your horse. You get details on the basics of equine nutrition and the types of food available to horses. You also get the skinny on dietary supplements and other special diet considerations, and you find out how to grow your own horse food.

Chapter 6

The Building Blocks of Good Nutrition

*M*ost people don't think much about their own nutrition. They eat what they want while trying to watch their weight. Fortunately, they're able to get most of the nutrition that they need from everyday foods.

Domestic horses, on the other hand, can't eat whatever they want. They're dependent on their owners and caretakers to provide them with foods that will get them the nutrition they need to stay healthy. The consequences of not doing so can be dire, which is why understanding equine nutrition is so important for horse owners.

In this chapter, we explain what horses need to eat and why. You discover the importance of water, protein, fats, carbohydrates, and roughage to the equine body, and you find out about essential equine vitamins and minerals. We also describe in detail why all these elements are vital if your horse is to stay healthy. Flip to Chapter 7 for specific information on different types of feed for your horse.

Drink Up! The Importance of Water in a Horse's Diet

Every living creature, without exception, needs water to survive. This is certainly true of horses, who need to drink anywhere from 10 to 20 gallons or more of water a day to keep their bodies working in good order. As much as 60 to 70 percent of a horse's body weight is made up of water.

Horses lose much of the water that they drink through the process of digestion and through urination, respiration, and sweating. This water needs to be replenished throughout the day, which is why providing your horse with fresh water at all times is vital.

Horses get their water in three different ways: they drink it, obtain it from moist food, and produce it internally as they break down fats, protein, and carbs during digestion.

Here are just some of the reasons why water is vital to your horse's body:

✔ Water is necessary for gastrointestinal health and function.

✔ The function of muscles and nerves is dependent on water.

✔ Horses who eat high-protein diets (such as alfalfa hay) require increased water to metabolize their feed. This is also true of horses who have a large amount of protein, salt, and potassium in their diet.

✔ Normal breathing expels water from the body, and that water has to be replaced.

✔ Nursing mares need water to produce milk for their foals.

Horses who don't get enough water are at risk of becoming seriously ill and even dying. If your horse loses about 100 pounds of her body weight in water, she's at risk for fatal dehydration. This is why it's vital that horses have round-the-clock access to clean, fresh water, and that they're encouraged to drink it.

Remember these points when providing water for your horse:

✔ Always have water available; you can provide automatic waterers, buckets, or troughs in your horse's enclosure. Make sure to check your buckets or troughs a couple of times a day to be certain that your horse has water.

✔ If you use automatic waterers, use a bucket style (as opposed to the bowl and paddle type) because most horses like this style better, and will drink more often.

✔ Check automatic waterers daily to make sure that they're working. Consider keeping a backup water source in your horse's stall if you can't check the system daily.

✔ Keep buckets, troughs, and automatic waterers clean and free of algae and debris. A good rule of thumb is to clean these devices at least once a week or more if they need it. (Consider locating them in the shade to cut down on the amount of algae.)

✔ If you're traveling with your horse and feeding her dry feeds like hay (as opposed to pasture grass), be sure that she has access to water for at least an hour afterward. You can offer water in a bucket during rest stops along your trip.

✔ When traveling with your horse, make sure that she gets enough water by soaking hay in a hay net before offering it to her. (This trick will help keep her hydrated, but it's not a substitute for offering water in a bucket.)

✔ Warm up your horse's water if the weather is cold; you can use a bucket warmer or a waterer equipped with a heater. Colic is more common in winter months because horses don't like to drink cold water.

✔ In the wintertime, ice can form in water buckets. If you live in a cold climate, use a waterer equipped with a heater, or break the ice throughout the day to ensure that your horse can get to her water.

You may notice your horse dunking her hay in her water. Although it makes a mess of the water, it's actually good for the horse's body because it provides her with moist feed. Coauthor Dr. Kate has even seen foals learn this behavior by watching their mothers do it.

If you have a horse who seems to drink too much, she may be sick, or she may be bored. Some confined horses consume lots of extra water to give themselves something to do. If your horse is drinking an excessive amount of water and urinating a lot, call your vet immediately. Her behavior may well be boredom but could also signal a metabolic problem, too.

Keeping Your Horse's System Working Right with Roughage

Without roughage, your horse wouldn't live too long. In the wild, horses graze for around 18 hours a day, eating various tough, fibrous plants that they find in their environment.

The equine digestive system was designed to process this type of material. Although human bodies would be hard pressed to digest this tough cellulose, horses are built to do just that. Without roughage and the fiber it provides, their bodies can't function.

What does fiber do?

Most people know what happens to their bodies if they don't get enough fiber. No doubt that's why bran muffins and high-fiber cereals have become so popular.

If people need fiber, horses need it a lot more. Fiber helps keep the intestines working properly, prompting normal motility that pushes particles of digested food through the system in an efficient manner. In other words, fiber helps your horse's intestines move food wastes through and out of his body.

Which foods are rich in fiber?

Horses who roam free have no trouble finding fiber-rich foods for their diets. The grasses, brush, and even tree bark that they encounter in their environment does the trick. Domestic horses, however, rely on their owners to provide them with the fiber they need.

The most important source of fiber for stabled horses is hay, whereas pasture-kept horses get their fiber from pasture grass. Each of these two sources provides significant fiber (in addition to providing necessary carbohydrates for energy, as we explain later in this chapter). They also satisfy the horses' innate and powerful urge to chew. Fulfilling that urge by feeding hay or allowing a horse to graze on good pasture makes for a happier, healthier horse.

Another feed with a lot of fiber is beet pulp. When soaked in water, beet pulp is a good choice as a source of fiber for senior horses who have trouble chewing hay. It's also great for horses suffering from COPD, because when soaked, it's free of dust. (See Chapter 11 for more details on COPD.) Horses seem to love beet pulp, and it provides almost as much fiber as hay does.

How much roughage should your horse have?

Your horse can't have too much roughage. The more roughage he eats the better. The only caveat is not to feed him so much that he becomes fat. Give your horse as much hay or pasture access as you can while still keeping his body at a healthy weight by providing the right balance of carbs, protein, and fat and by giving him plenty of exercise (see Chapter 5).

A good way to provide roughage without adding too many calories is to feed your horse grass hay. Grass hays in form of orchardgrass, Bermuda, or timothy can provide roughage and may not encourage your horse to put on weight.

Energizing Your Horse with Carbohydrates, Protein, and Fat

Your horse can't live by carbs, protein, or fat alone. All three of these vital nutritional components must be present for a horse's diet to be complete.

Carbs, protein, and fat are found in different sources of food in varying amounts. In the following sections, we look at these components, why they're important, and how your horse gets them.

Carbohydrates

Carbohydrates are the primary source for usable and readily available energy, and all horses need carbs to function. Carbs, in other words, are the primary fuel source necessary to keep the machine running! On the other hand, too many carbs can cause a lot of problems for horses, which is why it's important to know the best types of carbs around and the right amount to feed to your horse.

Discovering what carbs do

The building block of carbohydrates is glucose. In addition to providing the basis for carbohydrates, glucose components are also important for other roles, such as the manufacturing of glucosamine, which is so important for healthy joints. Brain function and hoof growth are also fueled by glucose.

The two basic types of carbohydrates are simple sugars, like glucose, and complex carbohydrates, like starches, which are found in pasture grass and grains. The latter must be broken down into simple sugars before their energy is released in a more easily usable form.

Horses who are exercising or growing, or who are in the last trimester of pregnancy or early in lactation, require more energy in their diet, which can be obtained through carbohydrates. An excess of carbohydrates can leave a horse with too much energy (often making her spooky and unmanageable), and in high doses, it can cause laminitis and other metabolic problems. (See Chapter 11 for more information on these conditions.) Horses who get more energy than they need through carbohydrates store the excess as fat.

Horses with a carbohydrate-deficient diet have to break down fats and proteins to use as energy — even for the most basic of metabolic functions. They become lethargic and can't perform well. They lose their body condition, and pregnant mares can abort. Stallions lose their sex drive, and youngsters show poor growth.

Choosing from the abundance of carbohydrate-rich foods

Foods high in carbohydrates are easy to find in the horse world. Because carbs are an easy source of energy, they're popular among horse people who want their horses to have some "oomph." Sources of carbohydrates include the following:

- **Grains:** Oats, corn, and barley are three grains that are high in carbohydrates.

- **Hay:** Alfalfa and orchardgrass can be particularly high in carbs, depending on when the hay was harvested. Hay cut at a later stage of maturity is lower in carbs than hay that's cut early.

- **Pasture grass:** Pasture grasses can be high in carbohydrates, depending on the species of plant, stage of growth, and environment. Cool-season grasses, such as bluegrass and tall fescue, produce sugars during photosynthesis, sometimes to excess.

- **Commercial feeds:** Certain commercial products known as "sweet feeds" and pelleted feeds can be high in carbohydrates. The molasses added to sweet feeds is a significant source of carbs in these products, as is corn.

- **Beet pulp:** A byproduct in the manufacture of table sugar, beet pulp is dried for storage. It's available as feed for horses in shredded or pelleted form, and is a good source of carbohydrates, although it can be deficient in vitamin A and selenium. (It should always be soaked in water before being fed.)

Your vet can help you determine the best carbohydrate to feed your horse based on her individual nutritional needs.

Figuring out how much to give your horse

Trying to figure out the right amount of carbohydrates to feed your horse can be complicated. The finer details of nutritional issues and corresponding energy production can make your head spin. To top it off, various sources of carbohydrates are available to your horse, and you want to make sure that you don't overdose her on carbs.

The good news is that you don't need to worry too much about deliberately adding carbs to your horse's diet. As long as you're feeding your adult horse a basic diet of good-quality hay or pasture grass, her carbohydrate needs usually will be met. (We discuss feeding hay and pasture grass in detail in Chapter 7.) Exceptions may be if your horse has an extremely fast metabolism, has a slow metabolism, or is undergoing very intense training and exercise. In these cases, your veterinarian can give you specific advice about what to feed your horse to more finely control her carbohydrate intake.

Proteins

Although horses aren't meat-eaters (those weird show horses who share hot dogs with their owners notwithstanding), they still need protein. An essential ingredient to proper equine nutrition, protein is necessary for a horse's survival. On the other hand, too much protein can cause problems. Understanding what protein does for the body and how much to feed is essential if you want your horse to be healthy.

Discovering what these building blocks do

Proteins are building blocks, and horses must have protein in order to construct new tissue. Muscle, hair, skin, hormones, and hooves — to name just a few parts of the horse — can be healthy only if a horse is getting enough protein.

Horses who don't get enough protein in their diet develop a rough haircoat and endure weight loss, decreased milk production (for lactating mares), and decreased energy. On the other hand, horses with an excess of protein in their diets drink too much water and urinate a lot. They sweat too much when exercising, which leads to dehydration and electrolyte imbalances. For this reason, too much protein can really be detrimental to a hard-working horse.

Getting protein from plants and grains

Fortunately, you don't need a degree in nutrition to figure out how to give your horse the proper amount of protein. All you need is to do a quick study of the protein level of available feeds.

Horses glean proteins from plants and grains. Different plants and grains have different protein contents. Proteins are made up of amino acids in various combinations, so all proteins are not created equal. That's why getting your feed from very reputable sources is crucial.

Here are the protein levels of common types of high-quality feed:

- ✔ **Alfalfa hay:** Quality alfalfa for horses has about 18 percent protein. Poor-quality alfalfa hay may have 14 to 15 percent protein.

- ✔ **Grass hay:** High-quality grass hay contains 7 to 12 percent of crude protein.

- ✔ **Soybean meal:** With a 44-percent protein content, soybean meal is a good source of supplemental protein when added to feed. This feed is usually most suitable for young horses and lactating mares.

- ✔ **Linseed meal:** This meal may be a good source of protein for horses who suffer from rhabdomyolisis (also known as tying up syndrome, azoturia, or myoglobinuria) because it contains selenium, which may be helpful in managing this condition in some parts of the country. (For details on azoturia, see Chapter 11.) Linseed meal may contain as much as 35 percent protein. However, it's low in lysine, so it shouldn't be a horse's only source of protein (this is especially true for young horses).

With all these choices, how do you know which type of protein-rich food to give to your horse? The best rule of thumb when deciding what protein-rich foods to feed your horse is to talk to your veterinarian, county extension agent, or local university nutritionist, if you have one.

Consuming the right amount of protein

A good rule to remember when dealing with protein and horses is that your horse should consume between 8 and 10 percent of her rations in protein. That rule is for adult horses. Young, growing horses — that is, horses who are younger than 2 years old — need more protein than mature horses. Lactating mares also need extra protein to help them produce milk for their foals. Young horses and nursing mares should have 12 to 14 percent of their rations in protein.

Your veterinarian can help you determine which feeds to use and how much you should give your horse to meet her protein requirements.

Old wives' tales abound in the horse world, and one is that mature horses in training or those getting a lot of exercise need more protein than idle horses. This isn't true! Although very active horses may lose a small amount of nitrogen in their sweat, they get all the nitrogen they need from grain energy sources needed to fulfill their requirements. To support this, many astute owners will tell you that grumpy, irritable horses calm down and feel better when their protein levels are at the correct level.

Fats

Fat is a dirty word in the rider's vocabulary. Too much of it makes a human portly, and that's not good for a horse's back. But when you're dealing with horse nutrition, fat is vitally important, as you find out in the following sections.

Letting fat do its job

The body uses fat to create energy. Fat also fosters good nerve and hormone production. Fat is also important for the functioning of all organs, and it helps keep the body from breaking down muscle tissue to use as energy.

Horses who eat fats are less likely to have digestive and metabolic problems, such as colic, laminitis, tying up, and stomach ulcers. This is especially true when compared to horses who are fed large amounts of grain.

Fats are the most calorie-dense form of energy, providing three times the number of kilocalories of energy than carbohydrates and proteins. That's why keeping a close eye on your horse's fat intake is important; you don't want her to become overweight!

Finding the best fatty foods for your horse

When you're feeding fat to horses, corn oil is the most economical way to add it. Although corn oil is somewhat messy, many horses love it. Some people prefer to give their horses rice bran oil, but we like corn oil because it has twice the calories per pound than rice bran products. That means that you can feed less of it and spend less money.

If you're looking to save money, you may be tempted to give your horse a combination vegetable oil containing soybean oil, sunflower oil, and canola oil. These lack the palatability of corn oil and aren't as good for your horse.

If you shop at a big box store that sells food items in large quantities, you can buy corn oil in big jugs for considerably less than you would pay at your local supermarket.

If you don't like the idea of handling oil every day, consider using food-grade stabilized rice bran. It's about 20 percent fat, and easily digested by horses. It provides an excellent source of energy. Rice bran products can be mixed into food or added on top of feed.

If you plan to feed commercial bran, you should know that at high levels, this feed can cause a mineral imbalance in your horse. The body has to compensate for this imbalance by taking calcium from its primary storage source: bones. This can result in a decrease in bone density that will in turn lead to an increase in fractures and injuries. It can also contribute to developmental orthopedic problems in young horses. To avoid causing a mineral imbalance in your horse, don't feed more bran than what's recommended on the label.

Another way to provide fat to your horse is through high-fat commercial feeds. These are often excellent in content (percentages vary among feeds) and palatability. However, after a certain percentage, fats require a process called "extrusion" to keep them from spoiling quickly and to remain palatable. You'll recognize these feeds because they'll remind you of dry dog food. Good extruded feeds can be more expensive but are worthwhile if your horse won't eat her fat any other way.

When storing fat-rich foods, be sure to keep them in a cool environment — they can easily become rancid in the heat. You'll be able to smell an "off" odor when fats get rancid, and most horses won't eat it.

Feeding your horse enough fat

Up until about 12 years ago, experts didn't think that horses needed much fat in their diets, and that too much fat was detrimental. Now experts say that horses can tolerate up to 20 percent of their total diet in fat.

Figuring out how much fat to feed your horse is easy. If you use oil, start with a ¼ cup per day mixed in a small portion of commercial feed or grain (see Figure 6-1), and work your way up to 1 cup over a period of one week, increasing in ¼-cup intervals.

Your horse doesn't need or want more oil than one cup per day, so adding more doesn't help her, and it won't hurt her. However, more oil per day may decrease the palatability of the feed (she probably won't eat it), and it may damage your wallet.

Figure 6-1:
Adding oil to
a horse's
feed.

If you prefer to use a commercial rice bran product or a high-fat commercial feed, follow the directions on the bag for how much to feed. Don't overfeed because your horse may start to get fat!

Understanding the Value of Vitamins

You probably already know that vitamins are important for people, and they're just as important for horses. The body needs these very small organic compounds for metabolic function, for the clotting of blood, to aid muscle contractions, for heart function, for body tissue growth, and for much, much more.

Too many vitamins can be toxic, however, so make sure that you have a thorough understanding of these nutrients and how they work before you start adding them to your horse's diet.

Telling the difference between different types of vitamins

Vitamins come in two types: water-soluble and fat-soluble. These two classes of vitamins are very different, and are processed differently in your horse's body.

Water-soluble vitamins

Water-soluble vitamins are required primarily as enzyme cofactors in metabolism. In other words, enzymes need water-soluble vitamins to perform their functions in the body. Horses easily excrete water-soluble vitamins from the body through the urine; these vitamins aren't stored for future use.

Here are the most important water-soluble vitamins for horses (all are present in good-quality hay and pasture):

- ✔ **Vitamin C:** Horses make their own vitamin C. Vitamin C is produced by the liver, and is also found in green, leafy foliages; fruits; and vegetables.

- ✔ **Vitamin B (complex):** The B complex vitamins include vitamins B1, B2, B5, B6, B9, and B12, and the horse's body produces them. They're byproducts of the gut's microbial fermentation.

  Some people give nervous horses B vitamins to calm them. These vitamins help only if the horse is so stressed that his body isn't producing enough on his own. Coauthor Dr. Kate has never seen vitamin B change behavior in a normal, healthy horse.

- ✔ **Choline:** This B vitamin helps metabolize fat, maintain good cell structure, and preserve normal nerve function.

Fat-soluble vitamins

Fat-soluble vitamins are difficult for the body to excrete and can be easily stored. This is a good thing in most cases, although if too much of a fat-soluble vitamin is found in a horse's diet, it can cause toxicity because the horse isn't able to eliminate the excess amount.

These fat-soluble vitamins are necessary for a horse's good health:

- ✔ **Vitamin A:** This vitamin is used for vision and the creation of epithelial cells (important cells that can be found in many different parts of the body). It's also necessary for normal bone metabolism. Vitamin A also plays an important role in reproduction.

  Signs of vitamin A deficiency are night blindness, brittle bones, poor haircoat, excessive tearing, and increased respiratory infections.

  Horses obtain vitamin A from their diet by ingesting its precursor, beta carotene. Carotene is found in high amounts in fresh green pasture, but it oxidizes very quickly, so the content decreases when hay is cured and stored for more than six months. The only hay that retains a fair amount of vitamin A after storage is alfalfa, and even then, it diminishes over time. Horses aren't very efficient in converting beta carotene to active vitamin A, so depending on your hay source, you may need to supplement (see the next section for more information).

- ✔ **Vitamin D:** This vitamin is obtained by exposure to sunlight, so horses who are stalled most of the time are at risk for vitamin D deficiency unless they receive supplementation. If a horse spends at least four to six hours a day in a paddock or pasture, he'll receive plenty of vitamin D.

  Vitamin D is important in the normal absorption and utilization of calcium and phosphorus. Deficiency in this vitamin can result in *rickets* (distortion of the bones) in young animals, and *osteomalacia* (softening of the bones) in mature horses. On the other hand, large doses or over-supplementation of vitamin D can lead to calcification of soft tissues.

- ✔ **Vitamin E:** A potent *antioxidant* (a compound that protects body tissue from damage during the conversion of food to energy), vitamin E is important in nerve function, as well as in other physiological functions in the horse's body. It's necessary for membrane stability and red blood cell integrity, and may be important in reproduction. A horse deficient in vitamin E can develop equine motor neuron disease, which is a rare condition of the nerve cells, and equine degenerative myeloencephalopathy, which is a degenerative nerve disease of the spinal cord and brain stem. Horses kept on pasture most of the year seldom develop deficient vitamin E levels.

  Vitamin E is usually present in ample quantity in natural feeds, particularly roughages, cereal grains, and especially in cereal grain oils like wheat germ oil. Vitamin E has a special relationship with the mineral selenium. The interaction between these two nutrients may be important in the management, treatment, and prevention of rhabdomyolisis (also known as azoturia or tying up). See Chapter 11 for more on this condition.

  Horses under stress and with heavy workloads may benefit from vitamin E supplementation, and horses with nerve problems or certain muscle function problems — like those that can result from West Nile virus and EPM — may also benefit from vitamin E supplementation. (For more details on West Nile virus and EPM, see Chapter 12.)

- ✔ **Vitamin K:** This vitamin is important for blood clotting. A product of gut microbial fermentation like vitamin E, vitamin K can also be found in some green, leafy plants.

  Horses suffering from a vitamin K deficiency develop bleeding disorders. Too much vitamin K may cause toxicity and can result in liver failure.

If you're feeding your horse a very high-fat diet for some reason, be aware that it may increase his need for higher levels of fat-soluble vitamins. Ask your vet whether this should be a concern with your horse.

Adding vitamins to your horse's diet

Go to any tack and feed store and you'll see plenty of vitamin supplements for the "performance" horse. In fact, a large segment of the equine products industry is devoted to various vitamin and mineral supplements.

Before you succumb to the marketing on the label, talk to your vet about how to provide the best diet for your horse given his individual circumstances. Your horse is best served if he gets all his vitamins from his diet.

A healthy horse on a good diet doesn't need extra vitamins. When water-soluble vitamins are provided in excess, horses just urinate them out. These vitamins aren't stored in the body, so feeding them to your horse may make you feel better, but unless your horse is extremely stressed (which may upset the happy GI tract leading to decreased microbial action), supplementation isn't necessary. Adding fat-soluble vitamins, which are stored in the body, can cause a problem, especially with vitamin A, when oversupplementation could affect the liver.

That said, added vitamins may be necessary in certain situations, like when a horse is growing, lactating, in heavy race training, or recuperating from a prolonged illness. In these situations, higher amounts of some vitamins can be useful. Still, meeting those vitamin requirements via the diet, if possible, is best.

If you're at all confused about whether to provide your horse with a vitamin supplement, talk to your vet. If he or she recommends adding vitamins to your horse's ration, you can mix them with a small amount of commercial pellet feed (see Figure 6-2).

Figure 6-2:
Adding
vitamins to a
horse's
feed.

Staying Strong with Minerals

Horses (and humans) need minerals to metabolize fats, proteins, and carbo-hydrates. They also need minerals for their muscles and nerves to function properly and for their bones to be strong.

Minerals come in two different forms: major minerals and trace minerals. Each serves a unique purpose in the equine body.

Major minerals

Major minerals, or macrominerals as they're also called, are found in larger quantities in the horse's body than trace minerals. These major minerals include the following elements:

- ✔ **Calcium:** Necessary for bone strength and repair, calcium is also needed in the horse's body for the function of cardiac muscles, cell membrane strength, glandular function, body temperature regulation, and blood clotting. Adult horses deficient in calcium can develop lameness or a softening of the bones; young horses can develop brittle bones that easily fracture. Older horses absorb calcium less efficiently than younger horses, so they sometimes need calcium supplementation pos-sibly in equal proportion to phosphorus.

- ✔ **Magnesium:** This mineral is important to bone strength and enzyme per-formance. Horses deficient in magnesium can experience nervousness and muscle tremors.

- ✔ **Phosphorus:** A close partner to calcium, phosphorus is required for healthy bones and teeth. It also aids in the function of cells and is vital for mares producing milk for their foals. Horses lacking phosphorus can develop lameness that shifts from leg to leg.

- ✔ **Potassium:** Horses need potassium, an electrolyte, to maintain the bal-ance of body fluid. Horses who don't get enough potassium can become fatigued, have weak muscles, and eat and drink less. Some potassium-deficient horses even show behavior changes and become spooky and restless.

- ✔ **Sodium and chloride:** These two elements together make salt, a vital mineral necessary to the horse's body function. Considered electrolytes, sodium and chloride are necessary for correct chemistry of the horse's body fluids. Horses who don't get enough sodium chloride tire easily, stop sweating, and experience muscle spasms.

Both of these minerals are easily lost through sweating and urination, so they must be supplemented in the form of a salt block (see Figure 6-3) or free-choice loose salt.

✔ **Sulfur:** Necessary to healthy hooves and coat, sulfur also helps in the metabolism of the B vitamins and other important elements in the horse's body.

Figure 6-3:
A salt block provides sodium and chloride.

Bob Langrish

With the exception of sodium and chloride, major minerals may not need to be supplemented to horses who are eating a good diet of water and quality hay, pasture, or commercial feed. If supplementation of minerals is necessary, your vet will let you know.

Trace minerals

Trace minerals, or microminerals, are so called because they're needed only in very small amounts in the horse's body. Although horses need only tiny measurements of these elements, they're still vital for the horse's health and well-being.

Trace minerals important to horses include:

✔ **Cobalt:** Closely tied to the function of vitamin B12 (which we discuss earlier in this chapter), cobalt enables the body to produce this important vitamin. Researchers haven't seen any problems in horses from too much or not enough cobalt, so horse owners have no need to supplement this mineral in healthy horses; your horse will receive enough cobalt from her feed.

✔ **Copper:** Creation and maintenance of the horse's connective tissue is dependent upon copper in the body. Copper also enables the horse's body to utilize iron and synthesize *melanin,* which is pigment in the body. Insufficient levels of copper can cause hind limb weakness and infertility. Horses usually get enough copper in their diets, although copper can usually be added in supplementation without risk of toxicity. Discuss this option with your veterinarian.

✔ **Iodine:** This trace mineral aids in the absorption of thyroid hormones, and is necessary for overall good health. Horses deficient in iodine can develop swollen thyroid glands; too much iodine can cause the same problem. Most horse feed contains adequate amounts of iodine, so supplementation isn't necessary. However, talk to your vet about a possible need to add this mineral to your horse's diet (particularly if you have a pregnant mare or foal) if feed grown in your area is lacking in iodine.

✔ **Iron:** Just as in the human body, iron is used to produce hemoglobin, a vital part of red blood cells. Fortunately, iron is plentiful in most hays and pasture grasses, and rarely needs to be supplemented. In fact, too much iron prevents the absorption of other minerals, such as zinc and copper, and creates a deficiency in these elements. Excess iron is especially dangerous to newborn foals.

That said, horses who have lost a considerable amount of blood can often benefit from iron supplementation. Supplement iron only if your vet has taken a blood test, and the results indicate that your horse has a need for this mineral.

✔ **Manganese:** A mineral used for the metabolism of *lipids* (a type of fat) and carbohydrates, manganese also helps the horse's body metabolize chondroitant sulfate, which helps joints stay healthy. This mineral is most important to growing foals, who can develop cartilage and bone deformities without it. Your vet will let you know whether your horse needs a manganese supplement.

✔ **Selenium:** Working in partnership with vitamin E, selenium is a powerful antioxidant, protecting cell membranes from free-radical damage. Normal, healthy horses need only a very small amount of selenium in their diet, and shouldn't be supplemented with this mineral unless your vet indicates otherwise. Selenium is present in most hay and pasture grass, although soil in some areas of the U.S. is deficient in it. In these situations, you may need to supplement this mineral.

Because horses' bodies easily become toxic if oversupplemented with selenium, make certain that your horse needs selenium before adding it to her feed or providing her with a mineral salt block that contains it. Your veterinarian can advise you on this.

✔ **Zinc:** Enzymes containing zinc help the horse's body metabolize the important dietary elements of carbohydrates and proteins. A lack of zinc in the diet may cause brittle hooves and a dull haircoat. Hay and pasture grasses contain adequate levels of zinc, so supplementing this mineral isn't necessary.

Chapter 7

Your Hungry Horse: Feeding Fundamentals

In This Chapter

▶ Exploring different hays and pasture

▶ Discovering other types of horse food

▶ Finding out how often and how much to feed

*Y*ou know that what you feed your horse is very important or you wouldn't be reading this book. But *what* to feed your horse — that is the question. Horse feeds come in a number of different shapes, sizes, and textures. Each one is significantly different in terms of nutritional value and palatability to the horse.

In this chapter, we describe all the feeds available to horses. You explore which types of feed are best for your horse given his age, condition, and workload. How much to feed your horse and how often will no longer be mysteries to you.

Hay Now! Choosing Hay for Your Horse

If you horse isn't on pasture (and most likely he isn't, simply because you don't have the option of keeping him on it), hay is the most important component of his diet, after water (see Chapter 6). For this reason, it's very important that you buy the best hay you possibly can. Because the quality of the hay you buy determines how much nutrition your horse gets, it's vital that you know how to recognize good hay.

Why choose hay for your horse?

Unless you have a pasture to graze your horse, hay is the best choice of basic feed for your equine companion. Quality hay provides the horse with all the carbohydrates he needs to function. It gives him plenty of protein, and just about all the vitamins and minerals that his body requires. It also provides vital roughage to his diet, which keeps his digestive system working properly. (See Chapter 6 for more about all these building blocks of equine nutrition.)

Hay is also less expensive than complete feeds (which we discuss later in this chapter), and it satisfies the horse's needs to chew. Watch a horse munching on hay and you can see how much he enjoys it!

Looking at different types of hay

Everyone knows that horses eat hay. But what is this mysterious stuff that looks like dried-up sticks but makes horses salivate?

Basically, hay is made up of plants that have been cut, dried, and baled. Each type of hay usually contains one or two different plants, depending on the bale. (We discuss different types of hay bales later in this chapter.)

You can buy three different types of hay: legumes, grasses, and cereals. Each type has different nutritional properties. Where you live, your horse's individual needs, and your veterinarian's advice will help you determine which hays to feed to your horse.

Legumes

Legume hays (see Figure 7-1) are rich in nutrients and provide plenty of energy to a horse's diet. The type of legume hay most available to you depends on where you live.

- ✔ **Alfalfa** is one of the most commonly fed legumes, and you can purchase it in many parts of the U.S., particularly the West. Most horses love it, although it has to be fed with some care because of its high calcium level in relation to phosphorus. You don't want to create an imbalance of these important minerals in your horse; doing so will risk the health of your horse's bones.

  An excellent source of protein and carbohydrates, quality alfalfa usually provides more protein than horses actually need — a whopping 18 percent. (Horses typically need 10 percent protein in their diets.) High protein content is especially seen in dairy-grade alfalfa, which is harvested to be fed to dairy cattle. Alfalfa that's cut earlier in the growing season has less protein, so it's more suited as feed for horses; your hay supplier can tell you when your hay was cut. (When horses get too much protein, they urinate a lot and can become unmanageable because of excess energy.)

✔ **Clover** is another legume hay that's often fed, and one that horses especially like. When eating it, they often select the most highly palatable clovers from the hay. This hay has a high energy content, and is a good hay for horses who get a lot of exercise. Different types of clover hay can be found throughout the United States.

Figure 7-1:
Legume hays are high in protein and calories.

Grasses

Grass hays (see Figure 7-2) are generally lower in protein content than legume hays, and also provide less lysine (an important amino acid) than legume hays. Some experts believe that you should feed both a legume hay and a grass hay together, although coauthor Audrey and many other horse owners feed their horses only grass hay and they do just fine.

Figure 7-2:
Grass hays have a moderate protein content and usually can be fed free choice.

The fiber content of grass hays is pretty high compared to other types of hays. These hays are usually lower in vitamin E than legume hays.

Common grass hays that make good food for horses include orchardgrass, coastal Bermuda, brome, bluegrass, fescue, and timothy.

- Orchardgrass grows tall in cool seasons. It offers 8 to 13 percent protein, depending on when it's cut. Coastal Bermuda has a 10 percent protein content. Brome has 12 percent protein, and bluegrass has 10 percent.

- Fescue has 11.8 percent protein, but be cautious when feeding it. Many tall fescue grasses contain a fungal endophyte (a plant parasite) that grows inside the plant but has no visible symptoms in the plant. This organism can cause reproductive problems in pregnant mares, abortion, poor milk production, retained placentas, and reduced growth rates in young growing horses. If you want to feed fescue, look for hay labeled "endophyte-free."

- Of all the grass hays, timothy is the highest in calcium and contains a greater amount of vitamins A and D. Timothy has a protein content of 7 to 11 percent.

All the grass hays mentioned here have good nutritional value and can be fed in unlimited amounts to horses, as long as it doesn't cause a weight problem.

Cereals

Cereal hays get their name from the grain heads that grow as part of the harvested plant. These hays aren't fed to horses very often because they can be hard to come by and don't hold their nutrition very long. (After the grain heads fall off as the hay matures, what's left is essentially straw, which has no nutritional value to horses.) Some horses rely on these hays for their prime source of roughage, however, because they can't eat legume or grass hays because of allergies or digestion problems.

Here are three popular cereal hays:

- **Oat:** Oat hay is the most commonly fed cereal hay and can be a good choice for older horses because of its lower protein level — 9.5 percent — when compared to legume and grass hays. (Older horses often have trouble metabolizing protein and produce large quantities of urine if they're fed a higher protein hay.) One problem with oat hay is that many horses eat only the grain heads and leave the stems behind.

- **Barley:** This hay has a protein level of 9 percent. It can be lower in nutritional value than some other hays. For this reason, feed this hay only if your vet recommends it. She may also suggest that a vitamin and mineral supplement be fed in conjunction with barley hay (see Chapter 6 for more information on vitamins and minerals.)

✔ **Wheat:** With a protein content of 8.5 percent, wheat hay is high in fiber and can be a good choice for horses who can't eat legume or grass hays. It can be lower in calcium than these other hays, however, so lactating mares and growing foals may need a calcium supplement. Discuss this issue with your veterinarian.

Distinguishing between different types of bales

Hay that has been harvested and prepared for sale comes in two different forms: square bales and round bales. Hay bales also come in small and large sizes:

✔ Small rectangular bales weighing 50 to 125 pounds are the most common bale size. These bales are great for most horse owners because they're easy to handle and transport. Small rectangular bales are divided up into individual flakes, which makes them easy to feed in small increments. (The weight of each flake varies considerably from bale to bale and among different hay types.)

✔ Large rectangular bales and large round bales are also available, weighing from 800 to 1,200 pounds. These huge bales are practical for horse owners who have a lot of horses to feed, and can help minimize cost and labor. These large bales are usually placed in a pasture or paddock inside special feeders made specifically for them so that they don't sit in accumulated rainwater. The feeders also help minimize waste by catching the hay that comes off the bale as the horses are eating. (We talk about basic feeders later in this chapter.)

Large bales made up of grass hay are a good choice for a group of horses. However, coauthor Dr. Kate doesn't recommend feeding big alfalfa bales to horses at all unless you can effectively keep the big bales dry and covered (alfalfa molds quickly in damp weather) and are willing to tear the bales apart for feeding. (Horses shouldn't have free access to alfalfa hay because they'll get fat!)

Keep the following in mind when you're feeding your horse from a bale: You don't know whether anything else is in that bale besides just hay. Foreign objects such as trash or even dead and decaying rodents are occasionally found in hay bales. You're more likely to find these potential dangers when you're hand-feeding small square bales, so you can discard that bale if needed. Consider this just another opportunity to prevent your horse from swallowing something that can be potentially harmful.

Evaluating hay quality

Picking up the phone and ordering hay from the feed store or just trusting the boarding stable to give your horse whatever it buys from its supplier is so easy. But if you really care about the quality of your horse's diet, you should get more involved by personally evaluating your horse's hay.

You should consider a number of factors when evaluating hay, including the following:

- ✔ **Color:** The ideal hay color is green. Beta carotene is greater when hay is green. A beige or brown color can indicate that the hay has been bleached and rain has leached nutrients after the cutting.

- ✔ **Texture:** The hay should be soft, leafy, and without lots of stems.

- ✔ **Condition:** It should be fresh, dry, free of dust, and without any trace of mold.

- ✔ **Age:** Buy hay that was harvested during the current year, if possible. (Ask you supplier for this information.) If you must buy older hay, be certain that it was properly stored in a covered and dry environment. (Many vitamins degrade with time, and old hay may not provide the amounts of vitamins your horse needs.)

- ✔ **Weed content:** Some weeds present in hay present no problems at all, and most hay bales contain some weeds. But too many weeds affect the palatability and nutrition of the hay you're feeding.

  Be careful not to mistake bright green weeds for alfalfa. Even though they're green, these weeds have a lower nutrient content than brown alfalfa.

- ✔ **Bug free:** Inspect alfalfa hay for blister beetles. Even just one of these tiny little beetles, which are sometimes accidentally baled in hay, can cause fatalities in horses. They're often found in alfalfa hay grown in areas that don't have a hard winter freeze. If your alfalfa comes from such an area, make sure that the hay producer sprays for blister beetles. (If you're buying your alfalfa from a feed store, ask whether blister beetle prevention was taken.)

Be prepared to see hay prices go up and down. The cost of hay varies greatly depending upon availability (hay costs skyrocket during drought years). You may pay anywhere from $3 a bale to $25 a bale, depending on where you live and what type of hay you're buying. Hay can quadruple in cost within a year when demand exceeds supply. Feeding poor-quality hay to try to save money can cost you plenty in terms of gastrointestinal upsets and poor health.

Hay and pasture help from a pro

A great way to learn about hay and pasture is through your county extension office. Extension agents — who can be found in every county in the country by looking in your telephone directory under "Government" — can show you examples of forages, and even possibly direct you to a local college that may have an animal husbandry course that has lots of great info.

Many extension offices offer regular seminars on how to live in the country, designed to educate new livestock owners about how to take care of their animals. At these seminars, you get to see the types of hay and pasture that are common in your area.

If you have your own horse property and plenty of storage, buy a year's worth of hay at a time, all from one source. Then, have your hay analyzed by your county extension agent for a small fee, and build your nutrition program based on your hay. The analysis tells you the amount of protein and total digestible nitrogen (TDN) in your hay. You find out how much "bang" you're getting for your hay buck. On the other hand, if you board your horse at a stable, you have little control over the hay your horse is getting. Some stables do allow owners to supply their own hay, so if you don't like the quality of the hay your horse is getting, discuss the possibility of supplying hay with management.

Storing hay

If you keep your horse — and your horse's hay — on your property, storing it properly is vital. Proper storage involves keeping it dry and free from dust and mold.

Water is your hay's worst enemy, so keeping it out of the rain is paramount. Store your hay indoors if you can. If you don't have a barn or garage where you can keep it, cover it with a tarp before it rains. Don't cover it with a tarp *after* it rains, however, because this encourages mold to grow. Instead, open the bales and spread the flakes out to dry. If you find mold on your hay, bite the bullet and throw it away. Feeding moldy hay can cause respiratory problems in horses, as well as colic (see Chapter 11 for more information about these issues).

When storing hay, keep it elevated off the ground where moisture can accumulate. Wooden pallets are great for this. They keep your hay off the ground, and can be found for free or minimal cost at many big box stores and home repair centers.

Grazing Time: Providing Pasture for Your Horse

If you have access to pasture, you and your horse are fortunate. Pasture is the best thing for your horse because it's the most natural environment for her. Horses evolved to graze, and pasture enables them to do that. Pasture that's well planted and maintained can also provide horses with excellent nutrition. However, keep in mind that poor pasture or toxic pasture is much worse than no pasture at all.

A variety of grasses can be grown for horses, including all the types also made into hay (which we discuss earlier in this chapter). If you have existing pasture and want to make sure that it's good for your horse, read on. If you're planning on growing and maintaining your own pasture from scratch, see Chapter 9 for details.

Why choose pasture for your horse?

When horses live the way nature intended them to, they spend many hours a day grazing. They walk around, slowly picking their way through the various plants in their environment, nibbling and chewing as they decide which pieces to eat and which to leave behind.

When you put your horse on pasture, you give her the opportunity to behave the way she was born to do. Eating and walking, eating and walking — this is what horses are really all about. The result of this natural environment is a happier, healthy horse. If you keep your horse on pasture, she'll be less likely to develop stable vices, leg problems, and digestive problems.

Surveying different types of pasture

Pasture grasses come in pretty much the same types as hay. Fescue, orchardgrass, Bermuda, bluegrass, and brome are all common hays seen in pastures, depending on which part of the country you're in.

As a general rule, grass is the only type of pasture that you want for your horse. Horses grazed on alfalfa and clover quickly become obese because of the higher calorie content of these hays. They're also at greater risk for developing colic and laminitis when they graze on pasture that's too rich.

Evaluating pasture

Before you put your horse out on a pasture (either grown on your property or provided by a boarding facility), you need to make certain that the grass is of the right quality. The plant species should be appropriate for horses, and no toxic weeds should be growing among the pasture plants. (You can find out about the grass quality by contacting your county extension agent.)

You also need to know how productive the pasture is. Vibrantly green, lush-looking acreage can be full of weeds and plants that your horse won't eat. Horses have been known to starve standing knee-deep in what an owner mistakenly thought was edible grass. If you aren't sure of the productivity of your pasture, ask your extension agent for help.

Pastures change with the seasons. Quick growth in the spring — with plants full of water after a lot of rain — has a different nutritional value than the same pasture in the fall with mature grasses that have concentrated sugars and nutrients. This latter growth, although more nutritious for the horse, can also be less palatable.

To make your late-season pasture grass more palatable, manage your pasture correctly all through the season. Keep manure piles down by removing them or spreading. Mow stands of mature grass. Practice good rotational grazing, and keep weeds under control at all times so good grass doesn't have to compete.

Switching your horse from hay to pasture

The equine digestive system doesn't take well to sudden changes in diet. So if your horse has been eating hay only and now has access to pasture, you need to make the change gradually.

Start by allowing your horse to graze for one hour a day on the pasture, while continuing to feed her a normal diet of hay. Do this for three days in a row. Then extend the grazing time to two hours per day for a few days as you reduce the amount of hay she's getting (talk to your vet about how much to cut back). Using this system, gradually work your way up to having your horse spend all day on pasture with little or no hay supplementation, depending on the quality of your pasture. (Your vet can tell you if your horse still needs hay.)

If horses aren't used to being on pasture, they sometimes gorge themselves when you first introduce them to this new type of feed. Watch to make sure that your horse isn't grabbing huge mouthfuls and not really chewing before swallowing. If she is, leave her on pasture for only 30 minutes a day to start with and go up in 30-minute increments.

If your horse begins to grow fat while she's on pasture, reduce the amount of time she spends grazing. Pasture grass can be richer in the spring when it's new, so though your horse may need to graze less in the spring to keep her weight down, she may be okay grazing all day in the fall.

Lush green grass can be a cause of colic or laminitis. In some areas of the country, many horses shouldn't be turned out on pastures during the early grass-growing season for more than 30 minutes per day, if at all. It may be safer to start acclimating your horse to the pasture when the summer starts and the pasture growth slows.

Considering Other Feeds

The staples of your horse's diet should be hay and/or pasture. You can add other feeds as well, depending on your horse's situation. Your veterinarian can guide you on which types of the following feeds, if any, you should give to your horse.

Grains for active horses

"He's feeling his oats!" You may have heard this expression, which harkens back to the days when horses were everywhere and cars had yet to be invented.

Oats and other grains like corn and barley have become synonymous with vigor in horses, and with good reason. These feedstuffs provide plenty of carbohydrates, which convert into energy in the horse's body:

   ✔ **Oats:** Of all the grains, oats provide the greatest nutritional boost. They're a good source of fiber and much less likely to develop mold or mycotoxins than other grains. Oats don't have to be processed at all for horses to get the available nutrition, and because they aren't processed, they don't spoil as easily as corn or barley.

✔ **Corn:** Corn is now the most popular type of grain fed to horses because it's inexpensive and provides a lot of energy. It's nutritious and very palatable to horses. It should be fed in moderation, though (your vet can tell you how much is right for your horse). Because corn doesn't have a hull, it's lower in fiber than oats, but it's also higher in density and digestible energy than oats. One pound of corn has twice the energy of one pound of oats.

Overfeeding corn can cause laminitis, colic, and diarrhea (see Chapter 11 for more information about these issues). Corn also is more expensive than oats and barley.

✔ **Barley:** Barley has the same protein content as grass hay and should be fed only in rolled or crushed form. The most widely cultivated of all cereal grains in the world, it looks similar to oats but is very hard and therefore more difficult for horses to chew. It's also less palatable than oats or corn. Buy barley that has been crimped or rolled because it's easier to chew.

Barley has more fiber than corn and more energy density than oats. However, less of its starch is digested in the small intestine, so you should feed it with caution to avoid founder. Your vet can tell you how much is right for your horse.

Grain may not be necessary to your horse's diet. In fact, if you don't do too much with your horse, he probably doesn't need grain included in his daily rations. Giving him grain gives him more energy, and if you don't ride him much, all that energy may be channeled into unwanted behavior (like spooking).

Complete feeds for the old and young

Complete feeds (see Figure 7-3) are commercially prepared diets that contain all the nutrients horses need to survive. These types of feeds are usually given to older horses. Senior horse diets, which are labeled specifically for use in older horses, are designed to meet the special needs of older horses who may have dental issues and require a diet that can be easily chewed and assimilated. (See Chapter 17 for details on caring for senior horses.)

Complete feeds are also used for weanlings and for horses who have certain medical conditions (such as equine metabolic syndrome; see Chapter 11) that require a closely monitored diet.

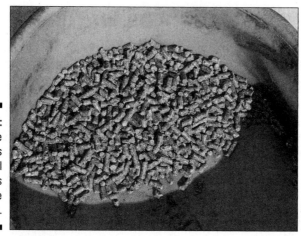

Figure 7-3:
Complete feeds contain all the nutrients a horse needs.

Some horse owners use complete feeds to mix with supplements (see Chapter 8) or medications (see Chapter 13). These feeds tend to be very tasty to horses, making them more willing to take their medicine if it's disguised within a bucket of complete feed.

Healthy adult horses shouldn't be fed an exclusive diet of complete feed. Even though these feeds are nutritionally complete, the horse's innate need to chew and biological need for roughage dictates that some kind of forage be a significant part of the horse's diet.

Before you give your horse a commercial feed, it's important to read the feeding instructions and nutritional information on the bag. Consult with your veterinarian and your feed dealer to know what you're buying and whether it's appropriate for your horse. For example, some senior feeds are formulated to include roughage and may need to be fed in greater volume to provide a horse with adequate forage intake. Other senior feeds are formulated to be fed in conjunction with pasture or hay.

You get what you pay for when it comes to commercial feed. The cheapest bag of feed may be just that. Many vitamins degrade with time, and feed that has been sitting in a warehouse before appearing at a discount farm supply store may not contain all the nutrition it once did. Also, cheaper prepared feeds tend to use cost-based rations rather than a recipe-based formulation; the ingredients listed on the feed tag can be included in any amount that will contain the listed amounts of protein, fat, and fiber if the feed were to be analyzed in a laboratory. Therefore, the actual ingredients may vary from one batch of feed to another.

Feeds for special circumstances

Over the centuries, horsemen have developed a lot of different types of feeds for horses. Each of these has different reasons for being fed, and may be of use to you and your horse in certain situations. Some special feeds include:

- ✔ **Hay pellets:** Made from either grass hay or alfalfa that's finely ground and pressed into ¾-inch pellets, this form of hay is a type of concentrated feed. It's an ideal choice when a horse is suffering from a respiratory ailment that makes him sensitive to the dust found in baled hay.

  Hay pellets (see Figure 7-4) are cheap to feed but shouldn't make up the main part of your horse's diet because they lack roughage and don't satisfy the horse's urge to chew. In fact, horses fed a diet of only pellets can develop stall vices like cribbing and wood chewing. (See Chapter 3 for more information on stable vices.) Pellets also aren't good for the horse's digestive tract, and when they're dry, they can cause choking; soak them before feeding.

- ✔ **Hay cubes:** Concentrated blocks of coarsely chopped hay, usually 2 x 1 ½ inches in size, are called hay cubes. They're easy to store and transport, and can be good for senior horses who have trouble chewing hay because the cubes break easily. (Some types of hay cube producers recommend soaking cubes in water before feeding to make them softer.) Horses with respiratory problems can benefit from a diet of cubes as well because they're less dusty than baled hay. Cubes are also good at putting weight on horses who have trouble keeping meat on their bones. Cubes aren't the ideal diet for a healthy horse, however, because they don't satisfy the horse's need to chew.

- ✔ **Beet pulp:** High in protein, beet pulp is a byproduct of the table sugar industry. The sweet stuff is removed from the sugar beet, leaving the sugarless pulp behind. Horses like beet pulp, and when soaked, it can make a good treat for mixing supplements or medication. Some people feed it to help put weight on horses who are perpetually thin.

- ✔ **Bran:** Bran is a popular treat for horses who live in cold climates. Horses love a warm bran mash on cold days and owners love to provide it. (Warm, soupy bran mixed with pieces of carrot and apple is the earthly equivalent of heaven for a horse.) Although bran is fine as an occasional treat, it's not beneficial on a regular basis. The hull of the grain left over after milling (usually wheat or rice), bran has very little nutritional value. It also can cause impaction if it's fed regularly and then abruptly discontinued.

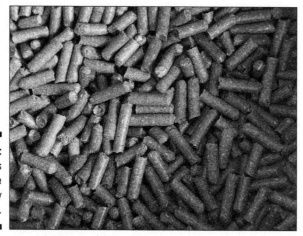

Figure 7-4: Hay pellets should be given only as a treat.

These other feeds are fine on occasion or under special circumstances, but should never take the place of hay or pasture as the basis for your horse's diet.

Feeding Your Horse Properly

If you want your horse to be healthy and happy, you should do everything you can to provide an environment that's as close to nature as possible. Horses are best off when they can live the way they evolved to do over time. When it comes to feeding, you have the opportunity to mimic the horse's natural environment in a few different ways, including providing feeding at the right frequency and in the right amounts.

The right frequency

Because horses were designed to eat for about 18 hours a day, the more often you can feed your horse, the better. The exact frequency of feeding depends on whether your horse eats hay or pasture:

- ✓ **If your horse is stabled and eating hay,** feed her at least twice a day — more if possible. Break up her daily ration into smaller portions so that she has less time between meals. Try to feed around the same time each day, too. Horses seem to have an internal clock that lets them know when it's feeding time, and they can become quite stressed if the food doesn't come when it's supposed to, especially if they're confined to stalls and don't have much to do all day.

✔ **If your horse is on pasture,** let her graze as much as possible. If your pasture has a shelter, she can be on it round-the-clock regardless of the weather. This is the most natural situation for a horse.

The right amount at each feeding time

For your horse's digestive tract to function at its best, she should consume a minimum of 1 to 2 percent of her body weight per day in long-stem dry matter, either pasture or hay. That means that the typical 1,000-pound horse should eat 10 to 20 pounds of forage daily.

If you aren't sure how much your horse weighs, buy a weight tape from your local tack-and-feed store. This tape allows you to measure your horse's girth and find her approximate weight. See Chapter 2 for details on figuring your horse's weight.

The weight of a flake of hay varies from bale to bale (see Figure 7-5), so it's important to get a sense of how heavy a flake is before you feed it to your horse.

Figure 7-5:
A flake varies in size, depending on the bale and type of hay.

In most cases, the amount of hours per day that your horse spends on pasture determines how much pasture grass she's consuming. Watch your horse's weight closely. If she's gaining weight, she may be getting too much pasture. If she's losing weight, she may not be getting enough to eat. Ask your veterinarian to help you evaluate your horse's condition when she's on pasture.

The right feeders

You see all kinds of feeders for horses on the market. The type of feeder you buy is determined in large part by your horse's enclosure. If you have your horse in a pasture with other horses and feed from a large bale, you need a big bale feeder. If your horse lives in a stall, you need a stall feeder.

Because horses are meant to eat with their heads down, using a feeder that enables the horse to eat close to the ground is best (see Figure 7-6). You don't want to put the hay directly on the ground because it encourages the horse to pick up dirt as she eats, which in turn can cause sand colic. (See Chapter 11 for more on this problem.)

Figure 7-6: Ground level feeders allow horses to eat in a more natural position.

Breaking down the significance of enzymes

Horses are nonruminant herbivores (they don't chew cud and they eat only plants), and derive their nutrition from forages. How? With the help of important elements called enzymes. They're responsible for helping the horse break down all that tough feed (have you ever chewed on a piece of hay?). The reason enzymes are important is a bit complicated, but if you're a horse owner, understanding the biology behind it is a good idea.

Here's how it works: Forages that horses eat have two carbohydrate components: soluble and insoluble. Soluble carbs are broken down into packets of energy by digestive enzymes that break bonds between the glucose molecules. The horse himself makes these digestive enzymes, which are very specific in the job that they do. When the enzymes break down soluble carbs, the carbs are absorbed in the small intestine along with minerals, vitamins, fats, and proteins. But the insoluble carbs, which the horse can't digest so easily, pass along into the fermentation vat known as the cecum.

Horses don't have the enzymes necessary to break down insoluble carbs, but they do have a great relationship with many different species of microorganisms that do have the enzymes that can break down insoluble carbs. Previously unusable food stuff can be used by both the microbe and the horse. The result of this fermentation is the production of energy packets called volatile fatty acids (or VFAs), certain microbial proteins, other digestive enzymes, and vitamins like vitamin K and B vitamins.

These microbe populations can be rather unstable, especially in horses who are stressed, or who quickly change from one diet to another as in the case of grain overload. These circumstances can cause changes in the microbial environment. And if the change is rapid and significant, a large number of these beneficial microbes die, often with dire consequences.

Here's an example of what can happen when the upset occurs: The resident microbe population is happily doing its job, digesting a diet of primarily hay with a small amount of grain. Suddenly, there's big change. The horse gets out of his stall, wanders into the feed room, and eats a large amount of grain. Some of the grain is digested by the small intestine, and a small amount of soluble carbs are absorbed, but because the horse's stomach is very small, the excess soluble carbs speed through the small intestine undigested and land in the cecum.

The microbes aren't prepared for this upset, but some bacteria thrive on the sudden change of food, and begin to multiply. The excess production of lactate by these organisms changes the acidity of the environment, causing death to a lot of other bacteria. When some of those bacteria die, they release endotoxins, which are absorbed into the bloodstream and can cause laminitis, colic, and — if severe enough — death.

Keeping your horse's enzymes balanced by making only slow and gradual introductions to new feed is vital. And because stress can cause an upset in the microbial population of your horse's digestive system, the use of probiotics in stressful situations can help keep your horse healthy. For more information on supplementing your horse with probiotics, see Chapter 8.

Feeders at ground level come in a variety of different styles, so simply pick one that appeals to you (you can ask your vet for advice on the safest types of ground feeders). Coauthor Audrey likes to feed her horses from big black rubber bins that are attached to a corner of the paddock.

Choosing to feed alone or in a herd

If your horse lives in a pasture or in a paddock with other horses, she's part of a herd situation. If she eats only pasture grass, you don't need to worry about whether to feed her alone or with the group because she's already eating with company. If your horse eats hay and lives in a large paddock with other horses, however, you need to decide whether you want to feed her separately. Although horses enjoy eating together, they also become territorial about their food. Because herds have a hierarchy, one or more horses inevitably become the low men on the totem pole and end up being chased away from the food.

If your horse is getting picked on when she tries to eat with the group — or if she's bullying another horse — it's a good idea to separate her at mealtimes. You can feed her in a stall and wait until she and the other horses have finished before returning her to the herd.

Chapter 8

Special Considerations for Your Horse's Diet

In This Chapter

▶ Exploring dietary supplements

▶ Rehabilitating horses with weight issues

▶ Feeding horses with allergies

▶ Changing behavior with diet

You know that hay or pasture is the basis of your horse's diet, and that you can add grain or other goodies if you so choose. (If you're not so sure, you can glean all this and more from Chapter 7.) But what if your horse has special circumstances? Can you do anything that's diet-related to help a horse with health or behavioral problems?

The answer is a resounding yes. In this chapter, we give you the lowdown on those dietary supplements that fill tack-and-feed store shelves. We also give you pointers on how to safely slim down a fat horse (or bulk up a skinny horse) and how to control equine allergies with diet. And last, but not least, we take a look at behavioral issues and how you can manage them with diet.

The Skinny on Dietary Supplements

If you've ever gone into a tack-and-feed store, you've seen The Supplements. They usually take up one or two entire aisles, and they have names and functions that you never even imagined would exist.

How are you to know whether your horse needs any of this stuff? And how are you to know how to shop for and feed supplements to your horse? We can help you with that — read through the information in the following sections.

Determining when supplements truly are necessary

Here's our philosophy on supplements: If your horse is generally healthy, if you spend your money on the best food for your horse (see Chapter 7 to find out what that is), and if you work and train her properly, you probably don't need any dietary supplements. (In fact, doing so may cause an imbalance in her body and even toxicity.) You need only one rule for the equine diet: Keep it simple.

Many people underestimate the activity levels of their horses; this can lead to not conditioning or exercising their horses enough to be competitive in whatever activity they like to do with their horses, such as showing, endurance, barrel racing, and so on. These folks try to make up the difference with supplements. No supplement is going to make a winner out of an average horse, or one who isn't in good physical condition. That said, if you want to try some supplements on your horse and see whether they improve her performance, keep flies away, or make her coat shine like a diamond, go right ahead. Just remember that certain vitamins and minerals can cause real problems if given to excess. (Read Chapter 6 to find out which vitamins and minerals can cause problems.)

Here are some situations where a horse may genuinely benefit from supplements (see the following section for the scoop on the different types of supplements we mention):

- ✔ **While in training:** Joint supplements may be useful because the horse's joints are being stressed. Antioxidants may be something to consider too, as long as you don't overdo the vitamin A. (See Chapter 6 for details on vitamin A.)

- ✔ **While under high stress:** Stress makes it difficult for the body to properly absorb nutrients. Horses undergoing extreme stress, like being shipped long distances or traveling extensively on a show circuit, may benefit from a vitamin supplement.

- ✔ **While pregnant:** The last third of a mare's pregnancy is very taxing on her body. Vitamin supplements designed for broodmares can be helpful at this time of gestation. (See Chapter 15 for more details on caring for pregnant mares.)

- ✔ **While nursing:** Nursing mares put out a lot of vitamins and energy to their foals in the form of milk. Vitamin supplements designed for lactating mares can help them stay in good condition during this time.

✔ **While eating poorly:** Horses who aren't eating much because they suffer from a chronic illness probably aren't getting all the vitamins they need. A supplement may be warranted in this case.

✔ **While eating marginal hay:** If you can't get good hay for part of the year because of a lack of supply due to weather or other issues beyond your supplier's control, you can supplement with vitamins and minerals. (Also consider using a good quality pelleted feed or hay cubes instead; we discuss these options in Chapter 7.)

✔ **While in the senior years:** Geriatric horses may benefit from vitamin and joint supplements. See Chapter 17 for more details on this.

✔ **While having hoof problems:** Horses with hoof problems (such as those in Chapter 11) may benefit from a hoof supplement containing biotin. First, be certain that you've ruled out any environmental causes such as overly dry conditions or stabling in shavings; both of these situations cause feet to dry out and become brittle.

✔ **While recovering from illness:** Horses who have been sick or suffering from an infection can benefit from supplements containing probiotics or prebiotics, especially if the horse has been on antibiotics.

- Probiotics contain the beneficial organisms that live in the horse's digestive tract and are necessary to proper function. Illness or the use of antibiotics can disturb the balance of these bacteria.

- Prebiotics are nutrients that encourage those beneficial bacteria to grow.

Your veterinarian can advise you about the use of probiotics or prebiotics in your horse.

If you're not sure whether you should be giving your horse a supplement for any of the preceding situations, don't hesitate to discuss your concerns with your veterinarian.

Surveying different types of supplements

Keeping track of supplements is difficult, because so much variety exists. Here are some of the most popular and useful types of supplement products that are out there:

✔ **Hoof:** Strong hooves are something that every horse owner desires, and you can find several supplements designed to make hooves grow tougher. They usually contain a type of vitamin B called biotin, which is believed to contribute to hoof growth.

- ✔ **Joint:** Supplements designed to help maintain healthy joints are probably the most abundant type of supplement on the market. Most of these products contain a combination of different ingredients, several of which may increase joint mobility.

  - Many joint supplements contain the compounds of glucosamine and chondroitin. Some also contain methylsulfonylmethane (MSM). We use joint supplements containing these ingredients because some of these products have been scientifically proven to work. Coauthor Audrey uses them for her senior Quarter Horse gelding, and coauthor Dr. Kate uses them for a number of her performance horses.

  - Other ingredients such as yucca and devil's claw, which are both natural anti-inflammatories, are sometimes used in joint supplements. Although no double-blind scientific studies have been done to prove that these ingredients help joints, enough anecdotal evidence exists to make adding these to your horse's diet a consideration.

- ✔ **Vitamins:** Just like humans take vitamins, so can horses. The difference is that if your horse is eating a quality diet of hay or pasture and has no special needs, she really doesn't need a vitamin supplement. However, your horse may need a vitamin supplement in certain situations, such as pregnancy (see the previous section).

Other types of supplements on the market include the following:

- ✔ **Allergy:** Horses can get allergies just like people do, and some supplements purport to help them with allergic symptoms. These supplements contain antihistamines, or all-natural ingredients designed to reduce inflammation. (We discuss other options for helping horses with allergies later in this chapter.)

- ✔ **Calming:** Supplements to help nervous horses contain anything from vitamin B to valerian root to L-tryptophan. All these natural ingredients have been shown anecdotally to relax the nervous system. Just be sure that your horse isn't nervous because of fixable issues like poor training, wrong diet, lack of exercise, or a stressful environment before you dose him with calming supplements.

  If you show your horse, be aware that some of the ingredients in these supplements will cause your horse to test positive on horse show drug tests, resulting in disqualification.

- ✔ **Electrolytes:** For horses who work hard and sweat a lot, electrolyte supplements are meant to replace electrolytes lost from the horse's body.

✔ **Fly control:** Natural supplements meant to keep flies at bay may contain powdered garlic. Garlic is purported to be unpleasant to flies, and horses who eat these supplements are supposed to be less attractive to the flying pests.

✔ **Skin and coat:** Every horse owner wants a horse with healthy skin and a glowing coat, and these supplements are designed to provide just that. They often contain different oils and minerals that are supposed to foster a healthy skin and coat.

✔ **Weight gain:** Some of these supplements, designed for underweight horses, contain high-calorie ingredients to help the horse gain weight. Others are made up of natural ingredients meant to promote healthy metabolism.

Supplements exist for just about every equine condition you can imagine. If your horse is in need of a particular supplement, your veterinarian will probably recommend one. If you see a supplement for sale that you think may be helpful to your horse, ask your vet about it.

Choosing a quality supplement

When you're shopping for dietary supplements, things can get tricky. Here are some guidelines:

✔ The Food and Drug Administration (FDA) doesn't control supplement labels on equine products, so determining the quality of the ingredients or the product is difficult. One way around this is to look for a seal on the label that says NASC. Short for National Animal Supplement Council, the NASC seal indicates that the ingredients in the product meet certain standards for quality.

✔ If you find that you can't clearly understand what's in the product or what levels of ingredients are inside without having to use a calculator, you should be concerned.

✔ Unrealistic claims as to speedy results or the effects of the product indicate that the manufacturer isn't being truthful. For example, don't trust a supplement that says it can cure something.

✔ Don't be fooled by higher and higher levels of active ingredients. Horses can assimilate only so much. The rest of the ingredients will be wasted — as will the extra money that you're paying for the higher dose.

If you aren't sure of the quality or quantity of a supplement that you're considering, talk to your horse's veterinarian. He or she is the best one to give you advice on this subject.

Feeding supplements to your equine friend

Most supplements are designed to be palatable to horses, who can be notoriously fussy about what they eat. Some supplements can be fed directly to the horse, added to pelleted feed, or given as a paste.

Follow the manufacturer's directions on the label when it comes to administering the supplement you want to give to your horse:

✔ If the label recommends that the supplement be a "top dressing" to feed, simply mix it with a commercial pelleted feed or hay pellets (see Figure 8-1).

✔ If the supplement is in a powder form, add it to a pelleted feed, mix in a little water, and stir the mixture before serving it to your horse (see Figure 8-2).

✔ A paste supplement calls for administering the paste directly into the horse's mouth with a syringe (see Figure 8-3). You do this by tying your horse securely by his halter and placing the tip of the syringe into his mouth. Depress the syringe plunger so the product goes into the horse's mouth and onto his tongue.

Figure 8-1: Some supplements come in pellet form and can be fed directly or mixed into feed.

Figure 8-2:
Use a small amount of a quality pelleted feed to mix with a powdered supplement.

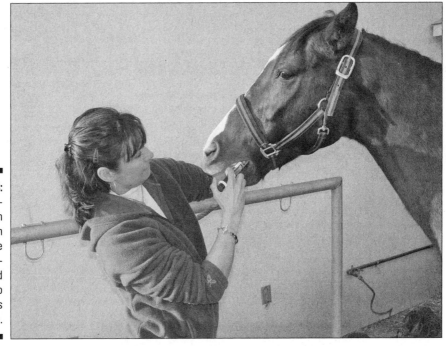

Figure 8-3:
Supplements in paste form must be administered directly into a horse's mouth.

The magic of good food

To illustrate how much a good diet matters to your horse's well-being (and to prove that you really don't need all kinds of supplements if your horse is being well fed), coauthor Dr. Kate tells a story of how she recently began riding with a new instructor to help improve her basic riding skills. The instructor has been everywhere and won everything at top levels in the American Quarter Horse Association world.

Upon arriving at Dr. Kate's 30-acre cutting horse ranch in Texas, the instructor was very impressed at how Dr. Kate's horses' coats gleamed even though they're out in the hot sun all day. The instructor wanted to know what kind of supplements Dr. Kate was feeding her horses.

When Dr. Kate showed the instructor the alfalfa and hay mix that she feeds her horses, along with the pasture they graze on, the instructor wouldn't believe it. After being at Dr. Kate's ranch for several weeks, she finally got it. Dr. Kate's horses get to be outside on pasture, and they're worked hard but they're not stressed. In short, Dr. Kate does everything that she and coauthor Audrey promote in this book. And it works.

Helping Horses with Weight Problems

Horses love to eat, no doubt about it. Put food in front of a healthy horse, and it's gone in no time. This penchant for chowing down serves the horse well in the wild, where food is scarce. But in captivity, when horses are given foods that are much higher in calories than the food that they'd find in nature, they can easily put on weight. Some horses are "hard keepers," however. This means that no matter how much they eat, they can't maintain a healthy weight. Both of these types of horses need specialized feeding programs.

Chubby equines

Being overweight is bad for your health, whether you're a human or a horse. Here are just a few dangers facing overweight horses:

✔ Too much weight on a horse puts considerable stress on his joints and can result in premature arthritis, or can aggravate existing arthritis and other joint problems. (See Chapter 11 for more information on arthritis.) Overweight horses can end up permanently unsound before their time as a result of their excess weight.

✔ Even worse than arthritis, overweight horses are at great risk for laminitis. This crippling disease causes the horse's coffin bone to rotate inside his hoof, rendering him lame, sometimes for life. (See Chapter 11 for more details on laminitis.)

✔ Overweight horses also are at risk of developing equine metabolic syndrome. (See Chapter 11 for more details on this illness.) Though much research is currently being done concerning this condition, a high starch/carbohydrate diet and subsequent development of insulin resistance is thought to be involved.

Horses who have too much poundage on their bones need help getting the weight off safely. Because the equine digestive system is designed to be constantly functioning, you can't just cut back solely on the amount of food you feed if you hope to take weight off your horse. You also need to change what you're feeding him.

Keep the following considerations in mind when you're dealing with an overweight horse:

✔ Some illnesses can cause a horse to gain weight no matter what he's eating. If your horse starts to become fat without an increase in his feed or a decrease in his exercise, contact your veterinarian before you change anything regarding his lifestyle. (In fact, be sure to talk to your vet before you make changes to your horse's diet for *any* reason.)

✔ If your horse is very overweight, ask your veterinarian to help you develop an exercise and feeding program for your horse. The vet should take into consideration the horse's current level of fitness, age, any soundness issues, and current body condition score. Flip to Chapter 5 for general information on exercising your horse.

See Chapter 2 for details on determining whether your horse is underweight, overweight, or at a normal weight.

Changing feed

If you read through Chapter 6, you know that certain types of horse food contain more fats and carbohydrates than others. If your horse is overweight, take a look at what you're feeding him:

✔ **Grains:** The first thing you should consider is grain. If you horse does only light or moderate exercise, and you're feeding him grain, that may be your problem right there. Grain — especially corn — is high in fats and carbohydrates, and can cause a horse to put on weight quickly.

A horse on a light or moderate work schedule likely doesn't need grain, so eliminating or reducing the amount may be the right move. (Talk to your vet about how much you should cut down.) If you're using grain to mix with supplements or medications, substitute a lower-carbohydrate option, such as a complete feed that's low in carbs and with no added molasses, and cut back on the amount you give.

✔ **Hay:** If your horse is eating legumes like alfalfa hay or clover, his weight problem may be a result of these higher-energy hays. Your horse likely isn't getting enough exercise to be eating this type of hay, so he needs something lower in carbs. A grass hay is a great substitution because it provides needed protein with fewer carbohydrates.

✔ **Pasture:** If your overweight horse is on pasture and you don't have another option as far as the type of forage that he's eating, consider confining him off the pasture for a few hours a day to see whether it helps him lose weight. (If you can't confine him, fit him with a muzzle for a few hours a day that will allow him to drink but not graze.) If he still doesn't lose weight, you'll have to keep him off the pasture even longer. To keep him from getting bored, feed him grass hay while he's confined.

The nutritional and caloric content of pasture changes with the seasons, so although your horse may get fat eating spring pasture 24 hours a day, that much fall pasture may not have the same effect on him.

Any changes you make to your horse's diet must be done gradually. Slowly introduce new feeds by making the new feed one-quarter of the horse's diet for the first three days. Then increase the new feed to one-half of the horse's diet. Maintain this amount for three days, and then add enough new feed to make it three-quarters of your horse's diet. If you're substituting a new food for one you plan to discontinue, continue this for three more days until you finally switch your horse over completely.

Decreasing feed

Cutting back on a horse's feed intake to encourage him to lose weight can be tricky. You don't want to deprive him of his intrinsic need to chew. You also don't want to create a situation where his stomach is empty for much of the day, because that can lead to colic, ulcers, and stall vices (see Chapter 11).

If you've already looked at what you're feeding your horse (see the previous section) and have determined that he's simply getting too much food, reduce the size of the portions you're giving him without cutting back on the number of meals he's getting. Another option is to decrease or eliminate any grain he's getting and to switch to grass hay or a grass-legume hay mix.

Use this method to determine how much to cut back on your overweight horse's feeding:

1. **Because the average 1,000-pound horse should get 18 to 20 pounds of hay per day, begin by gradually switching from the same amount of legume hay that your horse is currently getting to grass hay or a grass-legume hay mix; cut out any grains or concentrates that your horse is getting.**

   See how your horse does on this amount.

2. **If your horse continues to gain weight, cut him down to 15 pounds of grass hay or a grass-legume hay mix a day; if he maintains his weight but doesn't lose, cut him down to 14 pounds a day.**

Meanwhile, parcel this hay (whatever the amount) out into three to four feedings per day. Some horses eat more quickly than they ideally should. Horses in confinement — which is most horses these days — are especially bad about eating too quickly.

Weight loss should be gradual. *Do not* cut your horse's hay intake to less than 15 pounds per day (for a 1,000-pound horse). Horses fed minimal forage diets are likely under a significant amount of stress, predisposing them to developing gastrointestinal ulcers, colic, laminitis, and other diseases.

If your horse still doesn't lose weight after this feed change/reduction, contact your veterinarian.

Underweight horses

When it comes to weight issues, horses usually have more problems with being overweight rather than underweight. That said, some horses are known for being "hard keepers," meaning that it's tough for their owners to keep these horses at a high-enough weight.

If you have a horse who can't keep weight on, your first step is to have him checked out by a veterinarian. The vet should check the horse's teeth and talk to you about your deworming program (see Chapter 4 for general information about tooth care and deworming). He or she may then make some suggestions as to how you can boost the horse's calorie intake. This boost may involve giving the horse more of the same food, adding new foods, or changing the type of food altogether.

In some cases, horses can be hard to keep at a good weight because of genetic factors. Their metabolisms are such that they burn through calories at a higher rate than other horses and simply need more food to eat.

If deworming the horse, caring for his teeth, and increasing his feed don't solve the problem, the vet should follow up with a fecal exam and blood work to see whether a health problem is causing the weight loss.

Controlling Allergies with Diet

Horses get allergies just like humans do. Sometimes their allergies are airborne. Other times the allergies come from diet. Whether your horse's allergies are from what she's breathing, touching, or eating, a change in diet may help. (For more details on allergies, see Chapter 11.)

Recognizing signs of allergies

Horses show signs that they're allergic to something in different ways. These include:

- ✔ **Coughing:** When an allergen irritates a horse's airways, she coughs. This coughing may be intermittent or constant, depending on the severity of the allergy.

- ✔ **Loud breathing:** Horses can develop something called chronic obstructive pulmonary disease, or COPD (sometimes called "heaves"; see Chapter 11 for more information). Although COPD may not be caused specifically by allergens, it can be aggravated by them. Horses who have COPD breathe loudly, almost like they're wheezing. The loud breathing increases with exercise.

- ✔ **Hives:** Small itchy bumps that appear in a certain spot on a horse's body, or all over it, are hives. Hives can erupt when a horse comes into contact with something that she's allergic to, such as certain types of bedding or an insect bite. Breathing in allergens or eating something that she's allergic to can also trigger hives in horses.

- ✔ **Digestive upset:** Horses with allergies to food can get sick when they eat something that causes their immune system to overreact. One symptom of this may be diarrhea or loose stool.

If your horse shows any of these symptoms, allergies may be involved. Other life-threatening or contagious diseases may be involved, however, so a veterinary exam is recommended.

Checking out options for allergic horses

Horses who have allergies can benefit from changes in their diet. Depending on what your horse is allergic to, certain feeds can make a difference.

✔ Many horses who have allergies that affect their airways can benefit from eating feed that's low in dust. If your horse coughs a lot and your vet believes that she suffers from allergies, consider soaking her hay in a tub of water (enough to cover the hay) before you feed her (see Figure 8-4). Feeding the horse with a ground-level container is another good choice. Both methods reduce the amount of dust that wafts up her nose while she's eating.

Horses with allergic respiratory symptoms sometimes are forced to eat hay cubes or other types of complete feeds that are dust free. However, because horses need the roughage that comes with hay, we recommended feeding at least some hay, and soaking it first. Discuss this possibility with your vet.

✔ If your horse gets hives and your vet believes that the condition is being caused by food that she's eating, or if your horse gets digestive upset as a result of a food allergy, you need to find something for her to eat that doesn't trigger her immune system to overreact. Trial and error is often the best way to determine what food is most suitable for your allergic horse. Gradually switch your horse's hay or pasture to a different plant type and watch for an improvement in symptoms. For example, if your horse seems to be allergic to Bermuda, gradually switch her over to timothy to see whether that helps. If that doesn't do the trick, try another hay, such as orchard, or possibly alfalfa. Although food trials like this can be frustrating, if you persist, you may eventually find the right diet for your allergic horse. Your vet can help guide you through this process.

Figure 8-4: Horses with airborne allergies have less reaction to hay that's been soaked in water.

Affecting Your Horse's Behavior with Diet

You may have heard that children who eat a lot of sugary foods can become hyper. This is a classic case of how diet can affect behavior, and it applies to horses as well. Keeping horses calm requires a balance of food, exercise, and training. Overwork and/or stall confinement can actually make a horse seem more hyper when the actual problem is that the horse is nervous or stressed because he never gets any downtime.

That said, certain types of foods can cause horses to build up more energy than they can easily burn. The result is behavior that the average horse owner doesn't appreciate. The good news is that for many of these horses, a change in diet can literally change their personalities. (For the basics of handling misbehaving horses, flip to Chapter 3.)

Food-related misbehaviors

Most of the diet-related bad behavior seen in horses has to do with an excess of energy. Give a horse food that gives him gobs of energy and not enough exercise, and you have a recipe for disaster. Some horses are so affected by their diets that even hours of exercise every day won't calm them down.

Here are a few bad behaviors that can be food related:

- ✔ **Spookiness:** Ever ridden a horse who feels like he's going to explode out from underneath you? Who jumps at every sound and can't be consoled no matter how much you talk to him or try to distract him? Although many horses are just built to be spooky due to genetics or training, others may behave like this because they're getting too many carbohydrates.

- ✔ **Difficulty under saddle:** Some horses don't respond to training when being ridden. They can't seem to focus on the rider and want to do things like buck, run off, rear, or generally misbehave. Although most of the time this is due to poor training or riding, in some cases, it's the result of a diet that's way too high in carbohydrates.

- ✔ **Bad barn behavior:** If you've ever walked by a horse's stall in a barn aisle and had him come lunging at you, teeth bared, you know how unpleasant a cranky horse can be. Most horses who act this way are unhappy about something in their lives, or just don't like people, for whatever reason. Others are getting too many carbs and are crawling out of their skin with excess energy.

Not all horses react so violently to too many carbs in their diet, but enough do to make diet change one of the first recommendations vets and well-educated trainers suggest when clients express frustration with a horse's behavior.

Figuring out whether diet is the cause of bad behavior can be tricky. Discuss this possibility with your veterinarian before you look for other causes.

Changing your "hot" horse's diet

Take a close look at horses who are misbehaving for reasons related to diet, and you'll see that they're probably kept in stalls and are getting a legume hay (alfalfa in particular can make some horses high). Or, they may have a diet that includes grains, which are loaded with carbs. Another common ingredient in high-horse diets is *sweet feed,* a grain or hay mix or commercial feed containing molasses. The excess carbohydrates in each of these types of feed convert to sugar in the horse's body, which becomes unhealthy energy with nowhere to go.

Take these high-carb foods away from a "hot" horse and you just may see a change in personality. If you suspect that your horse may be one of these carb victims, cut out the grain and the sweet feed, and switch to a grass hay from a legume hay. Give your horse a month on his new diet to see whether it helps. If it doesn't, you may have a training or genetic issue. Get help from a professional trainer. (For details on how to find a good trainer, see *Horses For Dummies,* 2nd Edition, written by coauthor Audrey with Janice Posnikoff, DVM, and published by Wiley.)

Chapter 9

Growing Your Own Food

. . . .

In This Chapter

▶ Getting a grip on growing basics

▶ Discovering how to grow and maintain pasture

▶ Harvesting hay

. . . .

*I*f you're fortunate enough to have a lot of land at your disposal and are also a stickler about your horse's health and nutrition, this is the chapter for you! Growing food for your horses is a rewarding pastime, and your equine buddies will be happier and healthier for the experience. You'll save yourself a bundle of money on feed, too.

In this chapter, we tell you how to grow your own pasture and how to maintain it. We also educate you on the ways of turning that pasture into hay that you can store away for winter months. When you're done reading this chapter, you'll have a good idea of what's involved in being a self-sufficient horse owner.

Before You Begin: The Basics of Growing Food for Horses

Horses love pasture. It's not only good for them nutritionally, but it also satisfies their ever-burning need to graze. Wild horses are constantly browsing for food in their environment, and domestic horses who are robbed of this activity can suffer both physically and emotionally from this loss.

Of course, to grow good pasture (or good hay, for that matter), you have to know what you're doing. Your horse's very life depends on it. Fortunately, it's not that hard, and after you figure out how to do it, you'll find that it becomes an enjoyable part of your regular routine. In the following sections, we cover some basics for you to consider before you take the plunge and start growing food for your horse.

The benefits of growing food

The best thing about pasture is that it gives the horse a chance to do what comes naturally to him: graze! Because a pasture is the most natural environment for your horse, it's what he would prefer. So if you have a choice, let your horse graze on pasture instead of cutting it, or make it into hay, at least for part of the year. If you live in a cold climate where pastures just don't grow in the wintertime due to a deep freeze (and most people in the U.S. do), you'll have to feed your horse hay anyway for a part of the year. You can either grow that hay yourself or buy it from another source.

Additional benefits of growing pasture include the following:

- **Growing pasture saves you money on hay.** If you decide to cut your pasture and turn it into hay, you need the right equipment and manpower to get the job done. See the later section "Harvesting Hay for the Future" to find out exactly what this process entails.

- **Growing pasture is less work.** You don't have to feed your horses every morning if they're on fully sustainable pasture — they feed themselves.

- **Pasture saves you money on vet bills in the long run.** Pasture-kept horses have fewer problems with colic and lameness. You may even save time and money on training too. Horses who live in pastures have fewer behavioral problems than stall-kept horses.

A hard look at the responsibilities of growing food

Before you run out and plant a pasture, it's important to realize that taking on this venture requires considerable care and maintenance. You can't just turn your horse loose in a field full of plants and think that you have your horse on pasture. You have to make sure that the right plants are growing in the field, and you have to fertilize and irrigate the field, rotate the pasture, clean the pasture, and keep a close eye on it to make sure that it's producing the right type of nutrition for your horse. (Don't worry; we explain how to do all these tasks later in this chapter.)

Turning pasture into hay for your horse requires additional work. You need to cut, bale, and store the hay, which means you need the equipment to do these tasks or you must hire someone to do them for you. See "Harvesting Hay for the Future" in this chapter for more information on growing hay.

If you aren't willing or able to commit to this kind of workload, reconsider your ideas about keeping your horse on pasture. You can always go back to it later when the time is right.

Starting and Maintaining a Pasture

In order to grow a pasture and keep it in good shape, you have to maintain it. This maintenance takes work, so be prepared. After you take in all the information in the following sections, think long and hard about whether you want to get involved in this endeavor. It's rewarding, but it does require real commitment.

A new pasture can take a couple of years to mature enough to accommodate grazing horses, so be patient.

The stuff you need before you do anything

In order to successfully keep horses on pasture, you need some basic things. These basics include:

- **Land:** You can grow pasture on as much as 40 acres of land or as little as 40 square feet of land — and everything in between (see the nearby sidebar "Hope for the pasture challenged"). But you do need soil that's workable in order to pull it off. Ask your county extension agent to evaluate your soil for workability.

- **Fencing:** You need good fencing materials and secure gates if you hope to keep your horse safely in a pasture. You can use any type of fencing that's suitable for horses (pipe, no-climb woven wire, wood, PVC). Get the best fence that you can afford. Never use barbed wire for horses — they can easily become tangled in it and seriously injured.

Hope for the pasture challenged

Many people don't have room on their property for a proper pasture. You may be working with an acre or less of land, and just don't have room for one or two pastures to sustain your horse. If this is the case, don't despair. You can still give your horse the opportunity to indulge his natural instincts to graze. Simply create a small area that your horse can use as "pasture," even for just an hour or two daily.

When coauthor Dr. Kate lived in Las Vegas — which isn't an area that's known for acres of lush green pastures — she planted a 60 x 60 foot square area of Bermuda grass and watered it with a simple garden hose sprinkler. She let each of her five horses have about an hour daily in that area. When the pasture began to look overgrazed, she cut back on the time the horses spent there.

Because it was a small area, Dr. Kate rented an aerator once a year to keep the soil from becoming compacted and to make sure that it remained productive. She also kept the area fertilized and watered for optimum productivity. Even though it was only a small area, Dr. Kate's horses really looked forward to their grazing time.

> After your fencing is installed, you need to walk it frequently to look for holes, sagging, or any damage or problems that could be hazardous to your horse.
>
> ✔ **Irrigation:** Unless you live in a tropical rainforest, you have to water your pasture on a regular basis. Plan this out ahead of time. (See the section "Irrigating" later in this chapter for details.)

Make sure that you plan for all these necessities before you establish your pasture. You want to be prepared before the pasture starts growing.

Deciding what to plant

The types of forage you're able to grow depend on your geographic location, how much average rainfall you get, and which grasses are most resistant to local insect pests. (If you have an irrigation system, rainfall will be less of an issue for you when you're determining what to plant.)

Grow a combination of forages in your pastures so that your horse has a variety. Each species of grass will grow and be most productive at different times during the season. And if you add legumes to your pasture, in addition to grass, you fix nitrogen into the soil too.

To discover the best pasture grasses to grow in your particular area, consult with your USDA Cooperative Extension System agent. (See the appendix for the address of the USDA Cooperative Extension System office's Web site.) This individual can give you great advice about what grows well where you live, as well as what kind of treatment you need to give your soil for optimum pasture nutrition.

Letting your horse mow your lawn

Although it may be tempting to toss grass clippings to your horse after you mow your lawn, resist the urge! The size of grass clippings is too short for your horse to chew. The result is that the clippings can easily wad up into a ball in the esophagus and cause the horse to choke. Instead, let your horse mow the lawn for you with his teeth. Horse-proof your lawn first by looking for anything your horse could cut or scrape himself on, and make certain that you fertilize only with organic fertilizer. Don't use insecticides on your lawn, either. You may need to replace your sprinkler heads with industrial strength versions, but your horse will love you for the opportunity to help with gardening chores.

Preparing the ground

Before you can plant your pasture, you need to prepare the soil. Unless you have all the equipment on hand to do this, you may want to hire someone to do it for you (such as a neighbor who works his own pasture or a pasture maintenance service). Here are the general steps to follow:

1. **Till the soil with a plow or rotary tiller, and then work it with a mulcher.**

   Tilling aerates the soil and removes clumps of dirt.

2. **Level the field with a harrow.**

   The soil should be fine and without large clods or chunks of dirt before you plant the seed.

3. **Have your local county extension office test the soil.**

   You want to make sure that the pH level is just right for the plants you intend to grow before you put down that precious seed.

Seeding

Seeding a pasture isn't as easy as seeding a flower garden. You can't just toss the seeds out and hope for the best. (Actually, you could, but this technique would be wasteful.) Consider hiring an expert with the right equipment for this task if you're growing a pasture for the first time. Such folks include neighbors who are experienced with growing pasture or a pasture maintenance service.

Have an expert with the right equipment drill the seeds into the soil as they're planted. The best depth is from ¼ to ½ inch, although the ideal depth can vary from grass to grass. Get help from your county extension agent.

You may also want to consider planting a nurse crop, such as oats. A nurse crop helps the seedlings sprout by anchoring the soil and protecting them from the sun. (You plant the nurse crop seeds alongside the hay seeds.) You can harvest the nurse crop the next season, leaving the young hay exposed to light when it's ready.

The best time of year to seed your pasture is in the fall — the moisture in the winter and spring will help it grow.

Irrigating

Your pasture needs water in order to grow and survive. If you're lucky enough to live in a climate with a lot of rain, nature does much of the work for you. If you live in a dry climate, your pasture grass depends on you to keep it alive. How you choose to provide water depends on how big your pasture is, as well as your resources, time restraints, and personal preferences. Use the information in the following sections to help you irrigate your pasture in the best way possible.

Sticking to a few basic irrigation rules

Irrigating takes a bit of knowledge, but after you know the basic rules, you can water your pastures with success. Here are some rules to follow:

✔ Don't graze horses on freshly irrigated pasture because it damages the grass.

✔ Learn the water needs of your grasses, and don't over- or under-water.

✔ Test the quality of your water to ensure that it doesn't contain too much salt or too many minerals. Too much salt or minerals can store up in the soil and affect its fertility. Your local county extension agent can test your water for you.

✔ Irrigate early in the morning when wind and sun are low.

Getting water

If you have a tiny pasture, irrigation isn't too difficult. You can water your pasture the way you water your lawn: with sprinklers. But if you have a bigger pasture, you need a more sophisticated method.

Here are some methods of pasture irrigation. Choose the method of irrigation best suited to your pasture needs:

✔ **Sprinklers:** One way to water a large pasture is with multiple sprinklers hooked up to a traveling system. The system operates unattended and shuts off automatically when it's finished.

✔ **Flooding:** This method allows you to open a valve and flood the surface of your pasture with water. This calls for more labor than a sprinkler system because you have to monitor the water flow and shut it off before it reaches the end of the field. Also, if your land has slope, undulates, or is very sandy, this type of irrigation won't work very well.

✔ **Water reels:** Water reels are a popular choice for a lot of pastures, especially larger ones. The water reel moves through the pasture on its own, and can negotiate difficult terrain and work around trees and other objects.

Before you invest in an irrigation system, make sure that you have a reliable water source. You need from 5 to 20 gpm (gallons per minute) from a well or stream to effectively water a pasture.

Knowing how often to irrigate

Too much or too little water can stress your plants. Grazing plus stress from poor irrigation can leave you with sorry pastures.

The actual amount of water to give your pasture varies depending on where you're located. Information on pasture water use, also called *evapotranspiration*, is available at your local USDA Cooperative Extension System office. (See the appendix for full contact information.) This info can help you determine how often you should water.

The frequency of irrigation also depends on the kind of grass that you're growing. Find out how much water your crop needs by discussing it with your county extension office. Then, purchase soil moisture sensors to keep track of how wet your soil is, and to help you figure out when you need to water.

You can also figure how much to water based on the idea that many pastures should receive an inch of water every five days. If natural rainfall doesn't provide this much water, you need to provide it with irrigation.

The type of soil you have determines how much you should water, too. Loam types of soil hold more water than sandy soil, so they don't require as much irrigation.

Cleaning

Just because your horse is out to pasture doesn't mean that you don't have to pick up the poop! Keep your pastures clear of manure by breaking up piles or picking up manure at least once a week. Reasons for doing this include:

- ✔ Horses won't eat where they poop. Who can blame them?
- ✔ Internal parasites re-infect your horse if he's forced to graze near manure.
- ✔ Flies multiply if you leave manure lying about the field.

Either use a piece of equipment known as a drag to disperse manure piles (thereby breaking up parasite incubators) or use one of the newer vacuuming devices designed to pick up manure in pastures. You can find these devices at farming supply stores.

Fertilizing

If you want to keep your pasture grass nutritious, you need to fertilize it. Grazing depletes the grass of nutrients, and fertilizing pasture spares you the expense of having to reclaim soil that's been destroyed by improper care.

To know what kind of fertilizer to use for your particular crop in your area of the country, take soil samples. Your county extension agent can help you with this task and can also tell you how frequently to fertilize the type of pasture you've chosen. Keep in mind that if you want your pasture to be organic, you have to use only organic fertilizers.

Aerating

Horses walk while they graze, which is great for their legs. Unfortunately, it's not great for the pasture. All this walking compacts the soil and makes it more difficult for grass to grow and for soil to absorb water.

To combat this, you need to aerate your pasture on a regular basis. The frequency depends on your soil type, the amount of rainfall you get, and the number of horses you keep on the pasture. A county extension agent can help you determine the frequency rate. You can aerate the pasture yourself by investing in an aerator (the type you push for small jobs, or the kind you pull with a tractor) or by hiring someone who provides this service.

To help reduce the need for frequent aeration, don't graze your horses during or right after a rainfall. Give the pasture a chance to dry out. Grazing on wet ground increases the soil compaction rate.

Managing your pasture

In order to have continued good forage and healthy horses who get the nutrition they need, you need to manage your pasture. Maintaining a pasture is much cheaper than reclaiming one and starting from scratch. Here are some tips on how to best maintain your horse's pasture:

✔ **Take soil samples.** Taking soil samples of your pasture either in the spring or fall of each year is a wise maneuver. Have the sample analyzed by your local USDA Cooperative Extension System office so that you know the general health of your soil, and whether you need to add anything to it.

> ✔ **Practice rotational grazing.** Whenever possible, divide your pasture
> into at least two areas so that your horse can graze on one part while
> the other part "rests" for at least one season, depending on the type of
> grass you're growing. Resting enables your pasture to recover from
> repeated grazing.
>
> ✔ **Use weed control.** Practice weed control to keep your pastures healthy.
> Coauthor Dr. Kate doesn't use herbicides at all, but she controls weeds
> by mowing intensively before the weedy plants bud and go to seed.
> Eventually, the good grasses take over and crowd out the weeds. Yes, it's
> more labor-intensive, but it's better for the environment in the long run.

Harvesting Hay for the Future

Some people not only graze their horses on pasture, but also like to grow
their own hay. Growing hay is a lot of work, but it's rewarding. You save money
on feed, and you have the satisfaction of knowing exactly what your horses
are eating. You can even grow your hay organically to be sure that your horses
aren't ingesting any herbicides or pesticides.

Before you can start harvesting your own hay, you need to find out about
cutting, baling, curing, and storing hay.

Cutting hay in your pasture

The second cut of hay from a pasture during its second year of growth is usually
the best stuff to feed to your horse. Generally, during the first season, the hay isn't
mature enough. And the first cutting usually isn't high enough in quality to feed
your horse. (It's fine for cows, though, if you or your neighbors have any of those.)

The time of the season when you cut your hay is very important, as is the
weather. (When you cut your hay depends on the crop you're growing; your
county extension agent can advise you on the right time.) Too much rain can
result in wet, moldy hay, and weather that's too dry can leave you with dried-
out hay. Watch the weather and cut when the air is dry but not too hot.

Plant maturity is another issue tied in with the time of season to cut. Less
mature plants have more leaves than they do stems, so they're more nutritious.
On the other hand, they don't give as much yield as more mature plants. Again,
your county extension agent can help you learn the nuances of hay maturity
and nutrition, depending on the type of hay that you're growing and where
you live.

After the hay is cut, usually with a sickle-bar mower, it's left in piles called *windrows*. The hay sits and dries out in these windrows until it's ready for baling (see the next section). The amount of time it takes the hay to dry out depends on the level of humidity in the air at the time of the cutting. To help the hay dry, you can turn over the windrows a few times. (If you're inexperienced in cutting hay, have an experienced neighbor help you or hire a service to do the work.)

Baling and curing hay

When the hay in the windrows is dry, the baling process begins. In some parts of the country, you need to get up very early to get the job done. The morning dew helps keep the stems and leaves together during the baling process. In other regions, the hay has too much moisture in the morning and needs some time in the sun to dry properly for baling conditions.

Waiting until later in the day when it's hot leaves you with bales that aren't very good. In fact, they can be dangerous because harmful bacteria can grow inside them.

A hay baler, which is pulled by a tractor, determines the size of the bales. Most hay for horses is baled with a hay baler that yields bales weighing about 40 to 60 pounds. The hay baler compresses the hay into a bale, and then ties it together with baling twine. (You need someone with this equipment and experience baling to help you with this work. Hay baling services are available for hire.)

After you bale the hay, you may leave it out in the field to continue curing. This allows more of the moisture in the bales to evaporate before you move them indoors. This curing process can take anywhere from one day to three or more, depending on the weather and humidity levels.

Hay that's damp and kept inside is susceptible to mold, which can be dangerous to your horse's health. It can also cause the hay to start to ferment, which can lead to combustion, allowing the hay to catch on fire all by itself.

Storing hay

After your hay is baled and cured, you should store it indoors away from rain or snow. A three-sided building often is best for storage because it allows the hay to ventilate while still protecting it from getting wet and moldy.

If your only option is to store your hay outdoors in an uncovered area, be sure to cover it with a tarp to prevent it from getting wet. Check your tarp regularly too, to make sure that it doesn't contain any holes. If your hay gets wet, remove the tarp immediately and let the hay dry out as soon as you can by opening the bales and spreading the hay around. Leaving wet hay under a tarp encourages mold to grow.

When storing your hay on the ground, use wooden pallets underneath it to keep the hay from touching the ground, where moisture can get to it. Another option is to keep your hay in a barn loft so that you don't have to worry about the bales making contact with the ground.

Part III
Recognizing and Treating Illnesses

The 5th Wave   By Rich Tennant

"I'm hearing a lot. He either has intestinal problems or I've found your iPod Shuffle."

In this part . . .

In Part III, we explore diseases and conditions affecting horses. We start with a tour of the horse's body, followed by a description of the most common equine ailments and infectious diseases. We also give you a primer on first aid for horses, along with an introduction to complementary and alternative therapies.

Chapter 10

Introducing the Anatomy of a Horse

*Y*our horse is of course a beautiful creature on the outside, but did you know how awesome she is on the inside too? The horse has an amazing anatomy, designed to function in perfect harmony with her environment.

Knowing some of the details of how your horse's body works can help you take good care of your equine companion. It gives you a sense of what's happening when things are going right — and when things are going wrong.

In this chapter, we give you a tour of your horse's body. You discover all the important systems and how they work. You also explore the major organs, and other important stuff like teeth, ears, and hooves.

The Workings of Your Horse's Innards

Your horse's body is made up of a number of systems, each responsible for a different function. Put all these systems together and you have an incredible living creature known as the horse.

For your horse to stay healthy, it's vital that each of these systems functions properly and in conjunction with each other. In the following sections, we take a look at what goes on inside your horse's body and makes her tick. You can check out the details of these systems in the color section.

Start your engine: The cardiovascular system

The cardiovascular system — also known as the circulatory system — is one of the most important systems in your horse's body. This system is responsible for moving blood from one part of the body to another. It's essentially the engine that runs your horse's body, and it's the foundation for all other systems.

The cardiovascular system is responsible for moving nutrients, wastes, and gases to and from cells throughout the body. It's also responsible for stabilizing body temperature and body pH. It involves three different elements: the heart, the systemic circulation, and the pulmonary system. Arteries and veins are part of both systemic circulation and pulmonary circulation, and blood itself runs through everything.

Fortunately, cardiovascular ailments are rare in horses.

The heart

The equine heart is more than just a place where your horse's love for you resides. It's a four-chamber muscle weighing about 10 pounds that pumps blood throughout the blood vessels in her body. The equine heart is particularly powerful, as you might imagine, because it has the task of circulating blood through the horse's rather large mass.

The famous racehorse Secretariat was found after his death to have an abnormally large heart even for a horse (along with very large lungs). This is believed to be the reason he was able to run with such incredible speed.

The equine heart is very much like the human heart. It has left and right chambers, left and right ventricles, and a series of valves, veins, and arteries. The difference is that the horse's heart can pump about 40 quarts of blood per minute. That's a lot more than the human heart, which pumps only about 4 quarts in that same amount of time.

Pulmonary circulation

The reason for the circulation of blood in the horse's body is to spread oxygen to various parts. That oxygen comes from the air your horse breathes, and gets into the horse's blood through the lungs, or pulmonary system. Pulmonary circulation is the part within the cardiovascular system that sends blood to the lungs so that it can be enriched with oxygen before it goes to the rest of the body.

It works like this: Blood without oxygen (which is deep red in color, by the way) enters the right atrium of the heart and then moves into the right ventricle.

From there, it's pumped through the pulmonary arteries to the lungs, where it picks up oxygen. The oxygenated blood is then pumped out of the heart and into the rest of the horse's body.

Systemic circulation

While the heart works as a pump to move blood around your horse's body, the systemic circulation aspect of the cardiovascular system works to carry oxygenated blood from the heart to the rest of the body, and then back to the heart after the oxygen has been removed. A system of arteries, veins, and blood vessels moves blood throughout the body.

Essentially, the systemic circulation keeps the blood flowing, spreading much-needed oxygen to cells in different parts of your horse's body.

Arteries and veins

In order for oxygenated blood to be carried away from the heart, it needs a passageway. This comes in the form of arteries, which are flexible tubes. Some arteries are large, while others are smaller. They can be found in various areas of the horse's body (as you can see in the color section in the center of this book).

Veins are made up of blood vessels that carry blood with very little oxygen toward the horse's heart. From there, the blood is sent through special pulmonary arteries, where it gathers oxygen before returning to the rest of the body through the arteries.

Blood

You know what blood is, but do you know what it's made of? Whether you're talking about horse blood or human blood, the essence is the same. Both are made up of red blood cells, white blood cells, and platelets. These elements are contained in a protein-rich fluid called blood plasma. Here's more info on each:

- **Red blood cells** provide transportation of oxygen to different parts of the body, via the arteries.
- **White blood cells** help stave off infection from invading organisms.
- **Platelets** govern the consistency of the blood.
- **Plasma** serves to hold all the other components of blood together and provides immunoglobulins and clotting factors. If you were to separate the elements of blood in a test tube, a majority of what you'd see would be plasma.

Eat up! The digestive system

A very important system in the equine body is the digestive system. Horses are virtual eating machines, designed to consume food for nearly 18 hours a day. So, as you can imagine, their digestive systems are designed to work overtime.

The horse's digestive system consists of the mouth, pharynx, esophagus, stomach, pancreas, intestines, liver, rectum, and anus. Each of these body parts serves a distinct function in helping your horse's body obtain nutrients from her food.

When a horse's digestive system stops functioning properly due to illnesses or a particular condition, colic is often the first symptom. In Chapter 11, you find details on a variety of problems that affect the function of the equine digestive system.

The mouth

The process of digestion begins with your horse's mouth. The mouth not only provides entry to the digestive system, but also begins the digestive process.

When your horse chews her food, her teeth crush it into tiny particles. The food mixes with saliva and becomes moist, and then slips down into the esophagus through the pharynx.

The pharynx

Shaped like a funnel, the pharynx is a six-inch muscular sac in the area where the *trachea* (the tube that leads to the lungs) and the *esophagus* (the tube that leads to the stomach) meet. When your horse eats, her food passes quickly through the pharynx. After the food gets past this point, it can't go back into the mouth.

The esophagus

Next in the process is the esophagus, a tubular muscle that's nearly five feet long. It begins in the pharynx and feeds into the stomach. A wave-like process called *peristalsis* moves food that has been moistened with saliva down through the esophagus and into the stomach.

In the horse, the esophagus is a one-way street. The peristalsis can go only from the top down to the stomach. This is one reason why horses can't vomit.

The stomach

The next destination for the swallowed food is your horse's stomach, which is shaped like a J and pretty small, considering how big the horse is. (It can hold only from 5 to 15 liters at a time.) The entrance to the stomach is governed by the cardiac sphincter, a muscle that opens to allow food to come in, but it doesn't allow food to come out.

After the food reaches the horse's stomach, it's enveloped by digestive juices, which begin the process of breaking it down. The stomach then sends the food on to the intestines, where the majority of the nutrients are absorbed.

The pancreas

Some of the digestive juices that the stomach uses to begin to break down the cellulose material that your horse ingests come from the pancreas. Called *pancreatic juices,* these substances consist of enzymes that are alkaline in nature.

The pancreas also produces hormones, including insulin, which helps regulate blood sugar.

The intestines

The intestines are the most impressive part of your horse's digestive system. Your horse has 70 (or more) feet of intestine inside her abdominal cavity. The intestines absorb most of the nutrition from your horse's food.

The intestinal tract consists of the small intestine and the large intestine:

- ✔ The stomach empties into the small intestine, which contains the duodenum and the jejunum. Both the duodenum and the jejunum have a part in digestion; the duodenum breaks down food in the small intestine, and the jejunum absorbs nutrients from the food.

- ✔ The small intestine is connected to the large intestine (also called the colon) via the ileum. Microbes in the large intestine are responsible for breaking down the plant fiber ingested by the horse. Many of these critters are in part of the intestines called the cecum. The *cecum* joins the ileum on one side and the large intestine on the other.

  Without the amazing cecum, the horse wouldn't be able to digest its food. The comma-shaped bit of intestine can hold as much as 30 liters of fluid, and is considered part of the large intestine.

The liver

Your horse's liver is part of her digestive system; it converts amino acids into fat and glucose or glycogen, metabolizes ammonia, and keeps the horse healthy by purifying her blood like a filter. It serves several other functions: It stores glycogen, which is important in energy, and it synthesizes proteins found in blood plasma.

The rectum and the anus

After your horse has finished digesting her food, waste moves to the rectum, which is about one foot in length. From there, it goes to the anus, where it's projected out of the horse's body. That's when you come in, manure fork in hand, and clean it up.

Raging hormones: The endocrine system

If you've ever wondered where your hormones come from, wonder no more. The endocrine system — a series of small organs — produces the hormones in your body. Oh, and in your horse's body too.

The organs that make up the endocrine system are the hypothalamus, the pineal gland, the thyroid, the parathyroid, the thymus, the pituitary gland, the adrenal gland, the pancreas, and the ovaries or testes, depending on the gender of your horse. Each of these organs produces a different type of hormone. Hormones regulate all kinds of stuff in your horse's body, including adrenaline, thyroid, insulin, estrogen, testosterone, and progesterone, to name just a few.

As you probably know, hormones affect not only the way your body functions, but also your moods. This is true of your horse too. For example:

✔ Adrenaline kicks in when your horse spooks at something.

✔ If you have a mare, varying levels of estrogen and progesterone cause her to develop the equine version of PMS when she goes into season.

✔ If you have a stallion, you've no doubt seen his assertive attitude toward mares and sometimes life in general; this attitude is the result of testosterone.

Fighting off germs: The immune system

The immune system is a complicated series of protein types, organs, cells, and tissue, all interacting in a complex and elaborate way. The function of your horse's immune system is to protect her from viruses, bacteria, parasites, and any other foreign organism or material that may compromise her health.

Of all the elements that make up the immune system, white blood cells, also known as leukocytes, serve as one of the body's defensive linemen. When an outside invader enters the body, white blood cells attack the offending party and render it helpless.

The lymphatic system is another important part of your horse's immune system. A network of lymph nodes in your horse's body produces phagocytes, Pac Man-like cells that may remove bacteria and cancerous cells in the bloodstream.

When a horse's immune system becomes weakened, she becomes more susceptible to illness. The bone marrow doesn't produce enough white blood cells to combat invading organisms, and the lymph nodes don't produce enough phagocytes. The result is that the horse easily becomes infected by viruses or bacteria that exist in the environment. (Check out Chapter 12 for an introduction of common infectious diseases that may affect your horse.)

Sometimes the immune system becomes hyperactive, overreacting to foreign bodies and causing a problem as a result. Allergies are a good example of this problem. Horses who suffer from allergic reactions are victims of a hyperactive immune system that's overreacting to the pollen, dust, or other allergens in the horse's environment. (For more information on allergies, see Chapter 11.)

Strong stuff: The muscular system

Your horse is a pretty muscular beast, as you have no doubt noticed. In fact, her muscular system is one of the most incredible things about her. It's what gives her the ability to run like the wind, spin on a dime, and buck like a fiend.

More than 60 percent of your horse's body is made up of skeletal muscle. These muscles come in bundles, which are in turn made up of muscle fibers. These fibers contract to make the muscles move. Fascia, a fibrous tissue, covers the muscles. Muscles attach to one another through the fascia, and attach to bone through the tendons.

Tendons are important because they're vulnerable to injury and can render a horse lame if they're damaged. This is most true of the tendons found in your horse's legs. These include the common digital extensor, the lateral digital extensor, the deep digital flexor, and the superficial digital flexor. A tendon sheath protects tendons that extend over joints, and contains synovial fluid, which works as a lubricant.

Disorders of the muscles and tendons are one of the biggest issues for horses because they're athletes. Horses who are worked hard can damage muscles and tendons. See Chapter 11 for more information on muscle and tendon injuries.

Feeling sensitive: The nervous system

The most complicated system in your horse's body is easily the nervous system. You could say that the nervous system is a big part of what makes your horse who she is. So much of her personality and functionality are the result of workings in her nervous system.

Your horse's nervous system is made up of two subsystems: the central nervous system and the peripheral nervous system.

- **The central nervous system** consists of your horse's brain and spinal cord.
- **The peripheral nervous system** is made up of the cranial and spinal nerves, nerve ganglia, and the autonomic nervous system.

The central nervous system is largely responsible for your horse's behavior. It also controls your horse's senses, in conjunction with the peripheral nervous system. What your horse sees, feels, tastes, and hears is all deciphered by the central nervous system. The way she reacts to these stimuli is also a function of her nervous system. (Check out Chapter 3 for details on the connection between your horse's health and behavior.)

If your horse is nervous, does that mean that she has more nerves in her body than a naturally calm horse? No, but her nervous system may be more sensitive than that of a quieter horse.

Breathe in, breathe out: The respiratory system

If you ride your horse in any kind of performance event — or even if you just enjoy watching her gallop across the pasture — you can appreciate her glorious respiratory system.

Horses have pretty much the same respiratory organs and processes that humans have. The biggest difference is the size. Your horse's nasal passages are very long compared to yours. Her lungs are tremendous too, compared to a human being's lungs. This isn't surprising, of course, because such a large animal needs to be able to take in a lot of air.

When your horse breathes, she inhales air into her nasal passages with the help of her diaphragm. The air passes through her trachea, into her lungs via the bronchial tubes. Here, oxygen is taken from the air and transferred to the blood (see the earlier section "Start your engine: The cardiovascular system" for more information). The remaining carbon dioxide is exhaled back out through the nostrils.

Horses are susceptible to many of the same respiratory problems as humans, including allergies, chronic obstructive pulmonary disease, and pneumonia. For more information on respiratory problems, see Chapter 11.

Boning up on the skeletal system

The horse has a big skeleton, which serves several purposes. It provides a frame for the body, protects the organs inside it, and supports soft tissue.

Your horse has around 205 individual bones in her body. These include the following:

- ✔ Long bones, which help the horse move
- ✔ Short bones, which absorb concussion that's the result of movement
- ✔ Flat bones, which enclose the organs
- ✔ Irregular bones, which encase the central nervous system (which we discuss earlier in this chapter)

Your horse's skeleton is held together by tendons and ligaments. Tendons attach muscle to bone, and ligaments attach bone to bone. The joints are essentially the flexible parts of your horse's skeleton, which allow the individual bones to move independently of each other.

Cartilage is also part of your horse's skeletal system, and is located at the ends of your horse's bones. Cartilage is nourished by synovial fluid (joint fluid). Because it's pliable, it's often the first place to show wear and tear, even in your horses.

Horses are prone to skeletal injuries, which can be very serious because of the weight of the horse's body. Broken legs are difficult to repair, and fractured skulls are usually fatal. For details on conditions and injuries of the lower skeleton, see Chapter 11.

Wasting away: The urinary system

Ever heard the expression "pee like a racehorse"? Well, part of that term comes from the fact that racehorses are sometimes given diuretic drugs, which make them urinate a lot. The other reason for this expression is that horses have pretty big bladders!

The horse's urinary system is responsible for producing, storing, and eliminating urine. Urine is the liquid waste that the kidneys produce. The kidneys filter waste from the blood, as well as excrete and reabsorb water and electrolytes to help keep the body's blood electrolytes balanced. Horses have two kidneys, just like humans do, although the equine kidneys are much bigger. Each weighs almost 2 pounds.

The urine produced by the kidneys is mostly made up of water, and contains only a small portion of solid waste. After production in the kidneys, urine moves to the bladder and is excreted through the horse's urethra.

You can tell a lot about a horse by her urine. Horses with abundant, clear or light-colored urine are well-hydrated. Horses who have darker, shorter streams of urine may not be drinking enough water. A horse's urine may also change depending on what she's eating. And very copious, clear urine can signal a kidney or endocrine problem.

The good news is that kidney disease and urinary issues in general are pretty uncommon in horses. As long as your horse has plenty of fresh water to drink, she's unlikely to ever develop kidney or urinary troubles. Flip to Chapter 6 for more about the importance of water in a horse's diet.

Important Parts on the Outside of Your Horse

Your horse's internal organs and systems are pretty darn important, but what about all the stuff that you can actually see on the outside? How important is that? Well, very, of course. Without those external body parts, your horse couldn't function. Or at least not very well! In the following sections, we introduce you to some of the most important outside parts of your horse.

Figure 10-1 shows different parts on the outside of a horse's body. The terms in Figure 10-1 aren't anatomical (like those in the following sections); they're simply meant to help horse people identify different areas of the equine form.

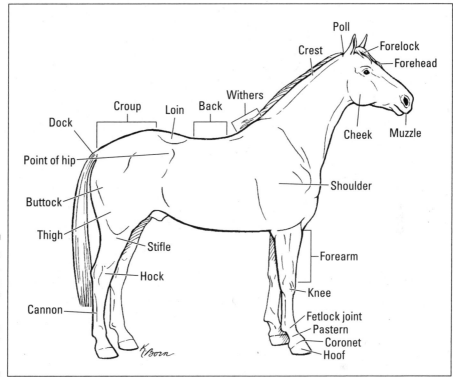

Figure 10-1:
Non-anatomical names of some of the horse's outside parts.

To serve and protect: The skin

The horse's skin is more than just a covering for his body. It's actually an organ — and the largest organ in your horse's body. Made up of different layers called the epidermis, dermis, and subcutis, the skin holds hair follicles, sweat glands, and sebaceous glands (see Figure 10-2).

The most important role that your horse's skin plays is protecting him from invasion by outside pathogens. The skin serves as a barrier, keeping your horse's vital organs from coming into contact with bacteria that could cause serious damage.

Your horse's skin also serves as insulation, keeping his internal organs from becoming too cold or too hot, in response to outside temperatures. And because his skin is sensitive to touch, it also protects him by keeping him apprised of possible dangers in his environment.

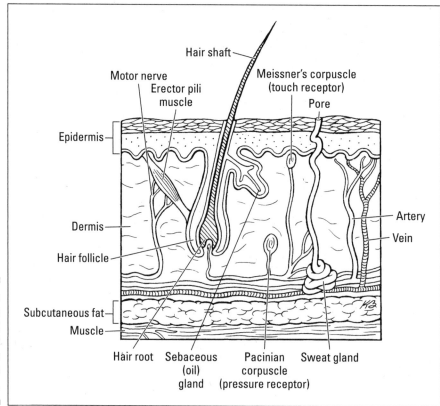

Figure 10-2:
The skin is considered an important organ in the horse's body.

When your horse's skin is damaged by trauma, it forms scar tissue as it heals. During the healing process, before the wound resolves into a scar, granulation tissue may be produced in significant quantities. Some areas of the horse's body are particularly prone to producing an excessive amount of granulation tissue when a wound isn't managed properly. Another common name for excessive granulation tissue is *proud flesh*.

Your horse's skin is susceptible to fungal and bacterial infections, as well as injuries. See Chapter 11 for more information on these kinds of problems.

Looking at the eyes

The eyes are the windows to the soul. This is true not only of humans, but of horses as well. The equine eye is very expressive, and horse owners who know how to read their horse's eyes become good at judging their horse's moods.

Although the eyes are a good way to determine your horse's state of mind, they're also highly functional external organs. The horse has a very large eye that's built very similarly to the human eye. The exterior of the eye has a cornea, pupil, iris, and sclera, just like the human eye, as well as upper and lower eyelids. Further in, the eye contains a lens, retina, optic disc, and optic nerve. Horses also have a third eyelid, which helps protect the eye from trauma. Figure 10-3 shows a side view and an anterior view of the equine eye.

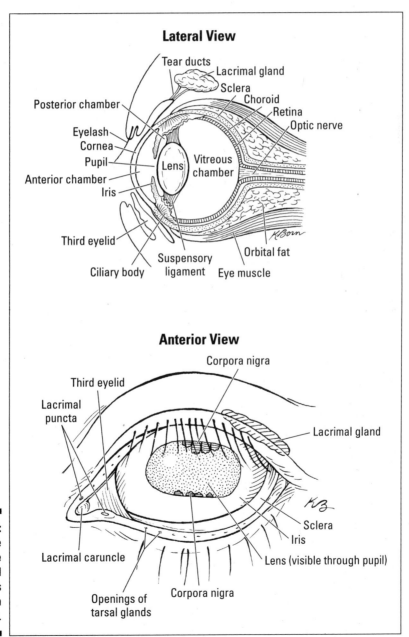

Figure 10-3: Horses have a large eye with good capabilities for seeing in the dark.

Your horse is equipped with better night vision than you are. He also has a very wide range of vision on either side of his head. On the other hand, he can't see well directly in front of his nose or directly behind him.

Unfortunately, several ugly conditions and diseases can affect equine eyes. Keeping a close eye on your horse's eyes is important because such problems must be treated immediately. See Chapter 11 for more details.

Listen up: The ears

The equine ear does more than just allow the horse to hear. It also provides a great way to judge how a horse is feeling at any given moment. Horses use their ears as tools of expression, and to send messages to other horses. (See Chapter 3 for an illustration of equine expressions, and take note of the ears.)

Besides mood gauges, your horse's ears are also functional — they detect sound. Because horses evolved as prey animals, they're astute at picking up noises that could possibly be a predator lurking in the bushes, or approaching in the distance. Watch a horse's ears swivel around to take in various sounds and you get a good sense of how these sound receivers really work.

The inside of your horse's ears are similar to yours (see Figure 10-4). They contain pinna, an ear canal, an ear drum, cochlea, vestibule, and semicircular canals. All these parts work together to collect sound from the environment and pass it along to the horse's brain for filtering. They also provide a source of balance and body position for the horse.

Horses are prone to a few different ear problems. Ear ticks can get into the horse's ear canals and cause head rubbing and much discomfort. Gnats can also bite the insides of the horse's ears and make them sore. In cold climates, the tips of a horse's ears can be lost due to frostbite.

If you suspect any problems with your horse's ears (he tilts his head, shakes it a lot, or rubs his ears on objects), contact your vet immediately.

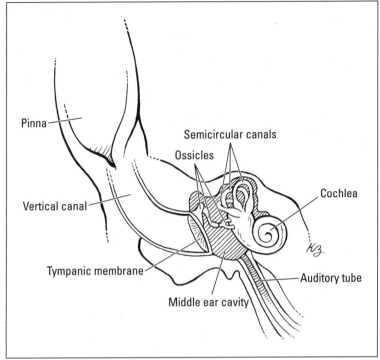

Figure 10-4:
The horse's
ears provide
him with the
ability to
hear sounds
at a
distance.

Taking a bite out of the teeth

You have no doubt noticed that your horse has a lot of teeth. Anywhere from 36 to 44, to be exact. They break down like this (see Figure 10-5 for the top and side views):

- ✔ Twelve of those are incisors, used for grasping and tearing food.

- ✔ Twenty-four of your horse's teeth are cheek teeth; they grind the food down into fine particles before he swallows it.

- ✔ Horses (usually only males) also may have four canine teeth, which are located between the incisors and the molars.

- ✔ Some horses have two wolf teeth, which are found just in front of the upper molars. Occasionally, horses have four wolf teeth, two upper and two lower.

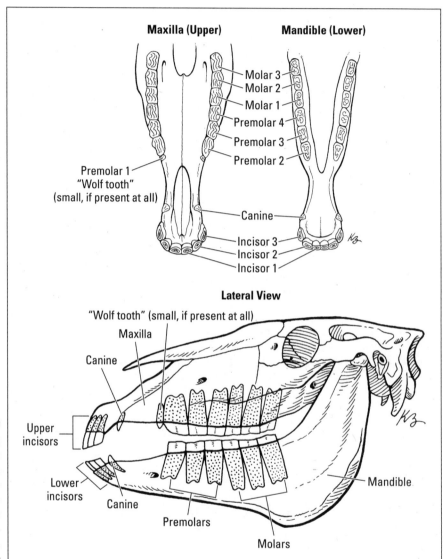

Figure 10-5:
The horse's
mouth
contains
anywhere
from
36 to 44
teeth.

Your horse's teeth grow continuously, and will do so throughout most of his life. This constant growth keeps the teeth from being worn down into useless nubs from all that grinding of tough plant material. However, in horses who are kept in domesticity, the fact that the horse's upper jaw is wider than his lower jaw creates a problem. The upper-outside teeth and lower-inside teeth have nothing to wear against as they grow, and ridges and sharp points result. These areas restrict the horse's normal side-to-side rotary chewing motion.

This restriction causes pain to the horse when he chews, and may cause him to drop his food. These sharp points can also cause sores, or ulcers, on the lining of the cheeks or on the tongue. Horses with this problem tend to chew their food abnormally or incompletely. They can be prone to choking, colic, or weight loss (see Chapter 11 for more about colic). These sharp points also hurt the horse when the noseband is tightened and when the bit hits the horse's teeth.

To keep ridges and points from getting to the point where they hurt your horse, you need to have his teeth filed — called floating or dressing the teeth — periodically. See Chapter 4 for more details on this procedure.

Step on it: The hooves

The expression "no hoof, no horse" is truer than we'd like it to be. Your horse's hooves are the foundation for his structure and his ability to move. If they aren't in good shape, neither is your horse.

Your horse's hooves are made of what's called cornified material, which is a tough, fibrous protein. The bottom of the hoof is made up of the heel, bars, frog, sole, outer wall, and white line. The hoof wall is divided into sections: the toe, quartet, and heel (see Figure 10-6). The hard, insensitive areas of the hoof — the heel, bars, frog, sole, heel bulbs, and the outer wall — are called the *hoof capsule,* and are made of *hoof horn.* The hoof capsule houses and supports structures such as the coffin bone, the very important hoof-shaped bone within the horse's foot. Between the coffin bone and the hoof capsule is tissue lined with blood vessels and nerve endings, called the laminae. (See Chapter 11 for more about the coffin bone and the laminae.)

A cool trick: Telling your horse's age by looking at his teeth

You may already know that you can tell a horse's approximate age by looking at his teeth. As a horse gets older, the length, color, shape, and markings of his teeth change. As the teeth grow, the surfaces also wear down and change their shape. Dark marks in the surface of the teeth — called *dental cups* — slowly appear and then disappear with age. The number and condition of dental cups visible in a horse's mouth may aid in determining the horse's approximate age.

A mark in the horse's upper incisors called the *Galvayne's groove* also helps determine age. The mark appears on the outside surface of the upper incisors after a horse hits about 10 years of age. As the horse ages, the groove expands downward. By the time a horse reaches 20, the groove extends all the way to the end of the tooth.

The function of your horse's hoof is not only to carry your horse's weight and protect it from excessive impact from the ground, but also to protect the coffin bone and laminae from damage. The frog portion of the hoof acts as a cushion that aids in the circulation of the lower leg.

When your horse stands or moves, weight is borne on different parts of his hoof, depending on the way that he's built and how he moves. Wild horses don't need to have their feet trimmed because they gradually wear them down as they move in their daily lives — as much as 20 miles a day. Domestic horses who are barefoot don't move as much as wild horses and therefore don't wear their feet down naturally. Horses who wear shoes can't wear down their feet at all. That's why domestic horses need their feet trimmed by a farrier. (See Chapter 4 for more information about hoof care.)

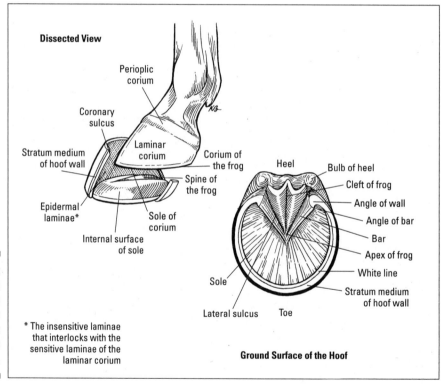

Figure 10-6:
The hoof is the foundation of the horse's body.

* The insensitive laminae that interlocks with the sensitive laminae of the laminar corium

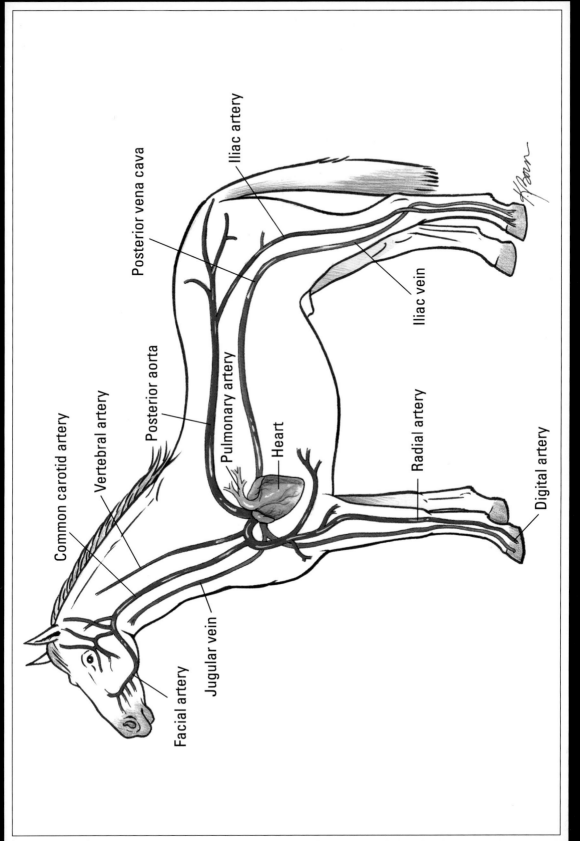

Common carotid artery

Vertebral artery

Posterior aorta

Pulmonary artery

Heart

Facial artery

Jugular vein

Radial artery

Digital artery

Posterior vena cava

Iliac artery

Iliac vein

The cardiovascular system — also known as the circulatory system — moves nutrients, gases, and wastes to and from cells throughout the body. It also stabilizes body temperature and body pH. See Chapter 10 for more information.

A horse's digestive system (viewed here from the left side) is made up of many different parts, each of which serves a distinct role in helping the horse's body obtain nutrients from food. Chapter 10 has the scoop on this system.

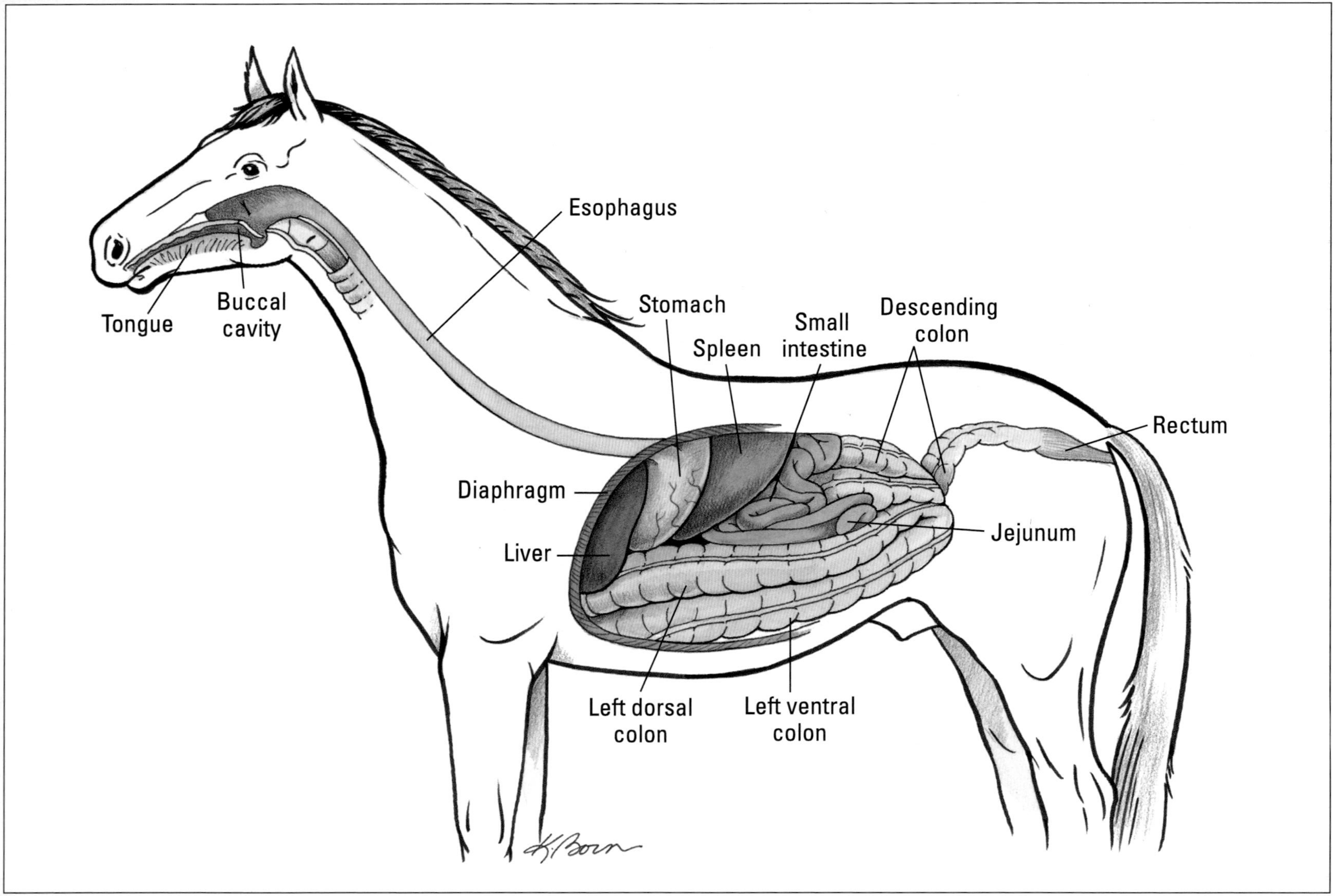

Esophagus
Tongue
Buccal cavity
Stomach
Spleen
Small intestine
Descending colon
Rectum
Diaphragm
Liver
Jejunum
Left dorsal colon
Left ventral colon

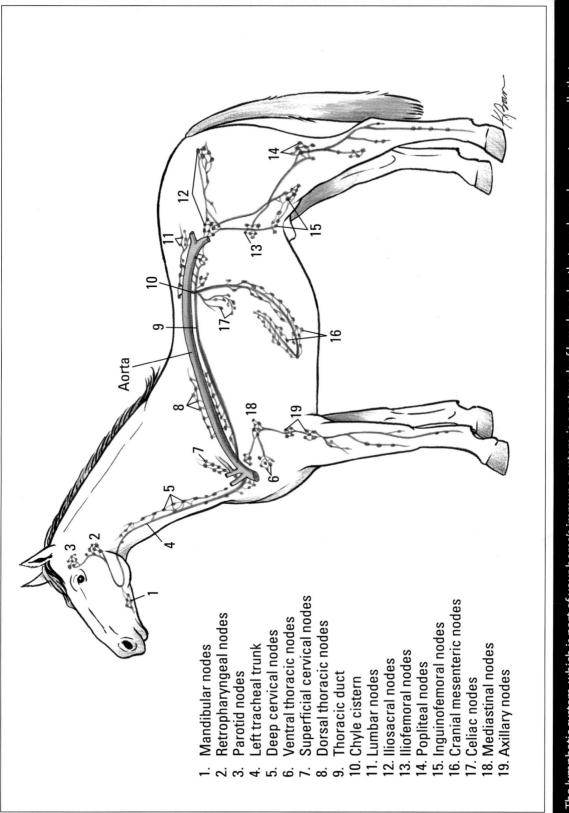

1. Mandibular nodes
2. Retropharyngeal nodes
3. Parotid nodes
4. Left tracheal trunk
5. Deep cervical nodes
6. Ventral thoracic nodes
7. Superficial cervical nodes
8. Dorsal thoracic nodes
9. Thoracic duct
10. Chyle cistern
11. Lumbar nodes
12. Iliosacral nodes
13. Iliofemoral nodes
14. Popliteal nodes
15. Inguinofemoral nodes
16. Cranial mesenteric nodes
17. Celiac nodes
18. Mediastinal nodes
19. Axillary nodes

The lymphatic system, which is part of your horse's immune system, is a network of lymph nodes that produce phagocytes — cells that remove bacteria and cancerous cells in the bloodstream. Flip to Chapter 10 for more about the lymphatic and immune systems.

A horse's muscles come in bundles, which are in turn made up of muscle fibers. Fascia, which is a fibrous tissue, covers the muscles. Muscles attach to one another through the fascia and to bone through tendons. Head to Chapter 10 for full information.

Nasolabial levator muscle

Canine muscle

Zygomaticoauricularis muscle

Obicularis palpebrum muscle

Subscapulohyoideus muscle

Splenius muscle

Cervical ventral serrated muscle

Cervical trapezius muscle

Thoracic trapezius muscle

Thoracolumbar fascia

Gluteal fascia

Superficial gluteal muscle

Semitendinous muscle

Femoral biceps muscle

Digital extensor muscles

Fascia lata

External oblique muscle

Thoracic ventral serrated muscle

Ascending pectoral muscle

Masseter muscle

Buccinator muscle

Brachiocephalic muscle

Sternomandibular muscle

Cervical cutaneous muscle

Subclavian muscle

Deltoid muscle

Brachial triceps muscle

Descending pectoral muscle

Carpal and digital extensor muscles

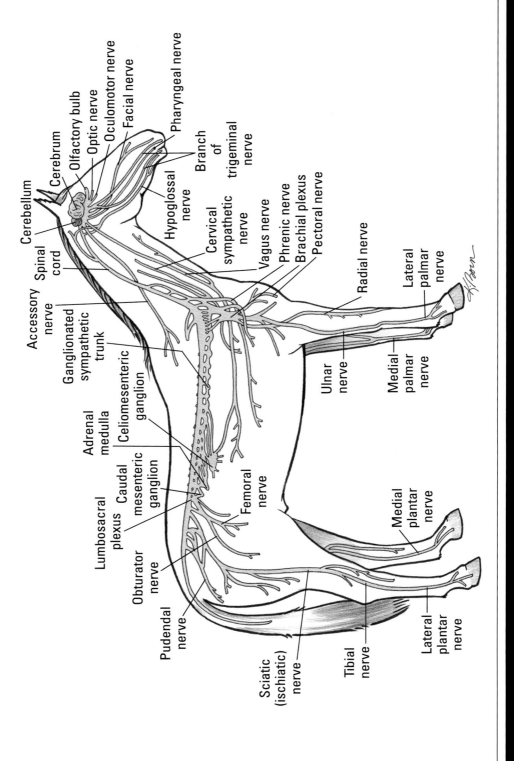

The most complicated system in a horse's body is the nervous system. The nervous system is made up of two sub-systems: the central

Horses have pretty much the same respiratory organs and processes that humans have; the biggest difference is the size. Flip to Chapter 10 for details.

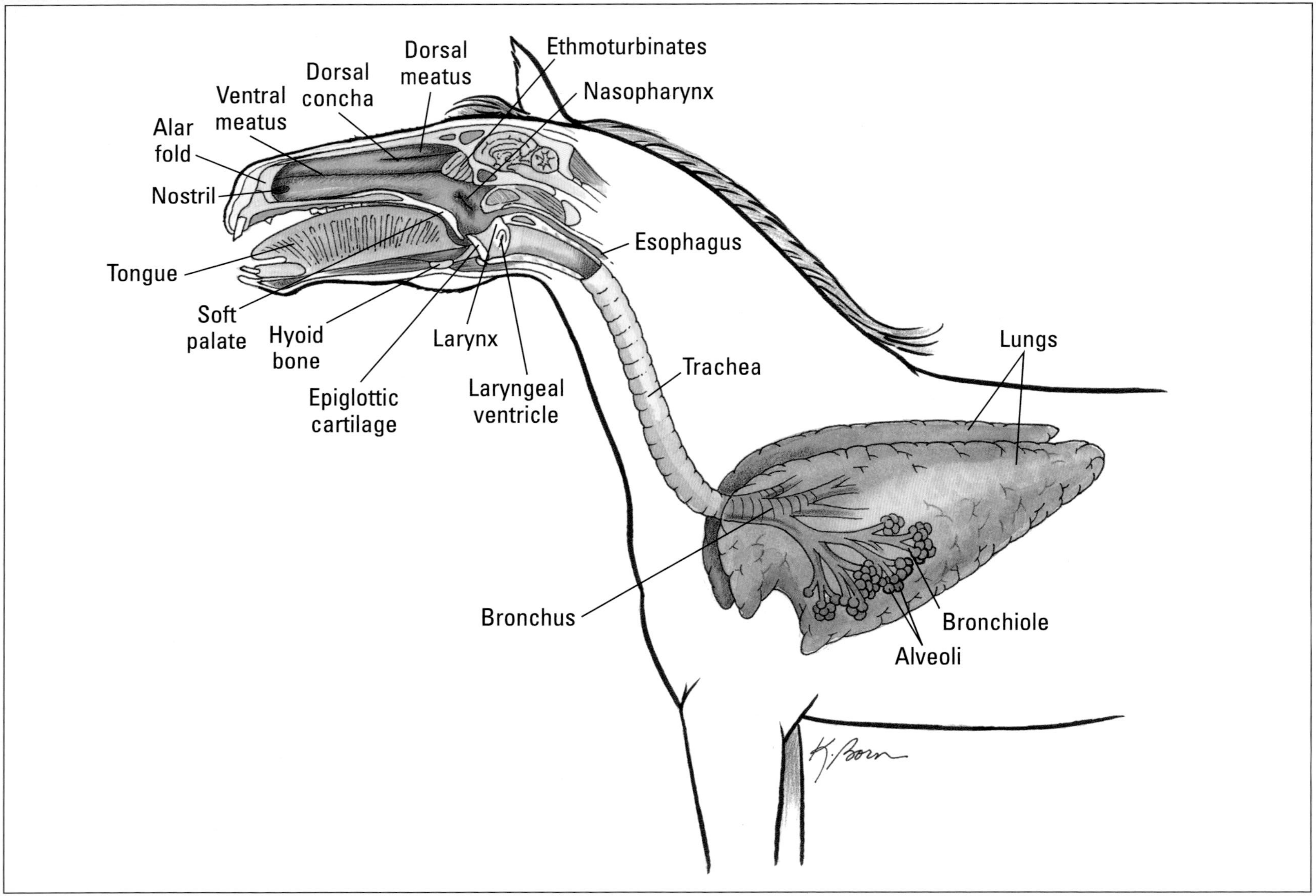

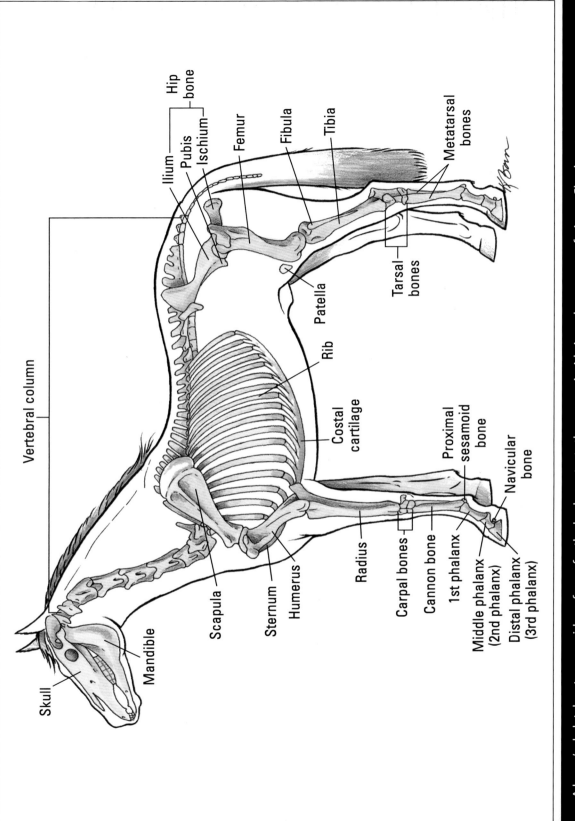

A horse's skeletal system provides a frame for the body, protects the organs inside it, and supports soft tissue. Check out Chapter 10 for more information.

The horse's urinary system (shown here in a stallion) is responsible for producing, storing, and eliminating urine, which is liquid waste produced by the kidneys. See Chapter 10 for more about this system.

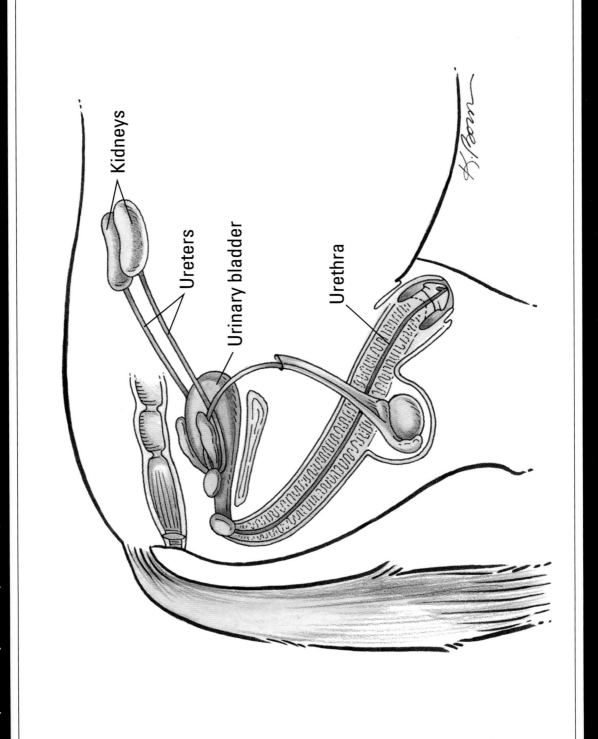

Kidneys

Ureters

Urinary bladder

Urethra

Chapter 11

Tackling Common Ailments

Considering how big, strong, and powerful horses are, it's amazing how prone they are to illness. Some people (like your authors, for example) believe that many of these problems are related to the way that humans manage horses in captivity. Wild horses don't suffer from most of these issues, in large part because they live the way nature intended horses to live.

In this chapter, we help you get a handle on some of the problems your domestic horse may unfortunately encounter. You find out about soundness and digestive troubles, which are the two most prevalent health issues for horses. You also discover illnesses affecting the horse's skin, eyes, respiration, and metabolism. Hopefully, when you finish perusing this chapter, you'll have a good handle on the kinds of conditions that your horse may be prone to.

Getting a Leg Up on Soundness Issues

One of the most widespread health issues in the horse world concerns soundness. *Soundness* refers to a horse's ability to move freely and without pain, at all the natural gaits (walking, trotting, and cantering), and to be free of any disease. Unfortunately, many horses become unsound at some point in their lives, and some become so permanently.

Recognizing unsoundness in your horse and understanding the various causes make it easier for you to help your veterinarian give your horse the help that he needs.

Arthritis

Arthritis is the most common cause of soundness problems in horses. Basically, arthritis is an inflammation of the joints. Horses tend to develop arthritis in their knees, hocks, and fetlocks (see Chapter 10 for an illustration of these parts of the horse). The joints become painful, and the condition tends to worsen over time.

Veterinarians recognize four different types of arthritis:

✔ **Degenerative joint disease (DJD).** The most common form of arthritis, degenerative joint disease develops as horses age. Horses who have been worked hard are most likely to develop this type of arthritis.

Most cases of DJD affect the hocks. The knees are the next most commonly affected joint, followed by the fetlocks and stifles. Horses with poor conformation and those who have worked hard in their lives are most susceptible to this condition.

Symptoms of DJD can include chronic stiffness and swelling around a joint, inability to perform activities that used to be easy, and bumps or swellings on the legs.

Your veterinarian has a few different treatment options available to tackle DJD. The goal with each is to stop the cycle of inflammation in the joint. Stopping the cycle may include injection of the joint with hylauronic acid. Other treatments may include corticosteroids, non-steroidal anti-inflammatories, and oral joint supplements containing glucosamine, chondroitant, and MSM. Alternative therapies, particularly acupuncture and Traditional Chinese Veterinary Medicine, have also proven helpful. (See Chapter 14 for details about alternative therapies for horses.)

DJD can't always be prevented, but you can help minimize the likelihood that this debilitating condition will cripple your horse. Keeping your horse's feet trimmed properly (see Chapter 4 for details), riding him on surfaces that provide good footing (such as a well-maintained riding arena or flat, rock-free trails), and not working him too hard, especially when he's not properly conditioned, can help stave off DJD.

✔ **Septic joint arthritis.** Septic arthritis occurs when the horse has an infection of the joint and the by-products of the infection and accompanying inflammation cause degradation of the cartilage. This degradation causes a change in the biomechanical properties of the cartilage.

An infected joint in an adult horse can be the result of direct trauma with an accompanying bacterial or fungal contamination. The most common causes of joint infections are puncture wounds, infection secondary to joint injections, and surgery followed by a generalized bacterial infection. Heat, pain, and severe lameness are signs of septic arthritis.

If your horse ever suffers a joint injury, call your veterinarian right away. Septic arthritis can be not only career-ending, but also life-ending.

Your veterinarian will treat this condition with antibiotics or another drug, depending on the type of organism affecting the joint. Arthroscopic surgery may also be necessary to treat the joint.

To help prevent septic arthritis, have your horse seen immediately if he experiences a joint injury.

✔ **Immune-mediated arthritis.** This type of arthritis is actually quite rare in horses. Experts suspect that immune-mediated arthritis is secondary to lupus erythematosis, an immune-mediated disease that causes the immune system to go haywire and destroy normal tissue. Although considered rare, coauthor Dr. Kate suspects that veterinarians may be diagnosing this illness more in the future because its existence is becoming more well-known.

Symptoms can include joint pain, lameness, lack of appetite, and fever. Treatment includes anti-inflammatory medications and chemotherapy drugs. Veterinarians don't know how to prevent immune-mediated arthritis.

✔ **Traumatic arthritis.** Traumatic arthritis is common and caused by repetitive injury or sometimes an isolated trauma to the joint. Horses who are worked too much and too hard can suffer from this type of arthritis. It's similar to DJD (see the earlier bullet), and viewed as the same by some veterinarians. It's usually treated with the same remedies.

Hoof problems

Issues that arise because of some insult to the hoof can cause problems for your horse. The good news is that these problems are fixable, and they're often preventable with good care.

Hoof cracks

Hoof cracks are just what they sound like: cracks in the hoof. They can begin from the coronet band and extend downward, or begin at the toe and go upward. Cracks that extend from the bottom up are most common, and may be due to poor hoof care. In these cases, the hooves become overly long, brittle, and dehydrated. (Chapter 4 has tips on good hoof care so that your horse can be clear of cracks.) Some cracks are secondary to a condition called seedy toe, where the hoof wall separates from the sensitive laminae — not a good thing!

The major types of cracks include the following:

- Hoof cracks that start from the bottom up may not be a big problem, but if your horse develops one of these, you need to determine why it occurred. Also, if the crack progresses and extends into the deeper structures of the foot, it can lead to a hoof abscess (see the next section for more information).

- Cracks that are consistently found at the quarters and heels of the hoof are a concern. The horse needs to be evaluated for poor conformation or poor shoeing or trimming practices.

- Hoof cracks that start at the coronet band and go down are usually caused by an injury or trauma, and result in a lack or unusual growth of horn at the injured site. You've likely seen a similar crack in people who have had an injury to their fingernail bed and forever after have a deformed nail.

Your veterinarian should treat any trauma to your horse's coronet band immediately. Deep infections or trauma to this part of the hoof can cause severe and permanent problems.

Common and simple hoof cracks often can be easily treated by a good farrier. A special shoe may be applied, and the horse may be limited to stall rest or only very light exercise while the crack grows out.

Hoof cracks are best prevented with good hoof care. Make certain that your farrier knows what he or she is doing. (For details on how to find a good farrier, see *Horses For Dummies,* 2nd Edition, by coauthor Audrey with Janice Posnikoff, DVM [Wiley].)

Hoof abscesses

A hoof may seem like a weird place for an abscess, but horses get them all the time. Hoof abscesses can cause severe lameness. Often, they start at the bottom of the hoof at the white line and work their way up into the laminae. They eventually break open at the coronary band and drain out. The subsolar abscess is usually caused by a puncture wound on the bottom of the hoof that becomes infected. Abscesses can cause sudden and severe lameness.

Veterinarians diagnose hoof abscesses by observing clinical symptoms and examining the limb. If the lameness is sudden and on only one leg, and if an increased digital pulse is present, an abscess is likely. Sensitivity to hoof testers may also point to an abscess.

To treat an abscess, your veterinarian may open it up on the sole of the hoof by using a hoof knife. By opening the abscess, the veterinarian enables it to drain out with the help of gravity. He or she then soaks the hoof in Epsom salts, or other drawing agents, because this helps draw out the pus from the abscess and reduce inflammation. The vet may also choose to administer anti-inflammatory drugs.

The prognosis for hoof abscesses is usually very good. Most horses recover fully in three to five days. (Figure 11-1 shows the treatment of an abscess.)

To avoid having your horse go through this unpleasant ordeal, keep your pastures free of nails and other debris that your horse can step on. Examine your horse's feet daily for nails and puncture wounds. If you find anything, contact your veterinarian immediately, even if your horse isn't showing signs of lameness.

Figure 11-1:
To soak a hoof for treatment of an abscess, ask the horse to stand in a pan of water and Epsom salts.

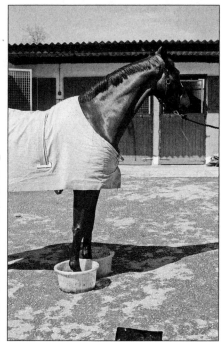

Bob Langrish

Laminitis

One of the strangest soundness problems that affects horses is laminitis. Also known as founder, this condition results when the lamina in the hoof are severely inflamed. This inflammation can lead to disruption in the attachment of the coffin bone to the hoof, allowing the coffin bone to rotate out of its normal alignment. The consequence of this rotation is tremendous pain in the affected leg. Figure 11-2 shows a normally aligned coffin bone, and Figure 11-3 shows laminitis.

Figure 11-2: A normal coffin bone maintains the same angles as the horse's hoof.

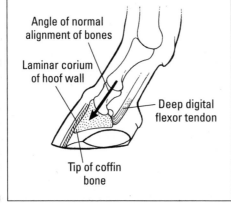

Angle of normal alignment of bones

Laminar corium of hoof wall

Deep digital flexor tendon

Tip of coffin bone

Figure 11-3: Laminitis causes the coffin bone to change angles within the hoof.

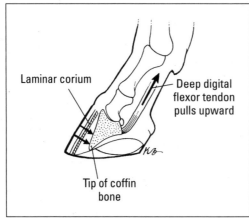

Laminar corium

Deep digital flexor tendon pulls upward

Tip of coffin bone

The causes

Laminitis occurs when the blood supply to the horse's legs is compromised. The tissue that lines the coffin bone, called the laminae, degenerates rapidly and the coffin bone slips out of its normal position.

A number of factors can cause the blood supply to the legs to short circuit. One of these factors is diet. Abrupt changes in feed or a sudden substantial increase in carbohydrates can lead to an imbalance of microorganisms in the horse's digestive system. Toxins are released from the digestive tract into the bloodstream, wreaking havoc in the horse's body.

Other causes of laminitis include:

- High doses or prolonged use of corticosteroids
- Obesity
- Bedding with black walnut shavings
- Severe colic (which we cover later in this chapter)
- Improper shoeing
- Retained placenta in mares after foaling
- Excessive exercise on hard surfaces (called road founder)
- Grazing on a lush pasture without gradual introduction (grass founder)
- Trailering long distances
- Any primary foot disease (any disease that affects the function of the hoof, such as an abscess)
- Any illness with high fever
- Any metabolic problem, such as Cushing's disease (we discuss these types of problems later in this chapter)

Laminitis is a complicated disease. At this time, researchers need more pieces to solve the puzzle. This condition is extremely serious and excruciatingly painful for the horse. To help manage this terrible disease, you need immediate attention from your equine veterinarian.

Certain equines are more prone to developing laminitis than others. Ponies and draft horses seem more likely to have problems with this illness than other horses. Also, horses who have foundered in the past are more likely to suffer a recurrence of the condition.

Diagnosis, treatment, and prevention

Veterinarians initially diagnose laminitis by observing the clinical signs of the disease. These signs include lameness, a painful stance (where the horse leans back on his heels while standing), increased digital pulses in the feet, and heat in the foot. X-rays can confirm coffin bone rotation and the degree to which it has occurred. Because coffin bone rotation may occur days to weeks after the initial onset of laminitis, X-rays on day one may show no rotation, while X-rays taken one week later may show significant rotation.

Treatment for laminitis may include anti-inflammatory drugs like phenylbuta-zone (bute), drugs to help dilate blood vessels, drugs to help thin the blood, antibiotics, and placing a special shoe on the affected leg or legs. Pain med-ication is important, too, because laminitis is excruciating for the horse. Acupuncture has also been shown to help in many cases.

The prognosis for a horse who's suffering from laminitis depends on the degree of rotation of the coffin bone. Many horses can recover from laminitis, although the damaged tissue in the hoof may take almost a year to grow out. In very severe cases, horses with laminitis are euthanized.

Horses recovering from laminitis need soft bedding or sand to help relieve their pain and pressure on their hooves. This soft bedding or sand is not only easier on the hooves, but also encourages the horse to lie down.

Because most cases of laminitis are diet related, this condition often is preventable with good nutrition. Pay close attention to what you feed your horse, and keep his weight down to a healthy level. (See Chapter 7 for infor-mation on how to feed your horse, and Chapter 2 for details about determining the proper body weight for your horse.)

If you even suspect that your horse has eaten too much of any good thing (he's gotten into the grain bin, for example), call your veterinarian immediately. Don't wait to see whether your horse develops symptoms of laminitis. Your vet can take preventative measures to try to prevent the development of laminitis.

To get a jump on laminitis, feel your horse's feet frequently so that you know his normal hoof temperature. Plus, ask your veterinarian to show you how to measure your horse's digital pulse so that you can check it yourself if you suspect laminitis.

Navicular syndrome

A small bone in the horse's hoof called the navicular bone is involved in various ways in navicular syndrome, which can render a horse unsound in his front legs (see Figure 11-4). Researchers believe that one cause of navicular syndrome is the degeneration of the navicular bone as a result of decreased blood supply. A more current theory on the condition suggests that it occurs as a result of excessive force on the navicular bone, causing abnormal bone remodeling. No one is sure how the problem arises, although many veterinarians suspect a genetic link because some types of lower leg conformation seem to be prevalent in horses with this condition.

To diagnose navicular, your veterinarian uses visible symptoms rather than X-rays. These symptoms include consistent reluctance to stand with weight on a particular leg and intermittent lameness. Nerve blocks and hoof testers can help your vet rule out other issues and make a diagnosis of navicular syndrome.

Navicular syndrome doesn't have a cure, but it can often be managed with special shoeing, drugs to help increase the blood flow to the navicular bone, intra-articular injections, and anti-inflammatory drugs. Some horses who suffer severely from navicular syndrome may be helped by cutting the nerves to the heel portion of the hoof. The horse can no longer feel the pain in the caudal portion of his hoof after this procedure.

You can help prevent your horse from developing navicular by providing him with good farrier care.

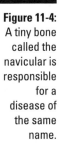

Figure 11-4: A tiny bone called the navicular is responsible for a disease of the same name.

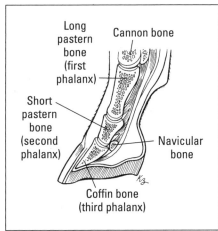

Long pastern bone (first phalanx)

Cannon bone

Short pastern bone (second phalanx)

Navicular bone

Coffin bone (third phalanx)

Osteochondritis Dissecans (OCD)

Osteochondritis dissecans is a mouthful, so most people call this condition OCD. A type of degenerative bone disease, OCD is basically a problem at the cartilage's cellular level, and starts when a horse is young and growing. The cartilage in the young horse's bones fails to ossify like it's supposed to — that is, it fails to turn into bone. So, instead of growing up like good cartilage cells should, they remain as cartilage. This happens at the growth centers of the horse's bones, so as the horse matures, this abnormal cartilage gets thicker and can separate from the underlying bone. It can also die, or wrinkle up and become flaps and little loose pieces of cartilage floating around in the joint capsule. (Coauthor Dr. Kate says that vets like to call these particles "joint mice.") These floating pieces of cartilage can make the joint very painful and cause lameness.

OCD is believed to have several causes. It's considered a developmental orthopedic disease (DOD for short), and can be caused by rapid growth in young horses, which is often caused by incorrect diet. Young horses who grow too fast because they're fed high-energy foods or have overweight mothers who produce overly rich milk can develop OCD, as well as other DODs. Genetics can also play a part in OCD, and some lines of horses show a greater tendency toward this condition.

Underfed young horses can also develop OCD. Poor-quality and low-quantity foods can lead to decreased bone growth, which puts additional stress on bones. Both lack of food and too much food can cause a mineral imbalance, which is believed to be behind OCD.

You can't always tell whether your horse has OCD. Although some horses display swelling of the affected area, others show no signs of it at all. Sometimes they become lame and sometimes they don't. The only definitive way to diagnose OCD is with the use of X-rays. If the OCD is giving the horse trouble, your vet may prescribe joint injections with anti-inflammatory drugs or simply prolonged rest. In cases that don't respond to conservative treatment, surgery may be in order.

The prognosis is good for some horses with OCD, especially after surgery in some cases. After the offending OCD is removed, the horse can often live a normal, active life.

Ringbone

An insidious lameness problem by the name of ringbone (technically known as phalangeal exostosis) is often diagnosed in horses. Ringbone is the development of extra bone in or around the joint and affects the pastern and coffin joints, usually in the forelegs. Low ringbone affects the coffin joint. High ringbone affects the pastern joint. High ringbone is worse than low ringbone because it causes more pain and lameness in the horse.

Ringbone often starts out slow and shows itself as mild lameness. Eventually more of the joint becomes involved with the disease, and the lameness becomes worse.

No one is completely sure why ringbone develops in some horses and not others, although certain factors seem to be involved. Those factors include the following:

- ✔ **Genetics.** When horses with ringbone are bred, their offspring have a tendency to develop the condition as well.
- ✔ **Conformation.** Horses who have very upright leg angles are more prone to the condition.
- ✔ **Poor hoof trimming.** Uneven trimming causes trauma to the joint.

One of the most common forms of treatment for ringbone is therapeutic shoeing. This involves special trimming and shoeing techniques that promote balance in the horse's feet. Anti-inflammatory drugs (taken orally or injected directly into the joint) can also help manage this condition, but can't cure it. Nutraceuticals designed to support the joints, acupuncture, and Traditional Chinese Medicine have also been shown to help.

Surgical treatment for ringbone calls for *arthrodesing,* which involves "freezing" (or fusing) the joint to make it nonfunctional while still allowing the horse to use the leg. Depending on the severity of the ringbone, this method may produce a good outcome, especially if the problem is in the hind limbs.

Unfortunately, when extensive bone growth with joint involvement has occurred, arthrodesing may be the only option. Even with this procedure, many horses still have some lameness.

The best way to help protect your horse from ringbone is to make sure that he gets proper hoof care from a reputable farrier. See Chapter 4 for more details.

Tendonitis

Tendonitis, or bowed tendon, is a common problem in hard-working horses. In fact, experts estimate that 30 to 40 percent of all performance horses have some degree of tendonitis.

Tendonitis is a condition that affects the lower foreleg. Some cases are acute, while others are chronic. Sometimes, tendonitis is a precursor to a fracture, back pain, or joint problems. It occurs when the tendons at the back of the leg (the flexor tendons) are strained or torn. Jumping and galloping, especially in deep footing, can cause a horse to develop tendonitis.

Tendonitis may be easy to spot. The horse acts lame, and the back of his leg may be swollen and hot to the touch. The condition and its relative severity can also be diagnosed by a veterinarian who's using ultrasound.

Veterinarians treat tendonitis by trying to reduce the inflammation. This treatment involves icing the leg, giving oral anti-inflammatory drugs, and resting the horse. A tendon takes a long time to heal, and horses who suffer from severe tendonitis often need six months to a year in order to recuperate. Stem cell therapy is being used to combat this condition, and so is shock wave therapy. Acupuncture and Traditional Chinese Veterinary Medicine have also been shown to help.

Whatever form of treatment you choose to treat your horse's tendonitis, it's imperative that the affected horse receive an ultrasound examination before returning to work. Ultrasound helps to tell the veterinarian whether the tendon has healed sufficiently enough to likely withstand the rigors of a normal exercise routine.

Bowed tendons can sometimes be prevented by following these guidelines:

- ✔ Make certain that your horse is receiving good hoof care from a qualified farrier (see Chapter 4).

- ✔ Ride your horse in footing that's not too deep, slippery, or muddy. (If you must ride in these conditions, keep your horse at a walk.)

- ✔ Rinse your horse's legs with cold water after a workout. (Coauthor Dr. Kate does this for all her horses to help keep their tendons healthy.)

- ✔ Make sure that splint boots, polo bandages, and leg wraps are properly put on. The wrong application of leg protection can actually cause tendonitis.

Trying to Stomach Digestive Problems

Horses are eating machines, designed by nature to spend most of their lives ingesting and digesting. Put them in an artificial environment where they're given foods that they wouldn't find in the wild, and then limit the time during which they can eat, and you have a recipe for trouble.

Digestive problems are one of the biggest veterinary issues in the horse world. The equine digestive tract doesn't always function well in the confines of domesticity. The result is a host of conditions that both horse owners and veterinarians face on a regular basis. (Flip to Chapter 10 for general information about a horse's digestive system.)

Diarrhea

Recognizing diarrhea in your horse is easy. Loose, liquid feces are a sure sign of it.

Diarrhea can be caused by any number of things, including an infectious agent (such as salmonella or clostridium bacterial diseases), Potomac Horse Fever (a bacterial disease), antibiotics, non-steroidal anti-inflammatory medication, blister beetle ingestion, poisonous plants, and a heavy parasite burden. Bowel strangulation or obstruction, peritonitis, and liver disease can also bring on diarrhea.

Before even trying to find the cause of the diarrhea, your veterinarian treats the condition to prevent dehydration and electrolyte imbalance. He or she also gives aggressive supportive care to help prevent your horse from going into shock or developing laminitis. In severe cases, your horse may have to be admitted to a hospital, placed in intensive care, and possibly put in isolation.

A condition called chronic diarrhea is any diarrhea episode that lasts longer than two to three weeks, with stool that's wet and unformed, but not completely liquid. The cause of this type of diarrhea is the same as the cause of acute diarrhea: parasites, internal issues (such as liver disease), salmonella infection, chronic peritonitis, inflammatory bowel disease, and unfortunately, cancer. Sometimes, nonspecific chronic diarrhea responds to a change in diet to grass hay.

Getting a specific diagnosis on chronic diarrhea can be challenging for your veterinarian, but it's important to ultimately get one. Hit-or-miss treatments may prolong the problem or, at best, be a temporary fix that may seriously delay resolution of the problem.

If your horse develops diarrhea, don't wait to call your vet, especially if your horse exhibits pain, fever, weakness, or lethargy. Diarrhea is a serious problem that should be immediately addressed.

Enteroliths

Imagine having a giant rock growing in your intestines. Horses who suffer from enteroliths have just that problem. A rock is literally growing inside them.

Enteroliths, also called "stones," form inside horses as a result of something that they may have eaten. Accidentally ingesting sand, hay bale twine, or a piece of wood starts the process. If the body fails to expel the foreign object, it becomes a *nidus* — essentially, it's like the pearl in an oyster. The horse's body tries to get rid of it while protecting itself, so it deposits mucous, minerals, and food around the object. That process, along with the normal peristaltic movements of the gut, turns the mass into a hard, rocklike ball.

Enteroliths are usually round, but they can assume other interesting shapes as well. Horses can pass very small enteroliths in their feces, or the stones can float around in the GI tract and cause impactions that can lead to fatal colic. (We discuss impactions later in this chapter.)

Some enteroliths can be seen on X-rays or felt by your veterinarian on rectal palpation. Most often, they're found with exploratory surgery. The enterolith must be surgically removed if the horse has any chance at surviving the impaction.

Horses living anywhere in the U.S. can develop enteroliths, but this problem is most often seen in the Southwestern states. California in particular has a very high incidence of enteroliths. Some experts believe that alfalfa hay, which is often fed to horses in California, combined with the high magnesium content of the state's water, contributes to the condition.

Because veterinarians aren't completely sure why enteroliths form, no one can say for certain how to prevent them. Some horse owners don't give their horses alfalfa for fear that stones may develop.

Gas colic

With all the fiber horses eat, it's not surprising to find out that they can sometimes suffer from gas. Colic can result when excessive gas production causes gas to become trapped in the cecum and large colon. This can be extremely painful to the horse. After all, just think about how you feel when you have severe gas pains. It's not fun.

Most cases of gas colic are simply the result of gas not being passed the way that it should. In other situations, gas colic can be a sign of an intestinal blockage or a twisted intestine. A gas-filled bowel can even rupture if the problem isn't rectified.

Horses with gas colic may paw the ground, roll repeatedly and kick at their bellies (see Figure 11-5 for a horse who's exhibiting some of these symptoms).

Figure 11-5: Horses express abdominal pain in a number of ways, including rolling on the ground.

Bob Langrish

Veterinarians treat gas colic by giving the horse an IV-painkiller. Vets recommend that you hand-walk your horse to help her pass the gas that's causing the problem. If this doesn't do the trick, your vet may opt to give your horse mineral oil or a laxative via a stomach tube. This can help stimulate movement of the bowel and allow the offending gas to pass.

If your horse is showing signs of colic pain, contact your veterinarian right away. It could be just a bit of gas, but it could also be something more serious.

To help prevent gas colic, make diet changes gradually in your horse.

Impactions

When a horse is *impacted,* dry manure has clogged up her intestines and stopped her from being able to defecate. Impactions are very serious in horses, and can be fatal if they're not treated quickly.

Impactions occur most often when a horse is fed tough, dry, forage with a lot of stems and not provided with enough water. Occurrences of impaction increase in the colder months because horses don't like to drink cold water — a good reason to keep your horse's water warm in the winter. Long stall rest or a long trailer ride can also be a contributing factor to impaction, because a horse's bowels work better with exercise.

A horse suffering from an impaction may show signs of colic, including pawing the ground, rolling repeatedly, or kicking at her belly. She may also be unable to produce manure.

Impactions are treated with large amounts of mineral oil passed into the horse's stomach through a tube in the nose. If this treatment doesn't make the impaction pass, the vet may give oral or intravenous hydration to the horse to help moisten the impaction and make it passable. If this tactic fails, surgery may be the only option for removal of the impaction.

If your horse must be confined for a period of time, ask your veterinarian for suggestions on how to prevent impactions in your horse. Soaking your horse's hay is one way to help decrease the likelihood of your horse becoming impacted.

Sand colic

If you ate your food off the ground, you'd probably end up with a belly full of sand. Well, that's what often happens to horses who live in areas with sandy soil. As they graze or munch on their hay, they accidentally ingest particles of sand.

The Southwestern states are most known for *sand colic,* which occurs when a significant amount of sand builds up in the horse's large intestine. It erodes the lining of the gut and can cause extreme pain, diarrhea, depression, weight loss, and decreased appetite.

Horses with sand colic are treated by being fed psyllium. The psyllium helps the sand move through the large intestine and out of the horse's system. Horses who don't respond to this treatment must have the sand removed from the intestine surgically.

Prevention is worth a pound of cure when it comes to sand. Here are some tips:

- ✔ If you live in an area with sandy soil, avoid feeding your horse directly off the ground. Use a feed bin, and put a stall mat underneath it. If some of the food spills out, your horse isn't eating directly off the ground.

- ✔ As a preventative for sand colic, give your horse 1 cup of dry psyllium every day for a week, mixed with a complete feed, oats, or another kind of grain mixture. This combination helps clear out any sand that may be lurking in your horse's gut before it becomes a problem.

Ulcers

Horses don't have long commutes or sales quotas to make, but they still get ulcers. In fact, 90 percent of all performance horses and horses in training have some degree of stomach ulcers. These gastric ulcers are caused by stress, frequent dosing of phenylbutazone or other non-steroidal anti-inflammatories, and certain diets, such as those lacking in adequate roughage.

Even baby horses can get ulcers, possibly indicating a bacterial link in some cases. Foals affected with ulcers grind their teeth, salivate excessively, have a decreased appetite, show pain after eating, and lie down more frequently than unaffected foals.

Adult horses with ulcers often show no signs of illness, although some are clearly uncomfortable. Frequent colic episodes may be a sign of possible ulcers. The gold standard to confirm the presence of a gastric ulcer in horses involves placing an instrument called an endoscope into the horse's esophagus and down to the stomach. By the time an ulcer is visible by endoscope, it's already causing the horse considerable discomfort because ulcers begin forming and are painful before they can even be seen with endoscopy.

Treatment for ulcers requires that the horse's stress be reduced, if possible. If the horse is being given phenylobutazone for a medical condition, alfalfa hay should be fed to help protect the stomach. Ulcer medication is also given to a horse suffering from ulcers. Drugs by the name of cimetidine or famotidine and omeprazole can help, and so can stomach ulcer protectors. Coauthor Dr. Kate also uses Traditional Chinese Veterinary Medicine to treat ulcers and has great success with it.

To help prevent gastric ulcers in your horse, feed her a diet high in roughage. If your veterinarian prescribes a regimen of phenylobutazone for a health issue, ask him or her about medication that can be given to your horse to help prevent ulcers.

Saving Your Horse's Skin: Examining Skin Disorders

Horses are big animals, so they have a lot of skin. They're also prone to a number of skin disorders. These problems are usually pretty obvious to the astute horse owner, and can sometimes be alarming. The good news is that, in most cases, skin problems aren't fatal.

Allergies

Horses get allergies just like people do, and sometimes symptoms take the form of hives, or urticaria. These hives usually appear as either small or large wheals (anywhere from half an inch to a few inches in diameter) that may or may not be itchy (see Figure 11-6).

Figure 11-6: Skin allergies in horses present themselves as hives.

Dr. Janice Sojka, Purdue University

Hives are usually brought on by hypersensitivity to drugs, feeds, insects, chemicals, molds, dust, pollens, or any number of other substances. With so many causative agents, finding the inciting culprit can be tricky. Your vet may want to do skin or other allergy testing, or even a food trial to attempt to find out exactly what's causing your horse's allergies.

The usual treatment is corticosteroids, either injected or oral. Determining and eliminating the causative agent is also part of the prescription.

Bacterial infections

Bacterial skin problems in horses are usually secondary to other problems that disrupt the protective barrier of the skin. These secondary problems can include trauma or injury, warm and humid weather, a dirty environment, and poor hygiene. Figure 11-7 shows a typical bacterial infection.

Figure 11-7: An example of a bacterial infection on a horse's skin.

Dr. Janice Sojka, Purdue University

A common bacterial skin problem in horses is called greasy heel, scratches, or pastern dermatitis, and is a condition involving the underside of the pastern or fetlock area. Like other bacterial skin problems, a predisposing factor — such as moisture or an abrasion — is usually to blame. Horses with white legs are most commonly affected. In some cases of pastern dermatitis, a fungus or mite is involved. Whatever the cause, your vet needs to make an accurate diagnosis for proper treatment and future prevention. (Treatment depends on the source of the problem.)

Another, similar problem in horses with white legs results when urine hits the ground and splashes onto the front of the hind legs. If it's not cleaned or rinsed often, it may also lead to a secondary bacterial infection that must be treated with antibiotics.

Fungal infections

Fungal infections can be more than itchy and painful to your horse, causing him to be irritable. Your veterinarian can use a Woods Light test to detect some fungal species, but a fungal culture or microscopic exam may be needed for diagnosis.

The most common fungal skin problem in horses is *ringworm,* which isn't actually a worm but a fungal infection that's highly contagious to other horses and humans. Called "ringworm" because the lesions often begin as small, round areas of hair loss — sometimes with raised edges — this infection relies on the presence of the fungal spores and skin abrasions to take hold (see Figure 11-8). It's most common during damp seasons, or when horses are kept in damp, dark conditions with poor hygiene.

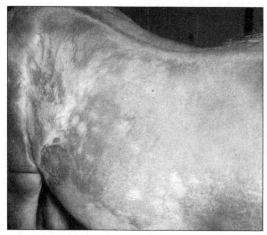

Figure 11-8: Ringworm starts as small areas of hair loss.

Dr. Janice Sojka, Purdue University

Most problems occur at the girth and saddle blanket areas, or the shoulders and neck — areas where horses sweat the most. Ringworm can also be spread by using dirty brushes, blankets, and other equipment on multiple horses.

Treatment for any kind of fungal infection is to avoid sharing grooming tools between horses and to clean all tools thoroughly in anti-fungal cleansers. Tack should be kept clean, especially girths and blankets. Horses affected by ringworm should be bathed with an anti-fungal shampoo recommended by your veterinarian. Vets may also give topical prescription medication to put on your horse.

Another common fungal infection of the skin is *rain scalds,* sometimes called rain rot. Technically called *dermatophilosis,* rain scalds are caused by a genetic anomaly that has properties of both a fungus and a bacterium. The organism responsible for rain scalds becomes active in damp weather and causes the most trouble in rainy seasons or in warm, humid climates.

The organism responsible for rain scalds enters the skin at a break. A bug bite or scratch is all that the organism needs to gain entry. Symptoms include areas of matted hair with crusty scabs on your horse's coat that look like paintbrush strokes. These areas show up primarily on the back, hindquarters, and thighs.

The best way to prevent rain scalds is to keep your horse dry in wet weather. Provide him with shelter to escape from the rain, and provide a waterproof blanket to wear during rainstorms. More severe cases may need veterinary treatment.

Sarcoids

Sarcoids are benign tumors of the skin. The most common of all equine tumors, sarcoids occur in horses of all ages but are most often seen in horses older than 7 years of age.

Most sarcoid tumors occur on the head, neck, limbs, and ventral abdominal area. The tumors can be solitary or occur in clusters, and they can be raised or flat in appearance. They can also look like warts, or large, firm skin masses, and usually come in one of two forms: flat and proliferative. (Figure 11-9 shows sarcoid tumors.) Some researchers believe that sarcoids are the result of a virus, although no conclusive evidence exists to prove this theory.

Figure 11-9:
Sarcoid tumors have a distinct appearance that sets them apart from other skin disorders.

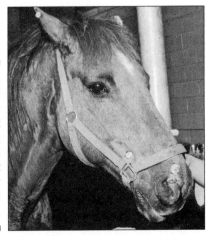

Dr. Janice Sojka, Purdue University

Sarcoids don't spread (metastasize) through the body the way that cancerous tumors do (we discuss skin cancers later in this chapter), but they can send out tentacles that spread into the immediate area, making some of them very difficult to eradicate. They can also be very persistent and locally invasive. Depending upon the location and size of the tumor, surgical removal is an option, but recurrence is common, even with very wide skin margins.

Sarcoids aren't usually life threatening except when they develop in areas of the body where normal function is affected. Sarcoids that develop on the anal area can be a particular hazard because they can grow large enough to prevent the horse from being able to defecate. Sarcoids around and in the eyes can also be dangerous. If they become large or invasive, the eye may have to be removed. That's why lumps or bumps near your horse's eyes warrant a visit with your veterinarian. When sarcoids occur in areas that come into contact with the saddle, girth, or other pieces of tack, surgical removal is often warranted.

Treatments for sarcoids include cryotherapy, immunotherapy, laser therapy, radiation therapy, and topical chemotherapy.

Seborrhea

Have you ever seen a horse with crusty skin on the front of his hind legs between the hoof and the hock? This condition can be maddening if you have a horse who suffers from it. No matter how much you wash his legs, you just can't get rid of the ugly crusts.

The technical term for these crusts is *seborrhea*. In most cases, seborrhea is secondary to another problem. (Primary seborrhea, caused by a genetic problem, is extremely rare in horses.) Also called cannon keratosis, secondary seborrhea may be the skin's response to the insult of bacteria, the contact of urine (in geldings, it splashes up and hits the legs), or even too much sun. The skin at the effected area may react by producing a greasy substance (see Figure 11-10).

You can buy over-the-counter shampoos to treat secondary seborrhea. These shampoos are labeled for such use, and can contain tar and sulfur, emollients, or mild sulfur-salicylic acid. The shampoo that you choose should be determined by which type of seborrhea your horse is experiencing. Treat seborrhea oleosa with a tar and sulfur shampoo. Seborrhea sicca may respond to emollient shampoos or mild keratolytic sulfur-salicylic acid shampoos. Your veterinarian may be able to tell you which type of seborrhea you're dealing with by taking a biopsy of the affected area.

To help prevent secondary seborrhea, keep your horse's hind legs clean by washing them every few days. If your horse has pink skin on his hind legs, consider putting sunscreen on them during the summertime.

Figure 11-10:
Secondary
seborrhea
causes
crusty skin.

Bob Langrish

Skin cancer

Every species of mammal seems to be prone to cancer, and horses are no exception. Unlike in humans, cancer of the lungs, liver, kidney, and other vital organs is uncommon in horses. However, horses are prone to skin cancers, which can cause a lot of problems, including death.

If you see a growth on your horse's skin that doesn't go away after a week or so, contact your veterinarian.

Melanoma

Especially common in older gray horses, melanoma is most often seen in Arabians and Percherons because of the large number of gray horses in these breeds. Three-quarters of these tumors are malignant, and they most often occur in the skin. They usually show up on the perineum (the area between the anus and the genitals), underside of the tail, around the eyes, and on the limbs. One form of melanoma occurs in young horses who are less than 2 years of age. This melanoma is usually benign, and usually is different from the melanomas of older horses.

Melanomas are usually under the skin and are black in color. Not all melanomas are black, however. The only way to know for sure whether a tumor is melanoma is through a biopsy.

Melanomas are most manageable when they're diagnosed and treated early. Removing these tumors surgically is the best way to prevent them from spreading further, but some veterinarians prefer to use cryosurgery. In some cases, vets opt to treat the tumor orally with a drug called cimetidine, which can bring about partial to even full regression.

Squamous cell carcinoma

This malignant tumor originates in the epidermal cells of the skin. It tends to develop in areas of the body in which some horses don't have pigment. These areas include the eyelids, nose, vulva, and penis. Chronic sun exposure is a primary culprit.

Squamous cell carcinoma may initially appear as warts or granulation tissue, and grows into raised, crusty lesions that don't heal. This cancer doesn't usually spread to the entire body, but it can be very locally invasive, especially in the eye, where it can spread into the tear duct or sinuses. Because this type of cancer can initially look like scar tissue, sarcoids, bacterial granuloma, or fungal granuloma, only a veterinarian can determine its true nature with a biopsy.

Squamous cell carcinoma can be treated with cryotherapy, radiation therapy, surgery, and various implants.

Watching Out for Eye Problems

The eyes are the window to the soul, and this statement is especially true of horses. Few things are sadder than a horse with eye problems. These conditions often are not only painful, but also very troubling to the horse. Because horses are prey animals, they depend a lot on their sight to feel safe.

All eye problems require immediate veterinarian attention. Most eye problems are quite painful, so your vet may perform a nerve block and/or sedate your horse before examining her eyes. The vet also may use topical anesthetic eye drops to lessen pain.

Coauthor Audrey lost her beloved Appaloosa mare Rosie to eye disease several years ago, and knows all too well how insidious eye problems can be.

Blocked tear ducts

Horses live in dusty, plant-filled environments, and sometimes their tear ducts become blocked as a result. Blocked tear ducts (technically called the nasolacrimal ducts) can make your horse's eye tear excessively, leaving her with a constantly wet face. It happens because dust or pollen plugs up the ducts, causes swelling, and keeps the tears from draining normally through the sinuses and out through the nose. This ailment is most common during allergy season and when the weather is hot, dry, and windy.

Bacteria can feed on the excess tears and cause itching and irritation. The itching and irritation, in turn, cause your horse to rub her face and possibly damage her eyes. This is why it's important to have your vet examine your horse if her tear ducts appear to be blocked. Your vet can clear the ducts, and also check to make sure that no other, more serious issues are at play.

If your horse develops blocked tear ducts, your vet may put a tube into the tear ducts by going through your horse's nose. He or she then flushes the ducts with solution to clear the blockage.

To prevent blocked tear ducts, try to minimize the dust in your horse's environment. If your hay is very dusty, soak it in water before feeding it to your horse. Water arenas and dusty paddocks during dry times of year.

Cataracts

Horses get cataracts just like people do. In horses, however, the condition can not only develop with age, but also be present at birth. If your horse has a large and diffuse cataract, you may easily see it. It presents itself as a gray colored pupil.

Congenital cataracts, which are present in newborn foals, may be removed by a veterinary ophthalmologist with the greatest likelihood of a successful surgical outcome. Acquired cataracts usually are secondary to another eye problem like ERU (which we discuss later in this chapter), but they may be the result of old age.

Cataracts can be present in one or both of a horse's eyes. They can affect your horse's vision because they prevent light from getting through to the retina. The maturity of the cataract determines how much vision the horse loses.

Several years ago, coauthor Dr. Kate's husband bought a 21-year-old gelding to be his first cutting horse. The horse had to be retired only two years later because of cataracts. He had trouble seeing at night, and couldn't be ridden in the evening unless a full moon was in the sky. Eventually, he became unsafe to ride at night at all.

Corneal ulcers

Corneal ulcers or abrasions are injuries to the surface of the cornea that result from injuries to the eye. Trauma, burns, chemicals, and even dirt or debris can cause corneal ulcers.

This condition is extremely painful, as are most eye problems. Untreated corneal ulcers can lead to other eye problems and loss of vision or the eye itself if untreated.

Veterinarians use a stain to determine the extent of the ulcer, and may manage the problem with ophthalmic antibiotics and ophthalmic atropine if bacteria are involved. Your vet may culture the ulcer to see what kind of bacterial or fungal agents may be destroying the cornea. Deep corneal ulcers that don't respond to medication may require surgical intervention.

Corneal ulcers are difficult to prevent, but they can be treated successfully if you catch them early. Pay close attention to your horse's eyes, and don't hesitate to call the vet if your horse is squinting, tearing, or rubbing her eye.

Equine recurrent uveitis (ERU)

Also called moonblindness or periodic ophthalmia, equine recurrent uveitis (ERU) is the most common cause of equine blindness. The condition comes and goes, and is primarily a problem in the acute phase.

Uveitits, which means inflammation of the anterior chamber of the eye, may be caused by trauma, a septic infection, certain bacterial or parasitic infections, or an immune-mediated disease. Some researchers believe that a genetic component may be involved as well.

In the acute phase, uveitis causes considerable pain, excessive tearing, and sensitivity to light (see Figure 11-11). The condition is treated symptomatically with anti-inflammatories and pain medications that may be administered topically, orally, and by injection. Acupuncture and Traditional Chinese Veterinary Medicine has also proven to be helpful.

If your horse is diagnosed with uveitis, you can manage the condition by keeping a close watch for symptoms, and instituting treatment immediately when the problem recurs. You want to initiate treatment immediately, because each episode may cause some degree of permanent damage to the eye. Good management of this condition often helps minimize the speed of progression of the disease.

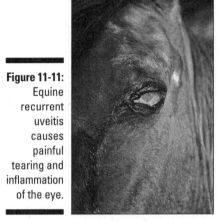

Figure 11-11:
Equine recurrent uveitis causes painful tearing and inflammation of the eye.

Bob Langrish

A Common Respiratory Problem: Chronic Obstructive Pulmonary Disease

Because horses are such athletic creatures, equine respiratory problems can create huge issues. Riding your horse in a show, competition, or even just on the trail is hard if he's having trouble breathing.

One of the most common respiratory diseases that's seen mainly in the older horse is COPD. Chronic obstructive pulmonary disease (COPD) is the equine version of asthma, and it causes a horse to have difficulty breathing in, and even more difficulty breathing out. COPD is also called recurrent airway obstruction (RAO) or heaves. This illness causes inflammation and spasms within the lungs. It's usually triggered by airborne allergies to mold, dust, and pollen, or by poor air quality.

Horses with COPD have shortness of breath during exercise, chronic coughing, and wheezing. They also often may develop a *heave line,* which is a line of developed muscle along the belly. It forms as a result of the horse's struggle to push air out of his lungs.

Just like some humans are born with a predisposition to asthma, some horses are born with a predisposition to COPD. To keep it from showing up in your horse, you can take a few precautions. These precautions include providing good ventilation in your horse's stall or keeping him in a pasture with shelter, giving your horse hay and bedding that's low in dust, and feeding your horse from a ground feeder to help him clear his nasal passages as he eats.

If your horse is diagnosed with COPD, your veterinarian may treat him with bronchodilators and/or corticosteroids. He or she may also suggest that you soak your horse's hay in water before feeding, or switch to pellets or hay cubes. Most horses with COPD do better when housed outdoors, because barn environments can be very dusty.

Surveying Other Systemic Problems

Issues that affect your horse's entire system are scary. Discovering that your horse is suffering from a systemic problem can be a frightening realization. Fortunately, veterinary science has made great inroads into diagnosing and treating these issues in the past 10 years, making it easier on affected horses and their owners.

Anhidrosis

"No sweat!" is generally something you like to hear — unless it applies to your horse. Some horses can develop a metabolic problem called *anhidrosis,* which is the inability to produce normal amounts of sweat.

The condition has a range of seriousness, from the extreme of a horse who has no ability to sweat, to a horse who simply produces less sweat than she should at certain temperatures and levels of exercise. The problem can be seasonal; some horses with this problem do fine in the cooler seasons, but have trouble when the weather heats up and humidity elevates.

Your horse depends heavily on sweating to regulate her body temperature. Sweat is critical so that evaporation can cool her down and keep her body temperature from becoming dangerously high. When a horse stops sweating, she tries to cool herself through an elevated respiratory rate or even panting, which isn't very effective. And the body temperature of a horse who can't sweat may elevate as high as 103 degrees Fahrenheit. (The normal body temperature for a horse is between 99 and 101.5.) Add exercise to the equation, and the horse's body temperature can go as high as 108 degrees. Brain damage is highly likely when body temperature exceeds 106 degrees.

Veterinarians believe that anhidrosis may result from a malfunction in the physiological or neural pathways involved in sweating. One theory is that the constant stimulation of sweat gland receptors wears them out, so to speak, and they quit responding. The problem is most common in the southern U.S., and especially in areas of higher humidity, but it can show up anywhere given the right conditions. Even horses who sweat normally can have episodes of anhidrosis, given the right set of circumstances of weather conditions, workload, and stress.

Your horse should normally cool off within 30 minutes after exercise. If your horse doesn't seem to be cooling off, check her rectal temperature. If it's above normal, and your horse is also breathing rapidly, has decreased energy, lethargy, and a lack of sweating, contact your veterinarian.

If your vet suspects anhidrosis, he or she may choose to test your horse to see whether the sweat glands are functioning properly. Anhidrosis has no proven treatments, but environmental adjustment (moving the horse from a hot, humid climate to a drier, cooler area of the country) tends to provide the best results. Some horses may be managed with misting fans, stall air conditioning, or by choosing to exercise them in the coolest part of the day. Horses with milder cases may respond to dietary supplements containing a combination of cobalt, vitamin C, L-tyrosine, and niacin. Some horses may benefit from methyl dopa and/or electrolytes. Other horses respond to acupuncture and Traditional Chinese Veterinary Medicine.

Treatment isn't 100 percent effective in all cases of this no-sweat conundrum. In cases where horses don't respond to treatment, house them in cool environments on hot days, making sure that they have plenty of shade and ventilation. They should be worked only at cool times of the day or at night during hot weather.

Exertional rhabdomyolysis (tying up)

Exertional rhabdomyolysis — more commonly known as "tying up" or azoturia — happens to some horses, often after extreme exercise following several days without much exercise, and while fed grain, especially high carbohydrate feeds. It may occur when a horse is overexerted when she's not fit to perform the work being asked of her. It can also occur when a horse is experiencing an electrolyte imbalance, heat exhaustion, or possibly a vitamin E deficiency.

The signs of exertional rhabdomyolysis include sudden hind limb stiffness or lameness, muscle cramping, refusal to move, and other distress, such as increased heart and respiration rates, sweating, and acting colicky. Veterinarians diagnose exertional rhabdomyolysis based on your horse's behavior, and through a blood test for elevated muscle enzyme levels. If your horse's creatine kinase levels are moderately elevated, the prognosis for recovery is good and the damaged muscle tissue will heal in a few months. In severe cases, horses can have a guarded prognosis for healing and future competition.

The possibility of exertional rhabdomyolysis makes it very important to carefully warm up your horse before exercise, and to gradually get her in condition for hard work.

Diet is extremely important for horses prone to exertional rhabdomyolysis. Limit starch in the diet, and avoid feeds that produce a grain high. (See Chapter 7 for more on how to feed your horse.) Diets developed specifically for horses with exertional rhabdomyolisis can be a huge help.

Metabolic problems

Horses are prone to several different metabolic problems. Each of these problems has a different origin, yet all are closely related. Diagnosis can be tricky, but finding out which one of these problems may be affecting your horse is important.

Although the solution to metabolic problems may be as simple as changing your horse's diet, any hormonal metabolic problem becomes more difficult to treat the longer it progresses. If you suspect any of the problems described in this section, have your veterinarian test your horse for a metabolic condition.

The following conditions are often difficult to differentiate, and ongoing research is constantly changing the equine veterinarian's understanding of these syndromes, diagnostic testing, and management:

- **Equine Metabolic Syndrome** (EMS) has, in the past, been called peripheral Cushings disease. Many horses who suffer from EMS are insulin resistant. Symptoms often appear in the form of fat deposits at the base of the tail and crest of the neck (see Figure 11-12). These animals are often prone to developing laminitis. Current recommended management of EMS consists of regular exercise and a low-carbohydrate diet (no pasture, a grass hay diet, little or no low carbohydrate grain, and balanced vitamin and mineral supplementation). If your horse isn't on pasture, she may need vitamin E supplementation.

- **Cushings syndrome** is more accurately referred to as pituitary pars intermediary dysfunction (PPID). Because a portion of the pituitary gland becomes unable to function properly, ACTH (a hormone) and blood cortisol levels are chronically too high. Horses who suffer from Cushings syndrome may also be insulin resistant, and they often have a long, curly haircoat (so they're often sweaty because they're hot). They're prone to developing laminitis, chronic infections, and loss of muscle mass (producing a pot-bellied appearance), and they may have increased water intake and urine output. This condition can't be cured, but many horses can be managed with drugs such as pergolide or cyprohepadine. Because much research is currently being done on this condition, your equine veterinarian may have newer, better information for diagnosing and treating this condition in the future.

✔ **Primary hypothyroidism** was once thought to cause many adult horses and ponies to develop cresty necks and excess fat at the tail head. Although many horses with this condition do have lower than normal blood thyroid hormone levels, many experts now think that this is a result of their overweight condition rather than a cause of it. Researchers found that horses who had their thyroid glands removed didn't develop this classic appearance. In addition to primary hypothyroidism, a congenital form of hypothyroidism is occasionally seen in foals.

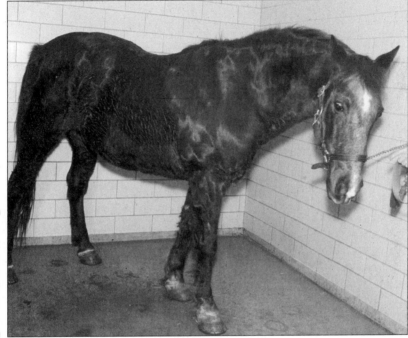

Figure 11-12: A fatty crest on the neck can be a sign of metabolic disease.

Dr. Janice Sojka, Purdue University

Chapter 12

Fighting Infectious Diseases

. . . .

In This Chapter

▶ Recognizing symptoms of infectious diseases

▶ Understanding diagnosis and treatment

▶ Preventing infectious diseases in your horse

. . . .

*H*orses are social creatures, and they have a host of infectious diseases that plague them to prove it! Passed from horse to horse or by a parasitic host, these diseases are dangerous and can be fatal.

In this chapter, we give you the basics on a number of common infectious diseases that can affect your horse. As soon as you see any suspicious symptoms, be sure to contact your veterinarian immediately for diagnosis and treatment. The good news is that vaccines and other prevention methods are available for many of these problems. After reading this chapter, you'll be motivated to keep your horse inoculated. (Flip to Chapter 4 for the basics of equine vaccinations.)

A Toxin Produced by Bacteria: Botulism

Most people have heard of botulism, the deadly disease that infects food and causes severe illness and often death. Although botulism is most often thought of as something that can show up in canned food, the disease is actually a problem for horses as well.

Horses are affected by the toxin that's produced by the bacterium *Clostridium botulinum*. These bacterial organisms are strict anaerobes, which means that they can't live in the presence of air. These organisms produce seven different types of toxins, and these neurotoxins cause very distinct symptoms. Protection from one type doesn't cross-protect for another.

Horses can be infected with the botulism toxin in three different ways:

> ✔ With any deep puncture wound or when a wound results in considerable dead tissue.

✔ When a rodent or other animal dies in a field where hay is cut and processed. The tightly compressed hay bales limit the amount of oxygen that comes in contact with the dead animal, creating a perfect growth environment for the oxygen-hating Clostridium botulinum. The horse accidentally ingests the bacteria when eating the hay or hay cubes.

✔ When the horse ingests bacteria that's living in pasture soil. After the horse accidentally swallows it, the bacteria begins to grow and produce toxins in the gastrointestinal tract. These toxins are absorbed from the gastrointestinal tract into the bloodstream. From there, it goes to the nerves throughout the body.

After a horse absorbs the bacteria, production of the toxin takes place within the horse's gastrointestinal tract.

Symptoms

Botulism causes weakness and paralysis. Muscles that are involved with standing and moving, as well as swallowing, are often involved first.

The first sign you may notice in your horse is the inability to swallow or a lot of drooling. The horse may not be able to get up after lying down, and he may begin to lose control of his muscles. In the early stages, this loss of control may cause extreme anxiety in the horse. You may also see his muscles quiver and tremble.

Affected horses may also fall abruptly when trying to lie down. The third eyelid begins to protrude, and the horse can't control his tongue. The internal muscles are also affected, and the horse can't control his bladder. His digestive system stops working properly. Finally, the diaphragm, which is the largest muscle involved with breathing, stops functioning, resulting in the horse's death.

Diagnosis and treatment

No specific diagnostic test for botulism exists, and blood work on affected horses is typically normal. Veterinarians make a diagnosis based on clinical signs. Although serum and feces can be submitted to a lab for toxin analysis, the vet will probably begin treatment immediately because time is of the essence when you're combating this disease.

Treatment involves giving the horse hyper immune plasma that's very high in antitoxin titers. However, because botulism types vary, the vet has to use plasma that's specific to the particular toxin that affected the sick horse.

Treatment is costly, and unfortunately, after the disease progresses and the toxin adheres to nerve cells, the antibodies are ineffective. Treatment is then aimed at providing intense nursing care for the horse until his body can make new neuromuscular transmissions and restore nerve function. This can take seven to ten days, and all the horse's bodily functions must be supported in the meantime. This support involves providing fluids, feeding the horse through a nasogastric tube, and giving him antibiotics to combat secondary infections.

Prevention

To help prevent botulism, inspect your horse's hay regularly for animal carcasses that may have been accidentally baled into it. If you find animal parts, don't feed the rest of the bale to your horse, and keep an eye on him for possible symptoms. Wound botulism can be prevented by calling a veterinarian right away if your horse seriously injures himself. Immediate treatment of the wound can help ward off botulism.

Affecting the Nervous System: Encephalomyelitis

Encephalomyelitis is a viral disease of the nervous system. Three strains of the same disease can infect horses. Called Western equine encephalomyelitis (WEE), Eastern equine encephalomyelitis (EEE), and Venezuelan equine encephalomyelitis (VEE), the illness can cause severe neurological symptoms and often death. EEE and WEE are most prevalent in the U.S., but VEE is becoming more common, especially in the South.

The virus lives in hosts like birds and rodents, and all strains of equine encephalomyelitis viruses are spread by blood-sucking insects, specifically the mosquito. A mosquito bites the host and then transfers the virus from the host to the horse by biting.

Symptoms

Symptoms of equine encephalomyelitis viruses can be lethargy, lack of appetite, and persistent fever. If the virus isn't successfully cleared by the horse's immune system after the initial infection, the disease can cause neurological behaviors such as circling, seizures, stumbling, and lethargy. As the disease progresses, the horse may begin head pressing (pressing the head against a wall or other object), become blind, and fall into a coma. Horses with VEE may have diarrhea or lethargy, or they may die before they show neurological signs. Pregnant mares who contract the disease may abort their babies. Some horses experience bleeding of the lungs.

EEE and VEE are especially deadly, and in severe cases that don't respond to treatment, the horse must be euthanized.

Diagnosis and treatment

The encephalomyelitis viruses may be diagnosed by blood tests, which isolate antibodies to the disease, along with clinical symptoms, or on postmortem testing.

No cure is known for equine viral encephalomyelitis, but veterinarians can provide supportive treatment for affected horses in the form of intravenous fluids, anti-inflammatories, and anti-diarrhea medications.

Prevention

Vaccinating your horse is the best way to prevent serious infection with encephalomyelitis. Your veterinarian can recommend a vaccine protocol that is appropriate for your particular area of the country.

Eliminating areas where mosquitoes can breed is another way to help control encephalomyelitis. Here are a few tips:

✔ **Remove standing water from your property.** Mosquitoes lay their eggs in standing water, and the larvae hatch and grow there. Eliminating water where the insects can lay their eggs can help reduce mosquito populations.

✔ **If you have a water trough for your horses, stock it with mosquitofish.** The fish will eat the mosquito larvae and reduce the number of mosquitoes that may bite your horse. Mosquitofish are often available at no charge from county vector control agencies.

✔ **Spray your horse with mosquito repellent during mosquito season, and try to keep her indoors at night** (or during the dusk and dawn mosquito feeding times) if at all possible. You can buy mosquito repellent designed specifically for use on horses at your local tack and feed store, in equine product catalogs, or on the Internet.

A Disease in Three Forms: Equine Herpes Virus (EHV)

The viral disease equine herpes virus (EHV), also known as rhinopneumonitis, has gotten more publicity lately because highly contagious neurological forms of the disease have become more prevalent. Horses transmit EHV to one another through direct contact or by coughing or snorting and releasing the virus into the air.

Symptoms

The symptoms of EHV depend on the form:

- The neurological form of herpes can start with mild fever, slight lethargy, and mild respiratory signs such as a cough.

- The respiratory form usually begins with a cough, fever, and nasal discharge. Many horses also develop a loss of appetite and lethargy, while some horses aren't affected much at all.

- The abortion form of EHV can be a silent and deadly killer. A mare infected with the virus in the last trimester of pregnancy can abort her fetus two weeks to several months after infection. Some foals may escape abortion but are weak and sickly and die soon after birth. Some mares show a respiratory infection, but many don't.

Diagnosis and treatment

Neurological EHV can show the same symptoms as many other neurological diseases discussed in this chapter, such as WEE, EPM, and rabies. You can help your vet make the proper diagnosis by maintaining good vaccine records and allowing him or her to perform the appropriate diagnostic tests. These include microscopic examinations of blood, nasal discharge, and tissue samples.

As with most viral diseases, no specific treatment exists for EHV. Most horses recover with good nursing care, and antibiotics may help treat secondary bacterial infections. Unless the horse's fever is very high, coauthor Dr. Kate prefers to let the disease run its course because the cyclical fever can be used to help monitor the disease's progress. Also, fever is part of the immune system's defense.

Prevention

The vaccines currently on the market are labeled to protect against the abortion and the respiratory forms of EHV, not the neurological form. However, it's important to vaccinate against EHV because cross-protection may occur. The vaccine will also stimulate your horse's immune system.

As with other diseases, horses involved in activities such as racing, training, showing, or transport are at an increased risk, not only due to exposure, but also because of stress on the immune system. Do whatever you can to reduce your horse's stress level (see Chapter 3 for help), and limit your horse's exposure to common water buckets at shows.

If you decide to breed your mare, be sure to ask your vet about proper vaccine protocols, and be diligent about protection so that your mare doesn't abort as a result of EHV. Chapter 15 has more information on breeding horses.

Equine Infectious Anemia (EIA)

Equine infectious anemia (EIA) is a disease that affects the blood. It's caused by a virus that's spread between horses by biting horseflies. It can also be spread by using needles, dental floats, and other contaminated equipment between horses. Infected pregnant mares can pass the disease on to their babies if they don't abort them first.

Symptoms

Horses with a serious case of EIA have a high fever, are lethargic, and develop anemia. They often develop *thrombocytopenia* (lack of platelets), which causes *hemorrhages* (heavy bleeding) to occur on the gums and elsewhere. They may also exhibit *stocking up* (swelling) of the lower legs and along the bottom of the abdomen.

The signs of EIA develop 7 to 30 days after exposure to the virus. Horses can die from EIA or become chronic carriers of the disease. These horses will have an intermittent fever and weight loss.

Diagnosis and treatment

The best test for EIA is something called the *Coggins test*. Because EIA is so serious and must be reported by law to state health authorities, blood for the

Coggins test must be drawn by a licensed and accredited veterinarian, and the sample submitted to a state-approved lab.

If a horse tests positive for EIA, he must be euthanized or quarantined for life because this disease has no treatment, and infection is permanent. The infected horse must be kept a minimum of 200 yards from any other equine. The virus lives for only 15 to 30 minutes in the horsefly, so keeping horses this far apart means that the virus usually dies before the infected fly can travel to get another blood meal.

After a horse is deemed positive for EIA, most states also require an obvious brand on the animal. Check with your veterinarian to find out your state's requirements for frequency of the Coggins test.

Before transporting your horse across state lines, check out the health requirements for transporting. Many large horse show and competitive venues may require a current Coggins test prior to competition. Some venues even want to see the paperwork before you can bring your horse on the grounds and unload. You may be asked to produce current negative Coggins paperwork at any time during any horse-related activity, so don't leave home without it.

Prevention

You'd think that with all this testing, EIA would have been eradicated by now. But unfortunately, that's not the case. To help protect your horse from EIA, follow these guidelines:

- ✔ Board your horse only at a facility that's vigilant about requiring proof of negative EIA status for all horses. (See Chapter 4 for more information about boarding your horse safely.)

- ✔ Never use any needle syringe more than once, and be diligent that equine professionals clean all instruments before using them on your horse.

- ✔ Make certain you know the EIA status of any horse you purchase.

Hitting the Respiratory System: Equine Influenza

Equine influenza is one of the most debilitating and highly contagious viral respiratory diseases to affect horses. Equine influenza is transmitted from horse to horse and through the air in particles that come from discharge released from the horse's nose. All horses can contract equine influenza, but younger animals are most susceptible.

Symptoms

Equine influenza can cause a high fever, lethargy, and a nasal discharge that starts out thin and clear, and can quickly develop into a thick copious discharge (see Figure 12-1). Affected horses often develop a cough.

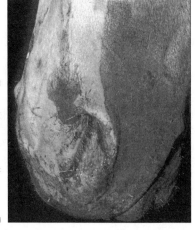

Figure 12-1: Significant nasal discharge is a possible sign of equine influenza.

Dr. Janice Sojka, Purdue University

Uncomplicated cases clear up on their own within a week, although a persistent cough may last several weeks. Complications and secondary infections can lead to pneumonia and persistent poor performance, especially if the horse is continually stressed and not allowed to recover completely.

Diagnosis and treatment

Veterinarians often diagnose equine influenza based on clinical symptoms. No cure exists for this illness, but good supportive care — such as intravenous fluids and drugs to control fever — can keep a horse from developing serious complications. Sometimes your veterinarian may recommend antibiotic treatment to deal with a possible secondary bacterial infection.

Prevention

The best way to prevent equine influenza is to vaccinate. Although not foolproof, the vaccine for this virus can go a long way toward keeping your horse from contracting this illness. The number of times per year that you should vaccinate depends on the amount of exposure your horse has to other horses as well as her age. Your veterinarian can tell you how often you should vaccinate.

A Common Neurological Disease: Equine Protozoal Myeloencephalitis (EPM)

Equine protozoal myeloencephalitis, or EPM, is caused by a protozoan called *Sarcocystis nerona* and is the most commonly diagnosed neurological disease in horses today. Many horses have been exposed to EPM, but not all horses develop the disease. Younger and older horses are more commonly affected, and horses who have never been exposed to the disease are more susceptible. In horses who have already been exposed, stress is thought to play an important role in developing clinical signs of this disease.

The opossum is the host of this disease. Birds can carry this nasty little parasite in their muscles. The opossums eat the birds and pass the organism out through their stool. Horses then get the disease from eating food or water that's contaminated with the opossum's feces.

Symptoms

The EPM protozoa affects the spinal cord and brain, resulting in a variety of symptoms, including incoordination of one or both rear limbs, stumbling, muscle atrophy, and other subtle to severe neurological signs, such as bucking under saddle, an inability to execute lead changes, and unequal stride length. Any signs of brain and spinal cord problems can also signal EPM, from paralysis to loss of bladder control and urine dribbling.

Diagnosis and treatment

At this time, the most definitive test for EPM requires examination of the cerebrospinal fluid (drawn from a spinal tap) in conjunction with clinical signs. Other tests are currently being developed.

Only a few approved products are on the market to treat this disease. The success of treatment depends on the individual horse. Some horses recover completely, while others retain some neurological damage for the rest of their lives. Recurrence of the disease is also a possibility.

Prevention

A vaccine is available for EPM, but it's somewhat controversial because it can give a false positive on tests for EPM in horses who are suspected of having the disease. Ask your veterinarian if this vaccine should be a regular part of your horse's protocol.

To help prevent EPM, keep water and feed sources clean and as free from contamination as possible. Keep trash covered in secure containers to avoid attracting opossums to your property. Remember though that any horse kept outdoors anywhere can be exposed.

Beware of Ticks! Lyme Disease

Lyme disease is more common in people and dogs than in horses, but equine veterinarians are seeing more cases in some areas — most frequently in the Northeastern U.S. This tick-borne disease affects different areas of the body. Ticks that are infected with an organism called *Borrelia burgdorferi* spread the disease to horses through their bite.

Symptoms

The symptoms of Lyme disease may include a stiff gait, shifting-leg lameness, fever, swollen joints, lethargy, and unwillingness to work. Incidents of equine recurrent uveitis (a chronic eye disease) and neurological problems have also been reported with Lyme disease.

Diagnosis and treatment

Lyme disease is tricky to diagnose because current tests can only indicate whether your horse has been exposed to the causative organism, not whether the horse has an active infection.

Because of the difficulty of this test, Lyme disease is usually diagnosed based on clinical signs and after other diseases with similar symptoms have been ruled out.

Treatment for Lyme disease is a regime of tetracycline, possibly given orally and by injection. In some cases, the disease is never completely eradicated from the body.

Prevention

As yet, no vaccine for Lyme disease is available. The best prevention is to keep your horse as tick-free as possible by keeping him stabled indoors if Lyme disease is a problem in your area; you can find out by asking your veterinarian. Groom your horse every day as well, keeping an eye out for embedded ticks; we provide details on ridding your horse of pests in Chapter 4.

A Fatal Neurological Disease: Rabies

Nearly everyone has heard of rabies, but most people don't know that horses can contract this disease. Rabies, which is alive and well all around the U.S., is caused by a virus that affects the nervous system. It's transmitted through the bite of an infected animal. When an open wound comes into contact with infected saliva, the virus gains entry into the body. Just about any type of wild mammal can transmit the disease to a horse, including a coyote, bat, or raccoon.

Symptoms

Infected horses may show classic symptoms such as hypersalivation, seizures, and other neurological problems, but they can just as often experience lethargy, colic, lameness, muscle twitching, or even abortion.

Diagnosis and treatment

The symptoms of rabies are similar to other neurological diseases, such as EPM (which we discuss earlier in this chapter), the equine encephalitis diseases (discussed earlier), equine herpes virus (also discussed earlier), and tetanus (which we discuss later in this chapter), so this disease can be hard to diagnose. In most cases, ruling out other possibilities is the best way to determine whether rabies is the culprit in a horse who's showing neurological symptoms. (A horse who's suspected of having rabies must be quarantined.)

No treatment exists for rabies in horses. The disease is almost always fatal, and can be definitely diagnosed only with a necropsy (an animal autopsy).

Prevention

To minimize the possibility of your horse contracting rabies, avoid attracting wildlife to your property by keeping trash containers well secured and keeping grain stores under tight control. But the best way to protect your horse against rabies is to vaccinate her. Talk to your veterinarian about the possibility of adding rabies to your vaccination program. Although rabies may be a relatively infrequent occurrence, the disease's frequency is increasing. Vaccination is a small price to pay for huge peace of mind.

A Nasty Bacterial Disease: Strangles

Strangles sounds nasty, and it is. Caused by the *Streptococcus equi* bacterium, this disease affects the lymph nodes. Strangles commonly occurs in younger horses between the ages of four months and five years. Older horses seem to be less susceptible, probably because their immune systems are more developed.

Strangles is transmitted from horse to horse, either by direct or indirect contact. A horse with strangles can contaminate a drinking trough, exposing all other horses who drink from that same trough. Horses can also pick up the disease from contaminated stalls.

The strep bug is a tenacious fellow! The bacterium can survive cold temperatures. In fact, freezing preserves it. It can live for three to four weeks in water that's been contaminated by nasal discharge. It can also live on wood, glass, and other surfaces for weeks.

Symptoms

Strangles causes fever, lethargy, and a thin, watery nasal discharge that eventually becomes very thick, and usually yellow. Horses usually start showing signs of the disease 7 to 12 days after exposure.

As strangles progresses, it often causes swelling at the throat area, where lymph nodes are situated between the jawbone and throat area. Affected horses may develop a harsh cough or noisy respiration, and a large abscess may form in the lymph nodes and then break open, draining the thick, ugly pus. Most horses recover, but some develop secondary infections or complications.

Approximately 15 to 20 percent of horses experience complications of strep infection, such as laryngeal inflammation and paralysis, and chronic infection of the guttural pouches (see Figure 12-2). These horses carry and shed the strep bacteria and may have recurrent episodes of coughing and nasal discharge. Other horses just carry the bacteria and aren't sick themselves, but can infect other horses.

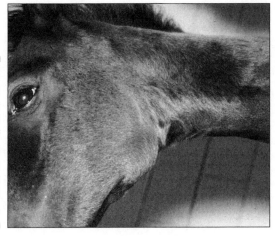

Dr. Janice Sojka, Purdue University

Figure 12-2: A horse with an advanced case of strangles may have a swollen guttural pouch.

Horses can also experience two very serious complications of strangles.

- ✔ One is purpura hemorrhagica, an immune system problem that causes severe inflammation of the blood vessels. Signs include swelling of the legs and hemorrhages on the gums and mucous membranes, and it may occur about three to four weeks after the initial infection.

- ✔ The other serious complication is "bastard" strangles, where the strep bug goes to the lungs, liver, kidneys, brain, or any other lymph node, and causes abscesses in the tissues of these areas. If these abscesses enlarge and rupture, the resulting infection and inflammation can be life-threatening.

Diagnosis and treatment

If your vet suspects that your horse has a guttural pouch infection, he or she will use an endoscope to view the guttural pouches, take a culture by doing a swab, and flush the pouches with antibiotics.

Treatment is supportive with isolated stall rest. The disease will run its course if the infection is mild. Severe cases with high fever and severe respiratory impairment from the abscess may require antibiotics, and even tracheostomy (a hole is cut in the trachea and a tube is inserted so that the horse can breathe through it). Vets disagree about how to treat the disease in its early stages, however. Using antibiotics as soon as the disease is diagnosed can prevent the formation of abscess, but prevent the horse from building a stronger immunity. This may result in a re-infection of the bacteria that remains in the environment. Coauthor Dr. Kate prefers to let the abscess form and rupture before giving antibiotics if necessary. (If the abscess doesn't open on its own, a veterinarian may have to lance and drain it.)

The serious complication of purpura hemorrhagica requires an aggressive approach and is considered a veterinary emergency. Treatment can include antibiotics, steroids to quiet the immune over-response, diuretics, leg wraps if necessary, and hydrotherapy, possibly in a hospital.

Prevention

Try to prevent strangles by isolating all new horses who come to your facility for at least two weeks.

Before you vaccinate your horse, ask your vet whether he or she recommends doing so based on your horse's level of exposure. Although vaccination may not prevent the disease completely, it may lessen the severity.

Never vaccinate a horse who is already showing signs of the disease, or any horse who has had strangles within the previous 12 months. These horses already have a high antibody concentration, and a vaccine could cause the horse to develop purpura hemorrhagica. If you have any question at all, ask your vet if taking a blood sample to check for a vaccine titer, or possibly a nasal culture, is in order.

You'd think that with modern science, strangles could be eradicated, but even the cleanest, best-run facilities have strangles outbreaks. Part of the problem is that even though vaccines are available, and horses who have had strangles infections develop some immunity, this resistance diminishes over time.

A Lockup of the Muscles: Tetanus

Tetanus, also called "lockjaw," is a serious and scary disease — and horses are particularly prone to it. Tetanus infection is caused by a toxin produced by the bacterium *Clostridium tetani*. This bacterium is commonly found in the intestinal tract of animals, and the spores can live in the soil for years. That means that it can be found everywhere in your horse's environment. Horses are also the most susceptible of all domestic animals to the tetanus toxin.

So how is tetanus transmitted? Horses are known for their predilection for injuries, even in the safest environment. Cuts and puncture wounds allow the bacterium to enter the tissues. Here, the bacterium releases its potent toxin. These toxins affect the neurotransmitters in the horse's spinal cord and brain, and the animal develops muscle spasms and can't relax.

Symptoms

The symptoms of tetanus include a stiff gait, muscle spasms, and protrusion of the third eyelid. Affected horses often jump violently when touched.

Diagnosis and treatment

A tetanus diagnosis is based on observing the horse's symptoms. Depending upon the severity of clinical signs when the horse develops symptoms, treatment focuses on locating and treating the wound, neutralizing residual toxin by administering an antitoxin, and providing nutritional and airway support if the horse's respiratory system is affected. Medication is also given to control muscle spasms.

Sadly, even with all possible intervention, tetanus in unvaccinated horses is always a very guarded to poor prognosis.

Prevention

Tetanus vaccine is one of the safest and most effective of equine vaccines. Every horse should be vaccinated against this disease.

Horses who are fortunate enough to recover from tetanus don't acquire future immunity and still require the vaccine yearly.

Attacking the Brain: West Nile Virus

West Nile virus has gotten a lot of press lately. The disease usually has serious effects on only two mammals: humans and horses. It attacks the body, infecting the brain and nervous system.

The virus was first detected in the U.S. in 1999 in Connecticut, and has since spread throughout the country. It can be an especially devastating disease, with up to 30 percent of infected horses dying or requiring euthanasia from complications of the disease. Of the survivors, approximately 17 percent have permanent neurological deficits.

Horses contract West Nile virus after being bitten by an infected mosquito. Birds are the main host of the disease. Mosquitoes bite infected birds, and then bite horses, transmitting the infection to them.

Symptoms

Horses infected with West Nile virus may experience either mild or severe neurological symptoms, including

- Lack of muscle coordination, stumbling, and weak limbs
- Partial paralysis
- Muscle twitching (especially around the muzzle)
- Hypersensitivity to sight or sound
- Head drooping
- Lethargy
- Falling asleep at inappropriate times, such as while eating

Symptoms usually appear seven to ten days after the horse is infected. Some horses also run a fever when they first start showing signs of the disease.

Diagnosis and treatment

Veterinarians diagnose West Nile virus by testing the horse's blood serum for antibodies against the virus. No cure exists, so treatment involves supportive care, such as intravenous fluids and anti-inflammatory drugs, to help the horse's body battle the effects of the organism.

Though not all horses who are bitten by an infected mosquito develop the disease, after a horse begins to show neurological problems, the prognosis for recovery is guarded.

Prevention

Regular vaccination is the best way to protect against West Nile virus. Most veterinarians recommend vaccinating twice a year for optimum protection. Vaccination protocol may depend on the climate and epidemiological status of the disease in different parts of the country.

Discourage mosquitoes from breeding on your property by getting rid of standing water and by adding mosquitofish to large water troughs and ponds.

Chapter 13

Staying Prepared with Equine First Aid

*H*orses have an amazing ability to hurt themselves. Maybe it's because they're such big creatures who are kept in relatively small confines. Or perhaps they're just naturally clumsy. (Coauthor Audrey recalls the story of a draft horse filly who once fell into her water trough and got her legs caught in a fence, all at the same time.) Whatever the reason, horses seem to get themselves in situations requiring first aid on a regular basis.

In this chapter, we show you how to prepare for a first-aid emergency. We give you instructions on how to deal with a variety of injuries and situations until your veterinarian arrives to save the day.

Gathering the Right Tools and Information for Emergencies

To effectively handle any equine emergency that may arise, you need to be prepared. That means you have to think ahead of time about how you might respond when your horse is in need, and you need to have the tools ready to do what's needed.

Before you do a thing, your first step in being prepared is having your horse vet's emergency number on hand and easy to find. Post it on your tack room door, put the number in your cellphone, and leave it for your horse sitter if you go away for the weekend. If you don't have your own trailer, have the phone number of an equine ambulance or friend with a trailer close at hand, too.

Staying aware of your horse's health

A big part of providing first aid for your horse is knowing when it's necessary. Discovering as much as you can about equine health will give you the knowledge you need to determine when your horse is in trouble and needs your help.

The following steps can help you develop a good working knowledge of horse health and prepare you for potential emergency situations:

- ✔ **Explore equine anatomy.** Memorizing the parts of the horse, where the major organs are located, and how the horse's body works will give you a solid background in how a healthy horse functions. (Chapter 10 is a great place to start.)

- ✔ **Know your horse.** Watch your horse when he's feeling well so that you can tell if something isn't right. Observant owners are usually the best judges of whether a horse is experiencing a health problem. (Chapter 2 lists the signs of a healthy horse.)

- ✔ **Find out about equine health problems.** Study up on the types of problems that can affect horses so that you're better able to recognize a health issue when it comes up. (Flip to Chapters 11 and 12 for a primer.)

If you become a knowledgeable horse owner in these areas, your veterinarian will love you for it.

Making the medicine go down

Unfortunately, horses aren't always cooperative when you try to give them their medicine. But we do have some tips and tricks that you can try to make this job easier.

If you're giving your horse a pill to swallow, disguise it. Grind it up and mix it with grain, applesauce, syrup, or even cake frosting. Experiment to see what works for your horse. (Never try to give your horse a pill without grinding it up first; he'll just spit it out.)

This trick also works with powdered medications. Some powdered medications are easily disguised in food. Others are bitter and require experimenting with added flavors. Powdered gelatin mix or a strawberry-flavored soft drink mix (like Kool-Aid) can often disguise unpleasant tasting powders.

To help your horse take liquid medicine, ask your vet about mixing it with pancake syrup or molasses in a syringe and depressing the syringe directly into the horse's mouth. If the medication is flavored, your vet may suggest that you mix it with some grain or pelleted feed.

Paste medications need to be administered directly into your horse's mouth. Depending on your horse, this will be either an easy task or a difficult one. Some horses let you put a syringe inside the corner of their mouths and allow you to inject the paste right in. Others fight you like a tiger to keep you from getting a syringe inside their mouths. If you have a horse who hates getting paste medicines, talk to your vet about getting the medication in an alternate form.

Assembling a first-aid kit

You can buy a complete first-aid kit at a tack store or through the Internet. Or you can put together your own by using a lunch pail or fishing tackle box. Keep the kit in your tack room or in your trailer if you travel with your horse. If you like to trail ride, consider putting together a small first-aid kit to take with you. The kit should fit in a saddle bag.

Include the following items in your kit:

- ✔ **Antibiotic ointment:** Triple antibiotic ointments are great for applying to minor wounds for protection against infection.

- ✔ **Antiseptic cleanser:** Chlorhexidine scrub is a good choice when it comes to an antiseptic cleaner for wounds.

- ✔ **Bandages:** Vet wrap bandages are good for applying pressure to leg wounds. They're available in tack stores, on the Internet, or through mail-order catalogs.

- ✔ **Cotton sheets or quilted wraps:** Sheets of cotton measuring 30 x 36 inches are good for wrapping injured legs.

- ✔ **Duct tape:** A roll of duct tape is useful in wrapping a hoof after a puncture wound.

- ✔ **Gauze pads:** Sterile, nonstick gauze pads are great for dressing small wounds, abscesses, and other breaks in the skin. They come in a variety of sizes.

- ✔ **Hand sanitizer:** If you can't find water to wash your hands, use a hand sanitizer before handling a wound.

- ✔ **Latex gloves:** These are handy if you have to handle an open wound on your horse.

- ✔ **Lubricant:** K-Y Jelly or another personal lubricant is good to have on hand for lubricating a rectal thermometer. (Petroleum jelly is not a good choice because it can irritate the lining of the rectum.)

- ✔ **Pocket knife:** A knife with a serrated edge sharp enough to cut is good to have because horses sometimes get tangled in ropes, wires, and their own tack.

- ✔ **Rectal thermometer:** A veterinary or human rectal thermometer is an absolute necessity. Knowing your horse's temperature before calling the vet helps give the doctor a better idea of what's wrong. (See Chapter 2 for instructions on taking your horse's temperature.)

- ✔ **Rubbing alcohol:** Rubbing alcohol is valuable as a disinfectant for rectal thermometers.

- ✔ **Scissors:** Scissors can be used for cutting bandages and cloths in an emergency.

✔ **Tweezers:** A splinter or cactus spine can be removed with a pair of tweezers.

✔ **Wound medication:** A wide variety of wound medications are available for use in a first-aid kit. These products help protect the wound, discourage flies from landing, soothe the skin, and promote healing. Ask your veterinarian for a recommendation.

Keep your first-aid kit up to date by replacing ointments, cleansers, alcohol, and lubricants every two years.

Considering the possibility of natural disasters

Unfortunately, catastrophic events such as hurricanes, floods, and wildfires have become all too common and have forced most communities to have evacuation strategies not only for people, but for animals as well. In the following sections, we explain the importance of planning for natural disasters and obtaining identification for your equine friend.

Making plans

Take the time to make a plan for any disaster that may strike your home, and know how to act on it if the time ever comes. The following points can help you evacuate and care for your horse in a disaster:

✔ Have a halter and lead rope available for every horse and have quick access to them.

✔ Plan a barn evacuation strategy in the event of fire. Your local fire department will be happy to help you devise a safety plan. You should also have a fire extinguisher in every barn and trailer, and be certain that each is in good working condition.

✔ Line up a ride for your horse well before a disaster strikes. If you don't have your own trailer, know who you'll call if you need to get your horse out of the area in a hurry.

✔ Don't wait until the last minute to evacuate your horses. Getting a horse out of danger quickly is usually very difficult. Heed voluntary evacuation warnings so that you'll have enough time to move your horse.

Securing permanent and temporary identification

Natural disasters like hurricanes, tornadoes, floods, fires, and even earthquakes can create situations where horses either escape from their enclosures or are deliberately turned loose in an effort to save their lives. Other horses are taken from their stalls or pastures by rescue workers and hauled to safety. If you're absent at the time of the rescue, you may have no way of knowing where your horse ends up.

You can mark your horse in permanent ways so that if disaster strikes, you're more likely to get your horse back. Here are some permanent ways to identify your horse:

- **Freeze brand:** A common and effective method of horse identification, freeze branding consists of a cold iron applied to the horse's neck. The freezing destroys the cells in the skin that produce color in the hair. The hair grows back white in the shape of the brand. (If your horse is white or gray, the hair doesn't grow back because the brand is held on longer, leaving an area of gray skin in the shape of the brand.) The brand provides a permanent mark that you record with a freeze-branding registry. Call your local brand inspector for a list of approved freeze branders in your area. (You can find brand inspectors by contacting your county extension agent.)

- **ID certificate:** Identification certificates for horses are available through some state agricultural offices. The identification certificate features line drawings with your horse's markings, brands, scars, and other identifying factors drawn in. The vet filling out the paperwork gives a written description of the horse and files the certificate with the state.

- **Lip tattoo:** If your horse is retired off the racetrack, he already has a lip tattoo. Or a veterinarian can put one on the inside of your horse's upper lip. Some people like this form of identification best because it can't be seen unless you lift up the horse's lip.

  Before you go this route, check with your horse's breed registry (if you have one) to make sure that their rules allow you to have your horse's lip tattooed. (Be aware that lip tattoos tend to fade and become unreadable.)

- **Microchip:** An electronic identification microchip is placed into a ligament in your horse's neck by a veterinarian. This tiny computer chip contains a unique number that corresponds to your contact information. This information is maintained electronically by a microchip-registering company. You can't see the chip, and it doesn't cause the horse any discomfort.

Even if your horse has permanent identification of some kind, adding a temporary ID is a good idea if you're preparing to evacuate because of an emergency. Rescuers will be looking for temporary identification on horses who have been separated from their owners, and this type of ID is easier to see. Here are some ways to identify your horse to help ensure that you get him back when the crisis is over:

- **Fetlock ID bands:** These bands attach to your horse's fetlock area and should contain your name, address, and a phone number where you can be reached during the emergency. (You can order these bands via the Internet.)

✔ **Hair ID:** Using clippers, shave your phone number into your horse's neck. You can also use a permanent marker for this if you don't have clippers available.

✔ **Halter tag:** Sold in tack stores and through equine catalogs, halter tags attach to the side of the halter. They're engraved with one or two lines — usually the owner's phone number and address. You can also use a luggage tag with your contact information and attach it to your horse's halter.

✔ **Photographs and record of identifying marks:** Take color photographs of your horse with you, along with notes on any identifying features such as scars, brands, markings, cowlicks, and anything else that sets your horse apart. Make sure that the photos show your horse from both sides and from the front and rear.

✔ **Tail ID:** A luggage tag with your name, phone number, and address and your horse's information can be attached to your horse's tail.

Braid the tag into the tail. Don't tie it to the dock of the tail because this can cut off circulation.

Approaching an Injured Horse

Few things are as scary as an injured horse. Horses are big animals, and their injuries are often dramatic. Injured horses are often scared and in great pain. They're sometimes panicky, too, especially if they're unable to get up or move.

To keep yourself and your horse safe during an injury emergency, you need to know the best way to approach and handle the horse. You can do a lot to help an injured horse, but you have to do it carefully or both you and the horse can suffer serious consequences.

One of the best things that coauthor Dr. Kate ever learned about emergency medicine was that in the event of an emergency, the first thing you do is take your own pulse. Why? It causes you to take a deep breath and gives you a moment to calm yourself. If you can't take your own pulse, or if your pulse is racing out of control, you won't do the horse much good.

Keep the following points in mind if you ever encounter an injured horse:

✔ **Stay calm.** It can be hard not to panic when you see a horse injured, especially if the horse is panicking too. But getting hysterical is the worst thing that you can do. Horses feed off your emotions, and if you stay calm, the horse is more likely to relax and allow herself to be helped. (By the way, Dr. Kate says that staying calm is easier for a vet because it's not the vet's horse experiencing the emergency.)

✔ **Call for help.** If you're alone, calm the horse down by staying calm and reassuring her, and then call for help right away. Ask someone to do that for you if you're with other people. You should call an equine veterinarian or even 911 if a horse is trapped and injured.

✔ **Put human safety first.** If a person also has been injured or if someone gets hurt trying to help an injured horse, help the person first before you attend to the horse.

✔ **Wash your hands.** If you need to handle a wound, wash your hands, use hand sanitizer, or put on latex gloves to prevent infection. (We explain how to handle wounds later in this chapter.)

Applying First Aid

Giving first aid to your horse depends on the situation. Do a bit of studying up on how to handle each of the following problems so that when an emergency hits, you're ready.

Wounds

Wounds come in several different types, and as you find out in the following sections, you need to handle each one differently when you administer first aid.

If your horse is bleeding freely from an open wound of any variety, try not to panic. Have someone call the vet while you apply first aid. Here's how:

1. **Assess the situation.**

   If you understand the type of bleeding that you're seeing, you can accurately gauge the seriousness of the situation.

   • If blood is spurting from your horse, your horse probably has severed an artery. In this case, take immediate action to stop the flow of blood.

   • On the other hand, if the blood is dark and oozing, it's coming from a vein. You should try to stop the bleeding, but this kind of blood loss usually isn't life threatening.

2. **Quiet the horse.**

   You need a cooperative patient if you're going to stop the bleeding. Talk to your horse and ask him to stand in one place because movement will make the bleeding worse. Keep everyone around you calm because hysterics will only upset the horse.

3. **Apply pressure.**

   Put pressure on the wound to help stop the flow of blood. Do this by wrapping a bandage around the source of the blood flow. If you can't do this because the affected area is too large to bandage, put a piece of gauze or another clean, absorbent material against it and press firmly. If you don't have a bandage or other material to press against the wound and the blood seems to be coming from an artery, use your bare hand to apply pressure to the wound. (Wear a latex glove if you can to avoid infecting the wound.)

4. **Add a tourniquet.**

   If you're dealing with a severed artery in the leg and applying pressure doesn't help stop the spurting of blood, make a tourniquet out of a clean towel or piece of cloth. Do this by wrapping the cloth around the leg above the wound (between the heart and the point of bleeding). Tighten the tourniquet and tie it until the blood flow stops. While waiting for a vet to arrive, loosen the tourniquet every 15 minutes for a few minutes at a time to allow blood to temporarily flow back into the leg.

Many wounds tend to happen on the legs. Know how to properly and safely wrap legs before you tackle this situation (Figure 13-1 shows a properly wrapped wound). If you wrap too loose, the bandage slips and can potentially slow down the blood supply. Wrap the leg too tight and your well-intentioned wrap could cause a bowed tendon. Ask your veterinarian to show you how to wrap a leg so that if your horse ever injures himself, you're prepared. (When coauthor Dr. Kate was in vet school, the students had to put bandages on each other's legs and wear them for several hours while attending classes. It was a great lesson, as you can imagine.)

Figure 13-1:
Clean and dress a serious wound just after it occurs.

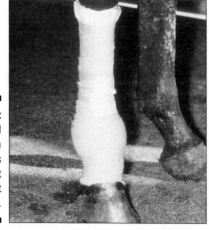

Dr. Janice Sojka, Purdue University

Abrasions

Abrasions are superficial wounds that usually result when a horse scrapes himself on something with a rough or jagged surface. Poorly fitting tack can also cause abrasions.

These types of wounds aren't dangerous in and of themselves unless they're particularly large and/or deep and become infected. You can prevent infection by handling an abrasion properly as soon as you discover the wound.

If your horse gets an abrasion that isn't too deep or large, you can handle it yourself with the following steps:

1. **If the abrasion is bleeding profusely, stop the blood by following the steps we give earlier in this chapter.**

2. **Cleanse the area with chlorhexidine scrub and apply antibiotic ointment.**

3. **Don't bandage the area.**

   You want the area to be exposed to the air to help ward off infection. Lower-leg abrasions are an exception; they can benefit from bandaging to prevent fly infestations.

4. **If the area becomes swollen, contact your veterinarian.**

Flies can feed and lay their eggs in a wound, so be sure to keep these pests away from any open sores on your horse's body. You can buy special wound cream that contains fly repellent at your local tack store or on the Internet. See Chapter 4 for more information about getting rid of pests.

Lacerations

If your horse cuts himself, he's suffering from a *laceration*. Lacerations can be shallow or deep, depending on their severity.

Take the following steps if your horse has a laceration:

1. **Flush the wound with water from a garden hose to get rid of foreign material like dirt or rocks.**

2. **If foreign material clings stubbornly to the site, use chlorhexidine scrub on a sponge to clean it gently.**

3. **If the wound is bleeding, apply pressure to stem the flow of blood (just follow the steps we give earlier in this chapter).**

4. **If the laceration is shallow, apply antibiotic ointment to the wound — don't bandage it — and let it heal on its own.**

If the laceration is deep (you can tell because deep lacerations bleed profusely and appear to go deep into the skin), don't apply ointment. Instead, contact your veterinarian right away.

Punctures

Puncture wounds are serious because they provide an avenue for bacteria to enter deep into the body. Nails and other sharp objects are the most frequent culprits for puncture wounds.

If your horse suffers a puncture wound, follow these steps for first aid:

1. **If the object is still embedded in the horse, remove it carefully and keep it; if it's embedded very deeply, have your veterinarian remove it.**

2. **If the puncture wound is on the bottom of the hoof, mark the area of the wound with a pen so that the vet can find it.**

3. **Don't try to stop the bleeding.**

   The flow of blood helps wash out the bacteria.

4. **Call a veterinarian right away.**

The danger of serious infection is real with a puncture wound, so you need a vet to come out and examine the wound. (Chapter 12 covers infections and their consequences in more detail.)

Fractures

Fractures are terrifying and serious injuries in a horse. The way that you handle first aid with a fracture can mean the difference between life and death for your horse.

When a horse fractures a bone — usually a leg — the initial injury is only part of the problem. As the horse struggles to stand or walk, further injury occurs.

If your horse fractures a bone, follow these steps:

1. **Have someone call a veterinarian immediately.**

2. **Immobilize the fracture site by keeping the horse as quiet as possible and keeping him from moving.**

   You can do this by staying calm, reassuring your horse with a soothing voice, and asking him not to move by saying "whoa."

3. **If a wound is present along with the fracture, control the bleeding by putting pressure on the area.**

   Clean the wound with water and bandage it to prevent contamination with bacteria. (Do this only if you can keep the horse quiet.)

4. **Don't attempt to transport the horse before a veterinarian arrives to splint the broken bone.**

Poisoning

Unlike dogs and cats, horses don't routinely get into poisonous household cleansers and antifreeze. They can still eat toxic substances, however, usually in the form of plants growing along the trail or in the pasture. (See the nearby sidebar "Problem plants" for a long list of threats.)

You may not know that your horse has eaten a toxic plant until he starts to exhibit the symptoms of poisoning. The symptoms depend on the type of toxin ingested. Some common poisoning symptoms include

- Colic (this ailment is explained in Chapter 11)
- Neurological symptoms like staggering
- Refusal to eat or drink
- Diarrhea
- Lethargy
- Poor coat and body condition that worsens over time
- Abortion of foal
- Profuse sweating

The symptoms of poisoning are similar to many other illnesses, so your veterinarian will need to determine the cause if your horse is exhibiting any of these behaviors or conditions. If you see one or more of the noted symptoms, call your vet immediately; treatment depends on the type of poisoning that has occurred.

Bites

Horses live outdoors and sometimes come into contact with other animals. These meetings can result in a horse being bitten. The consequences of a bite depend on the type of animal and the seriousness of the bite, as you find out in the following sections. If your horse is bitten, take steps immediately to deal with the situation.

Spiders

Two species of spiders can cause painful and serious bites in horses: the black widow and the brown recluse. If your horse is bitten by one of these spiders, you'll probably see a wound that starts as a dime-sized lump and gradually grows larger as the hair falls out. The spot is sore to the touch, and your horse may even start rubbing it on fence posts or the walls of his stall. Eventually, the lump opens up and a thick greenish pus begins to ooze out.

Problem plants

As a horse owner, you need to know the most common poisonous plants in your area. Watch out for these plants in your pasture or along the trail. If your horse eats one of these, contact your veterinarian right away:

- Arrowgrass
- Asters
- Azalea
- Black locust
- Black walnut
- Boxwood
- Broomweed
- Buckwheat
- Buttercup
- Castor bean
- Clover
- Cotton
- Fern palm
- Fescue
- Fitweed
- Ground ivy
- Hemlock
- Horse chestnut
- Hydrangea
- Indian paintbrush
- Lantana
- Larkspur
- Locoweed
- Lupine
- Mesquite
- Milkweed
- Mistletoe
- Mountain laurel
- Oak
- Oleander
- Onions
- Rape
- Red maple
- Rhododendron
- Snakewood
- Squirreltail grass
- Tobacco
- Wild cherry
- Yew

If you discover a bite wound on your horse, follow these steps to provide him with relief:

1. **Call your veterinarian.**

   You need a vet to treat the bite, which has become infected. Your vet may administer antivenin (if the wound isn't too old) and/or antibiotics, and may perform minor surgery to remove damaged tissue.

2. **Don't let your horse rub the bite.**

   While waiting for your vet, keep your horse from rubbing the area by tying him in a place where he can't rub.

3. **Remove food from your horse's reach (providing him with water is okay).**

   Take your horse's food away from him in case your vet needs to give him a sedative or anesthetic for the surgery.

Where one spider lurks, many others can be found. Search out black widows and brown recluses in dark corners. Get rid of clutter where these spiders can hide.

Snakes

Most snakes found in the U.S. are harmless. That said, you do have about 25 poisonous species to worry about. The most common of these is the pit viper. Species in this family are the rattlesnake, cottonmouth or water moccasin, and copperhead. Each can deliver a bite that can make a horse very sick. It's a good idea to find out what each of these reptiles looks like so that you recognize them if you see them on the trail. (The easiest way to know what these critters look like is to do a simple Internet search.)

If you happen to run across one of these snakes, go around it, giving it plenty of room. These snakes usually coil as a warning before they strike, and rattlers shake their noisy tails. If you happen to see a viper in this position and you can't pass at least 30 feet from it, turn your horse around and go the other way. The snake will probably leave the trail after you're gone, and you can go back several minutes later to see if it returned to the brush.

If your horse accidentally steps on one of these snakes or gets bitten on the face by one because he lowered his nose to investigate, follow these tips and try not to panic. Most snake bites aren't fatal, although they can cause lameness, swelling, and plenty of discomfort.

- ✔ **Try to keep your horse from moving.** The more he moves, the faster the venom will circulate through his body. (This is if the snake injected venom in its bite — not all bites contain venom.)

- ✔ **Call for help, either with a cellphone or by sending another rider ahead.** If you're alone and don't have a phone (or can't get cell service), tie your horse to a tree and go get help. If this isn't feasible, slowly hand-walk your horse to get help.

- ✔ **If you trail ride frequently in an area where pit vipers are common, consider carrying two 5- to 6-inch long pieces of garden hose in your saddle pack.** If your horse is bitten in the face, inserting the hose pieces into his nostrils will keep them from swelling shut.

✔ **Don't put a tourniquet above the bite, cut the wound, or try to suck out the venom**. These methods are old wives' tales that will do more harm than good.

Other animals

Your horse may tangle with just about any kind of animal when out in a pasture, but the most common altercations are with other horses. If your horse is bitten severely by another horse, let the wound heal on its own with just an application of antibiotic ointment. Keep flies out of it as it heals with a combination wound cream/fly repellent. Make certain that your horse is up to date on his tetanus vaccine because the wound can become contaminated with the tetanus organism that's widespread in the horse's environment. (See Chapter 12 for more information about tetanus.)

If your horse is bitten by another type of animal, like a dog, cat, coyote, or raccoon, call your veterinarian immediately. These types of bites are prone to infection, and antibiotics may be warranted.

Choking

When a horse chokes, it's not the same as when a person or even a dog or cat chokes. Food doesn't block the horse's airway — instead it blocks his esophagus and makes him unable to swallow.

You can tell that your horse is choking if he coughs and salivates with his head down while watery food comes out of his nose and mouth. He may also back away from his food, act anxious, and/or swallow repeatedly.

If your horse is choking, call the vet right away. Food trapped in the esophagus can cause irritation that often results in scarring and permanent damage or may actually rupture the wall of the esophagus. The scarring causes the esophagus to narrow, which means that the horse is more prone to choking in the future. While you're waiting for the vet, don't allow your horse to have access to any food or water.

Burns

It's rare for a horse to experience a burn, but it sometimes happens. Horses can be singed in a barn or brush fire, accidentally electrocute themselves, or get a very bad sunburn.

✔ If your horse receives a burn from an open flame or from an electrical wire, contact your vet immediately. While waiting for the vet to arrive, run cool water over the burned area.

✔ Sunburn is the most common type of burn seen in horses and tends to happen more often to horses with pink skin. The muzzle and nose are most prone to this, although horses with pink skin on their backs can also get sunburned. A sunburned horse can benefit from an application of aloe, which helps soothe the skin. It's best to protect your horse before he becomes sunburned. A thick, zinc oxide ointment can shield the area and prevent it from burning. Some people simply use a strong sunscreen lotion to keep the sun from burning sensitive skin. Ask your veterinarian to recommend a sunscreen suitable for use on horses.

Another option is to keep your horse indoors during the day. Or you can fit your horse with a sun-blocking *fly mask*. If your horse has a pink muzzle that tends to burn, purchase a mask that extends down the nose and covers the delicate area.

Heat stroke

When horses work hard in hot weather, they're prone to heat stroke — especially if they're unfit for the task that they're performing. Heat stroke occurs when a horse is unable to cool his body temperature because of increased exercise and hot, usually humid weather.

If you see any of the following symptoms in your horse, he may be suffering from heat stroke:

✔ **Sweating stops:** Even though the horse is exerting himself, he stops sweating.

✔ **Heavy breathing:** Your horse is breathing more heavily than usual at rest and may even try to breathe through his mouth.

✔ **Fatigue:** Your horse becomes tired and has trouble continuing with his exercise.

✔ **Stumbling:** Just walking is difficult for a horse with heat stroke, and the horse begins to stumble.

If you notice any of these signs in your horse, stop all activity and contact a veterinarian immediately. While you're waiting, work on getting the horse's body temperature back to normal by pouring cool water on his body, especially around the head and neck and on the inside of the legs. By cooling the blood flowing though these areas, you can bring down the overall body temperature. Try to move the horse into the shade too.

If your horse is diagnosed with heat stroke, give him a couple of weeks of rest before asking him to work again.

Knowing When to Call the Vet Immediately

If something is wrong with your horse, should you automatically call the vet? That depends on what the problem is. You can handle some issues yourself, or at least provide first aid before the vet comes.

Some situations are serious, though, and require an immediate call to the vet. If your horse has one or more of these symptoms, call your vet for help:

- **Bleeding:** If your horse has significant bleeding, apply pressure to stop the flow as we describe in the earlier section "Wounds." Then call the vet.

- **Bloody urine:** If blood comes out when your horse urinates, she may have an infection or bladder injury.

- **Choking:** If your horse coughs and salivates with her head down, and watery food comes out of her nose and mouth, and she acts anxious, swallows repeatedly, and/or backs away from her food, she may be choking. (We discuss choking in more detail earlier in this chapter.)

- **Colic:** Signs of colic may include profuse sweating, repeatedly lying down and getting up, pawing, standing with her legs outstretched, rolling, and/or biting at the abdomen. Take away the horse's food and hand-walk the horse until the vet arrives. (For more information on colic, see Chapter 11.)

- **Diarrhea:** Severe, liquid, foul-smelling diarrhea is an emergency.

- **Difficulty breathing:** Horses who are breathing rapidly, coughing repeatedly, or have noisy, raspy breath need to be seen by a veterinarian.

- **Fever:** If your horse's temperature is significantly above 101.5 degrees Fahrenheit (38.6 degrees Celsius) or below 99 degrees Fahrenheit (37.7 degrees Celsius), call your veterinarian right away. (We explain how to take your horse's temperature in Chapter 2.)

- **Inability to stand:** Staggering, falling, or not being able to get up signals an equine emergency.

✔ **Injury:** Deep wounds that expose the bone are emergencies, as are puncture wounds. Infected wounds also demand a call to the vet.

✔ **Irritated eye:** If one or both of your horse's eyes becomes teary or is held partially or completely closed, contact your vet. Other signs of serious eye problems include the white part of the eye turning red, sensitivity to light, a cloudy surface, or the inability to see in the dark. (See Chapter 11 for the basics on eye problems.)

✔ **Pain:** A horse showing pain in any part of her body should be seen by a vet.

✔ **Refusal to eat:** This is a serious sign of illness.

✔ **Straining:** Straining to defecate or urinate with little or no result may indicate a serious intestinal or urethral blockage.

✔ **Swelling:** Swelling in any part of the body requires a call to the vet.

Chapter 14

Checking Out Complementary and Alternative Therapies

. . . .

In This Chapter

▶ Discovering different types of nontraditional therapies

▶ Finding out how to choose a practitioner

. . . .

*Y*ou've no doubt heard about alternative therapies in relation to human health. Well, many of these same therapies are available for horses too. Really!

Alternative medicine is called alternative medicine because that's just what it is: an alternative to conventional medicine. In recent years, different types of alternative therapies have grown in popularity, both in human and veterinary medicine. That's because, in many cases, they work.

Your authors believe that alternative therapies work well when used in conjunction with conventional medicine or in place of traditional therapies when these therapies haven't proven helpful. In a nutshell, we want you to understand and hopefully embrace alternative medicine but still rely on conventional veterinary medicine, too. We use many of these therapies on our own horses, and coauthor Dr. Kate practices them. So you're in good hands in this chapter! Here we explain the different types of alternative medicines available to horses and what kind of problems these therapies can address. We also show you how to find a trustworthy practitioner. You'll know a thing or two about what you can do in addition to conventional veterinary medicine after you finish this chapter.

Working with your primary-care veterinarian as a veterinary healthcare team will help your horse get the best integrative and comprehensive care. Your veterinarian should remain your horse's primary care provider and provide all conventional (or Western) medical and surgical needs and diagnostics that your horse may need.

Understanding Which Treatments May Help Your Horse

Alternative medicine comes in a variety of treatments. Although scientific studies have shown some of these therapies to be useful, the success of others is based on anecdotal evidence. In the following sections, take a look at the different types of alternative therapies available for horses to get an idea of what's out there.

No one therapy can cure every disease or condition, but some of the therapies in the following sections can surely help. They can work to complement traditional treatments or as a substitute for traditional practice.

- In the first case, alternative therapies can be used in conjunction with traditional treatment. For example, a horse with a tendon injury can be treated traditionally, and then acupuncture can be used to help the horse heal faster.

- In the latter case, we recommend that you go this route only if you try traditional therapies and don't find success with them.

Acupuncture and Traditional Chinese Veterinary Medicine

Acupuncture is probably the most well-known alternative therapy. This ancient Chinese practice has taken hold in the Western world, both in human and veterinary medicine, and with good reason: It works. Acupuncture goes hand in hand with Traditional Chinese Veterinary Medicine (TCVM), another ancient practice.

In the narrowest sense, *acupuncture* is the application of small-gauge needles to various points on the body in order to cause physiological responses in the treatment of almost any disease or condition. It can be especially useful for relieving pain.

In a broader sense, acupuncture is an ancient procedure used in TCVM for the treatment of whole-body conditions. TCVM is an entire medical system that also includes food therapy, herbal prescription medications, massage therapy (known as *tui-na*; we discuss massage in more detail later in this chapter), and addressing emotional/behavioral and environmental issues.

According to acupuncture theory, electrical life energy, or *Qi* (pronounced *chee*), travels through the body in very specific pathways called *meridians*. Acupuncture points act as valves along the pathways, which the acupuncturist can manipulate with needles to change the energy flow, help balance that energy, and promote a healing response. Horses' bodies want to be healthy — this natural inclination toward health is how you can fight or, better yet, *prevent* disease. Western medicine has a more mechanistic view of health, reducing disease and illness to specific cellular and molecular systems.

If you're wondering right now how your horse is going to feel about having needles stuck in her, take heart. The needles are usually small enough that horses experience minimal pain. However, the needle stimulation can cause warmth, tingling, or numbness, which can be slightly discomforting to some horses. Most don't seem to notice the individual placement of needles during their session. Many horses become very relaxed or sleepy and may continue to sleep for hours after their treatment. Others may feel energized and may have increased energy and activity. These responses signal neurological or hormonal changes or pain relief brought about by the treatment.

Because TCVM (including its most common component, acupuncture) is an entire preventative and therapeutic medical system in itself, you can use it as a supportive or adjunct therapy for a vast number of diseases and problems and not just for pain control. For example:

- ✔ Veterinarians have reported favorable acupuncture results in the treatment of cardiovascular disorders, chronic respiratory conditions, skin disorders, gastrointestinal problems, allergies, reproductive disorders, immune-mediated problems, musculoskeletal diseases, neurological disorders, and disc disease, as well as behavioral problems in horses.

- ✔ It also helps support the care and recovery of cancer patients, often improving their quality of life during treatment.

- ✔ Emergency veterinarians may even use acupuncture to help stop or control seizures and to aid in cardiac CPR.

Using the other components of TCVM in addition to acupuncture can increase your horse's chances for health and recovery.

- ✔ Food therapy is very important and, as practiced in TCVM, very specific for each individual patient. For example, an older horse showing a certain pattern of disharmony in the body would be given more barley in his diet.

- ✔ Chinese herbal prescriptions are very specific prescription medications used to treat disease imbalances. They aren't over-the-counter substances.

- ✔ The practitioner may also teach you how to perform massage or acupressure procedures to help your horse at home.

Aromatherapy

Aromatherapy is the therapeutic use of plant essences, or *essential oils*, for healing. You can use aromatherapy alone, but many people commonly use it in conjunction with massage therapy (which we discuss later in this chapter) and other bodywork techniques. Aromatherapy is most commonly used to calm and relax horses.

Some plant oils have inherent antibacterial, anti-inflammatory, and healing properties. Other oils are used for their aromatic properties, which supposedly affect healing and well-being. The essential oils used in aromatherapy come from flowers, leaves, bark, and the fruit of plants. They usually have a very strong scent.

Aromatherapy works like this: When the potent scent molecules from the plant essences are inhaled into the body, they're read by the limbic system of the brain, which then triggers the endocrine system to release various neurochemicals that cause varied responses in the body. For example, essential oil of lavender seems to exert a calming effect on animals and people.

Aromatherapy is generally very safe, although some oils can render a horse disqualified in a drug test for a competitive event. Camphor, menthol, and thymol are absorbed systemically and can cause positive reactions in drug tests. Some oils are also very irritating and can cause sensitivity reactions if applied to the skin of some horses.

Flower essences, such as the popular Bach flower essences available in health food stores, are distillates of flower blossoms or plants that are believed to have powerful harmonizing effects on animals. They're frequently used for behavioral, emotional, and stress-related issues. One of the most common Bach flower essences is Rescue Remedy, which some horse owners feel helps to alleviate anxiety in their horse during situations such as trailering and weaning. In fact, some competitors not only give Rescue Remedy to their horse prior to competition, but also take it themselves to help calm preshow jitters.

Chiropractic

You've no doubt heard of chiropractic for humans. Believe it not, chiropractic is used quite a bit on horses too. *Chiropractic* is the use of manipulation of the spine, joints, and specific anatomic regions of the body to cause a therapeutic response. It uses controlled forces applied to these areas to improve neurological and physical function.

The theory behind chiropractic is that spinal and joint dysfunction can affect the normal physiological function and balance in healthy horses. The health of the spine and all associated structures — including the vertebrae, nerves, blood vessels, muscles, and ligaments — is involved. Chiropractic care is an excellent therapy to help horses heal from injuries that often involve secondary compensatory problems; these problems result when one part of the body is injured or weak and another part becomes overworked or injured trying to compensate.

Veterinary chiropractors perform adjustments to the spine and joints to correct any improper alignment and restore normal range of motion, and thus restore health and relieve pain. Most horses don't seem to mind chiropractic adjustments. Some even seem to enjoy them. A good chiropractor will take care with a horse's painful areas, using gentle techniques to reduce pain before making an adjustment to the horse's spine.

You can find chiropractors without veterinary degrees, but coauthor Dr. Kate recommends that you use only veterinary chiropractors for your horse because their veterinary knowledge is key in properly assessing your horse's healthcare issues. They also know when chiropractic care is the best option for your horse or whether you should use conventional care and diagnostics. We give you the scoop on finding trustworthy practitioners later in this chapter.

Homeopathy

Homeopathy is a healing system developed by Samuel Hahnemann in the late 1700s in Germany. In this form of healing, extremely diluted forms of particular substances are given to a patient to promote healing. Some of these substances include arnica montana, chamomilla, and nux vomica.

Proponents of homeopathy say that this therapy treats the patient, not the disease. Each horse is diagnosed and treated on a specific, individual basis. For example, two horses with a similar diagnosis of degenerative joint disease would both be treated conventionally with a drug called bute and possibly other drugs or procedures. But with homeopathy, the veterinarian would consider the individual differences in each horse's underlying disease processes, and he or she would treat each horse differently.

Homeopathic practitioners look to restore the balanced state of the patient's *vital force*. Hahnemann's theory is that disease manifests when there's a d isruption of that vital force. When the integrity of the vital force is restored, so is the animal's health, and the disease is cured. Hahnemann believed in thoroughly assessing all aspects of a patient's health issues for clues to determine the disruption of the vital force and prescribe a specific remedy.

You can dilute homeopathic remedies to a strength of only 1:10,000. Although such a dilution contains an almost imperceptible amount of the original substance, homeopaths maintain that shaking the solution appropriately between dilutions to add energy has a positive effect on a patient. The exact dilution of the remedy is also determined by the individual patient.

Horses can drink the remedy if it's added to their water, or they may eat the remedy in solid form after it's mixed with some grain.

If you want to treat your horse with this type of therapy, seek out a qualified, experienced veterinarian who's trained and certified in veterinary homeopathy. (We explain how to find a practitioner later in this chapter.)

Laser therapy

If you (or your horse) have had any surgery within the last five to ten years, the surgeon probably used a surgical laser to expedite the procedure and cause less trauma. You probably had a faster and less painful surgery and a quicker recovery, thanks to the laser.

Although surgical lasers are extremely high-powered, using low-powered lasers to reduce tissue swelling and shorten healing time for numerous soft-tissue problems and injuries is becoming common. These low-light lasers are believed to help healing by utilizing electromagnetic radiation that's transformed into amplified light beams. These beams can penetrate the skin and some muscle tissue and may stimulate the release of neurotransmitters, which in turn can enhance cellular functions without producing heat.

The most common application for low-light laser therapy in horses is treating tendon and ligament problems. Some practitioners use laser therapy to manage the pain that comes from navicular syndrome and arthritis (see Chapter 11 for more information on these ailments). It may also facilitate the healing of wounds.

In addition, some acupuncturists use laser therapy to stimulate acupuncture points that may be too difficult or dangerous to needle in a horse who won't stand still for treatment. (We discuss acupuncture in more detail earlier in this chapter.)

By the way, the word *laser* is actually an acronym for Light Amplification by Stimulated Emission of Radiation. Who knew!

Magnetic therapy

You've undoubtedly seen folks at horse shows wearing those interesting necklaces and bracelets made of magnets. Many people who wear them swear that these magnets have pain reducing and healing powers. Proponents claim that certain parts of the body respond positively to magnetic fields. This notion has caught on to the point that every horse publication and equine supply catalog has at least one advertisement for magnetic therapy products. You can find these products for horses in hock wraps, blankets, and even headbands. For humans, you can find jewelry, mattress pads, and even socks.

Although most healing benefits of magnetic therapy are believed to be a result of initiating cell membrane stabilization in tissue that has been disrupted, some believe that magnets also reduce pain. Magnets help to stimulate hoof growth and treat navicular problems, laminitis, and thrush. Magnetic leg wraps supposedly speed healing, generate heat, and increase blood flow by rearranging the ions in the blood stream. They also treat tendon and bone problems. However, many conventional scientists don't believe these claims because no double-blind studies have been conducted to prove them.

Electromagnetic therapy is the use of pulsating electromagnetic energy via electrical current. In addition to the previously mentioned applications, veterinarians also use this form of magnetic therapy for fracture healing.

Massage therapy

Massage therapy comes in many different forms. It's great for relaxing horses and for increasing their circulation. It can also help ease muscle soreness and stiffness. Massage therapy can be helpful after strenuous exercise to help muscles get rid of waste products like lactic acid.

Massage therapy also facilitates bonding between owner and horse. People who routinely massage their horses notice health problems with their animals early, when treatment can be quicker, easier, and less expensive. Coauthor Dr. Kate believes that all horse owners can benefit from studying even the most basic massage techniques so that they can use them on a regular basis to enhance their horse's well-being.

You can use different types of strokes with various massage therapies, each with specific applications. And massage can also include the use of liniments and essential oils.

A popular type of massage for horses is *equine sport massage therapy*. Designed to increase circulation, relax muscle spasms, relieve tension, enhance muscle tone, and increase range of motion, this type of massage is most popular on performance horses.

Another technique often categorized as massage is T.Touch. Developed by horsewoman Linda Tellington-Jones, the technique involves circular movements of the fingers and hands on various parts of the horse's body.

The theory behind this technique is that cells in the body retain memory of injury or pain. The movement to the skin applied through the T.Touch method helps reset the body's cellular memory, thus eliminating the pain or emotional issue associated with that part of the body.

T.Touch is used for a variety of purposes, including muscle stiffness and soreness, as well as pain in any part of the horse's body. Behavior issues arising from fear, anxiety, and lack of confidence can also be treated with this method.

Nutraceutical therapy

A *nutraceutical* (the word comes from a combination of *nutrition* and *pharmaceutical*) is a dietary supplement that supposedly has benefits that go beyond nutrition effects but aren't quite in the category of a drug. Although some would classify nutraceuticals as alternative treatment, the use of these compounds has grown so dramatically that you'd be hard-pressed to find a conventional veterinary practice that doesn't carry at least one of these products.

The good news about nutraceuticals is that they aren't regulated as drugs, so they're easier to get. The bad news is that their effectiveness hasn't been conclusively proven. The claims and benefits are mostly anecdotal and theoretical. Plus, not all nutraceuticals are created equal; the difference in quality of ingredients can vary because little standardization exists.

Horse owners have so many nutraceuticals to choose from that picking the right one can make your head hurt. You see nutraceuticals in a wide range of prices, along with an even wider range of ingredients. They can be found to help manage a wide range of conditions, including allergies, arthritis, and hoof problems.

On the market you can find some excellent nutraceuticals that coauthor Dr. Kate has personally used through the years on her patients, and she believes that these animals have benefited from them. But she also thinks that, in most cases, your horse can get along fine without them if you have an excellent equine healthcare program in place. Remember: Nothing will turn old Dobbin into the next Secretariat.

Nutritional therapy

Certain diseases can benefit from nutritional therapy, which is basically the use of food to help control the disease process. Some examples of equine illnesses that you can manage with nutritional therapy include hyperkalemic periodic paralysis (HYPP), which is a genetic disease affecting the muscles; pituitary pars intermedia dysfunction (PPID), or Cushing's disease, which is a metabolic condition; equine metabolic syndrome (EMS); and insulin resistance (IR). (See Chapter 11 for details on the last three ailments in this list.)

For example, in horses with HYPP, veterinarians instruct owners to give the affected horses feeds that are low in potassium; examples include alfalfa, timothy, Bermuda grass hays, beat pulp, and oats. In fact, owners can find proprietary feeds made just for HYPP horses.

If your horse is diagnosed with an illness that you can manage with nutritional therapy, your veterinarian will instruct you on how to best feed your horse.

Physical therapy

Physical therapy comes in many different shapes and sizes. Everything from *craniosacral* work (moving the spinal and cranial bones to treat the central nervous system) to hyperbaric oxygen therapy to therapeutic ultrasound falls under the heading of physical therapy. More traditional physical therapy focuses on veterinary sports medicine and rehabilitation after surgery.

Some veterinary schools have started offering postdoctoral courses for rehabilitative physical therapy in response to the demand created by an increase in equine surgeries and more intense equine competitions.

An example of one type of physical therapy is therapeutic ultrasound. (This isn't the same ultrasound that your vet uses to check for pregnancy or tendon lesions — that's diagnostic ultrasound.) This type of ultrasound is a form of acoustic energy, and is used to increase the metabolic activity in the cell that the sound wave passes through or near. Although topical application of heat affects skin (like those chemical heat packs), deep-tissue ultrasound can penetrate as far as 5 centimeters into muscle tissue to aid in healing.

This form of ultrasound provides pain relief, softens calcium deposits, softens or reduces scars, increases joint mobility, and can increase tendon elasticity. For this reason, it's a favorite form of physical therapy for some veterinarians.

Because deep-reaching ultrasound units can cause burns very deep in the tissue, only therapists working under veterinary supervision should apply this type of therapy. (See the next section for details on searching for a practitioner.)

Another type of physical therapy for horses involves mobilizing and stretching the muscles that have become strained or inflexible. Stiffness and restriction of muscle movement of different areas of the body can cause pain for a horse. Physical therapy that focuses on increasing mobility works in part by causing a reflex in a part of the horse's body that allows whatever muscle has become tense to automatically relax.

Physical therapists use their hands to gently trigger these reflexes. They can also encourage the horse to stretch the muscles herself. If the horse has a problem in her neck, for example, the therapist can get her to voluntarily stretch her muscles by offering her a treat in a way that makes her move her neck a certain way.

Qualified and skilled equine physical therapists can do wonders to help a horse who's suffering from pain related to muscle stiffness and soreness. If you think that your horse may benefit from physical therapy, discuss with your veterinarian the possibility of having her treated by a physical therapist.

Finding a Practitioner

When choosing an alternative or complementary therapy practitioner, you should use the same degree of care that you use to select your regular veterinarian. (We detail how to find a vet in Chapter 4.)

You also need to make sure that the person you're considering is truly qualified to practice the type of alternative or complementary medicine that he or she is advocating. The person should have completed extensive training in the therapy and not be someone who just hung up a shingle. Also, be wary of a practitioner — even a licensed veterinarian — who claims to practice a little bit of many different types of therapies. The expression "jack of all trades, master of none" comes to mind in this scenario.

To help you find a good practitioner, ask your regular veterinarian who he or she would recommend — assuming your vet is open-minded to alternative and complementary therapies. Ask the person you're considering a lot of questions about the particular therapy that you're pursuing. Good questions include the following:

 ✔ What are your training and credentials?

 ✔ How long have you been practicing this modality on horses?

 ✔ How many treatments will my horse need?

 ✔ What is the cost of this treatment?

 ✔ How long will my horse need to recover?

A good alternative or complementary practitioner will be honest in his or her opinion about whether a certain therapy can help your horse. Run fast if someone claims to be the next big thing or guarantees results.

Some types of alternative or complementary practitioners are certified by or are official members of organizations in their relevant field. Certification or membership helps to guarantee that the person has been trained in the chosen technique. If you're considering a veterinary chiropractor, a homeopath, or an acupuncturist for your horse, verify that the practitioner is certified by or is a member of his or her respective organization. (You can find contact information for these organizations in the appendix.) Some states require licenses for alternative practitioners. Contact the professional organization for the modality that you're considering to find out whether your state requires licensing.

Part IV
Horse Care for All Stages of Life

The 5th Wave — By Rich Tennant

"He just can't get around anymore."

In this part . . .

Chapters in Part IV provide you with information on your horse's health from birth to old age. We describe how to breed your horse and how to care for the newborn foal. You also discover the best way to manage your horse's senior years, and, finally, how to say goodbye.

Chapter 15

Breeding Your Horse

In This Chapter

▶ Understanding the basics of equine reproduction

▶ Figuring out whether to breed your horse

▶ Looking at different breeding techniques

▶ Walking through the stages of equine pregnancy

▶ Bringing a baby horse into the world

*O*ne of the great joys of horse ownership comes with breeding your own foal. Determining which stallion to put with your mare can be a fun and exciting activity. And caring for your pregnant horse can be very rewarding.

In this chapter, we give you a primer on horse breeding: how the equine reproductive system works and how to provide the best care to your mare during pregnancy and foaling. Because breeding your horse is a huge responsibility, we encourage you to make sure that this is something you really want to get into.

Equine Reproduction 101

The equine reproductive system is truly incredible when you take a close look at it. How a baby horse comes to be is just amazing. Studying the mechanics of how it all works will help you understand this miraculous process.

The female horse's system

When it comes to reproduction, mares have a lot in common with human females. That's because both are mammals and both usually give birth to only one baby per pregnancy.

The mare's reproductive organs are located inside the pelvic and abdominal regions of her body. The external reproductive organs include the vulva and the teats, the latter of which deliver milk to the foal. The internal organs include the vagina, the cervix, the uterus, two uterine horns, two fallopian tubes, and two ovaries. (Figure 15-1 shows the female reproductive system.)

When a mare breeds, semen enters the vagina, passes through the cervix, and moves into the uterus. The stallion's sperm make their way into the fallopian tubes, where they make contact with a ripe egg that has been released from one of the ovaries. This fertilized egg moves down through the fallopian tube into the uterine horn, and then to the uterus, where it attaches to the uterine wall. The embryo inside the egg develops into a fetus, and 11 months later the mare gives birth to a foal. (We describe the development of a fetus in detail later in this chapter.)

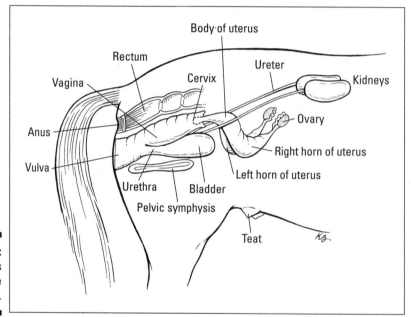

Figure 15-1:
The mare's
reproductive
system.

The male horse's system

Just as mares have many reproductive similarities to human females, so stallions are similar to human males.

The stallion's reproductive organs include the external sheath, penis, and testicles. Inside the penis is the urethra. Sperm is manufactured inside the stallion's testis, located within the testicles, and then stored in the epididymis. It's released from the epididymis into the vas deferens. Seminal fluid is created in the ampulla, which is part of the vas deferens. The seminal vesicles, prostate gland, and bulbourethral glands make up the remainder of the accessory sex glands of the stallion. They contribute the seminal plasma, gel portion, proteins, and various enzymes that make up the remainder of the semen. These components mix with the sperm, and at the moment of ejaculation, the semen is transported through the urethra and out through the penis opening. (Figure 15-2 shows the male reproductive system.)

Figure 15-2:
The stallion's reproductive system.

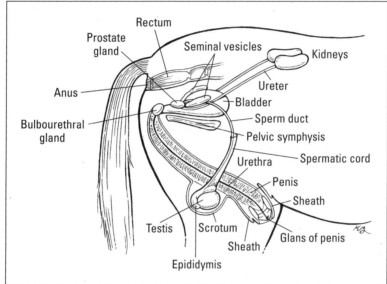

Rectum
Prostate gland
Seminal vesicles
Kidneys
Anus
Ureter
Bladder
Bulbourethral gland
Sperm duct
Pelvic symphysis
Urethra
Spermatic cord
Penis
Sheath
Testis
Scrotum
Glans of penis
Sheath
Epididymis

The breeding process

In terms of the actual act of breeding, horses are just like most mammals. The mares cycle at certain times of the year, are receptive to breeding when they're *in season,* and don't conceive again until they birth their foals.

The particulars of horse breeding are different from those of many other mammals — although rabbits also have a lot in common with horses in this department. In the following sections, we take you on a tour of the finer details of breeding season and cycles.

The breeding season

Mares typically come into heat in the springtime and go in and out of *estrus* (the time when mares are receptive to stallions) throughout the summertime. In the fall, the cycles of estrus in many mares end until the following spring.

The equine breeding season is dependent upon the number of daylight hours, which trigger the pineal gland to signal the hypothalamus (the pineal and hypothalamus are glands in the brain) to begin the hormonal changes that set a mare's breeding cycle in motion. In nature, this is all well-planned in order to have breeding and foaling occur during the best weather conditions, primarily from May to July.

However, some people want their mares to foal early in the spring because many breed registries officially consider all foals to be one year old on January 1st. To produce a foal shortly after that January date, they must breed the mare in the prior February or March because she takes 11 months to gestate. The folks put their mares under lights to simulate the longer days of spring and bring the mares into estrus. (Some breeders also put the stallions under lights at this time of year in hopes of increasing their sperm counts.)

Breeding cycles

Mares are *seasonally polyestrous*, which means that they have recurring estrus cycles during the breeding season until they become pregnant. In general, average mares have single estrus cycles that last from 21 to 23 days. During that time, the mare is receptive to the stallion for 4 to 7 days. This is called the period of estrus. During the remaining 14 to 15 days, she isn't receptive to the stallion.

Equine PMS

Many mare owners are painfully aware when their mare is cycling. Some mares never seem to have problems when they cycle — they act and perform like real ladies. Some mares, however, have pain in the back area where their ovaries are located, and are stiff and sore. This causes them to perform well below par. And mares exhibit what has become known as *witchy mare syndrome.* These cantankerous females show behavioral issues ranging from pinning their ears to kicking trailers apart.

For this reason, many mare owners elect to give their mares hormones that shut down their normal cycles. Although this sounds like a great and simple solution, you need to know that doing so can affect a mare's reproductive capabilities later on.

Before you elect to use any hormonal manipulation on your mare's estrus cycles, please collect all the facts and get several opinions from different veterinarians. Hormones that affect your mare's cycles are potent and can have side effects. Also, oral preparations must be handled with extreme caution because they can have adverse effects on humans.

Typically, mares ovulate 24 hours before the end of estrus. The average gestation is about 340 days — or 11 months — with some degree of variation on either side.

Possible reproductive problems

When left to their own devices, horses seem to reproduce rather efficiently. Human interference can sometimes reduce the natural equine efficiency for reproduction, and that's when breeding problems arise. The following sections list additional reproductive problems that humans can't control.

Female problems

Mares can develop breeding problems for a number of reasons beyond the control of their human handlers:

- **Age:** A mare's fertility declines with age, and getting an older mare — that is, one 18 or older — pregnant can be challenging. Senior mares may begin to cycle later in the breeding season and cycle less frequently. The mare's aging eggs may not be as viable as a younger mare's, either. Also, an older mare's uterus may not function as efficiently as that of a younger mare.

  As mares age, they may have anatomical changes that necessitate a procedure called a Caslick's. In this procedure, the vet sutures the vulva two-thirds shut to keep the mare from contaminating her reproductive tract with feces. (This measure may be necessary in some younger mares who have a vulvar anatomy that predisposes them to uterine infections.)

- **Scarring:** Mares that have been bred numerous times can also experience scarring of the reproductive tract. This scarring can challenge fertility, as can multiple or large uterine cysts, which may affect implantation.

- **Infection:** Chronic uterine infections can also affect a mare's fertility and are one reason why mares should have cultures prior to breeding. A culture can reveal a uterine infection that needs treatment before breeding.

- **Hormone imbalance:** Mares can also develop hormonal problems. If a mare has any metabolic imbalances, such as Cushing's syndrome, she may be less likely to become pregnant. Also, some mares don't produce enough *progesterone* — the hormone primarily responsible for maintaining pregnancy.

Male problems

Stallions also have their issues with fertility, although they're often not as complex as the problems seen in mares:

- ✔ **Age:** Stallion fertility also declines with age. Sperm count diminishes, and the sperm produced may be abnormal or less motile.

- ✔ **Low sperm count:** Not all stallions are created equal. Some stallions just don't produce as many sperm as others. Also, some stallion semen doesn't lend itself to artificial insemination because it doesn't fare well in the shipping or freezing processes.

- ✔ **Low libido:** Some stallions just aren't in the mood. These boys usually turn out to be stallions who haven't spent much time around mares. Research shows that stallions with low libido develop a stronger drive if they're more frequently exposed to the gentler sex.

Determining Whether You Should Breed Your Horse

Breeding sounds like great fun, and it can be. But it's also a huge responsibility. If you want to breed your horse so that you can have a cute baby around the barn, you need to realize that you're taking on a huge responsibility. And when all is said and done, breeding is still a crapshoot. You can never know for sure what you're going to get. In the following sections, we explain the responsibilities of bringing a foal into the world and the considerations you should think about before breeding your mare. (We don't discuss how to breed a stallion in this book because only experts in breeding should be handling stallions for this purpose.)

Before you bring another horse into the world, remember that many horses end up unwanted and suffer sad fates, either at the slaughter house or living out their lives in neglect. Unless you plan to keep the horse that you breed forever, realize that you may be contributing to the unwanted horse population.

Understanding the responsibilities of having a foal in the family

Bringing another life into the world comes with a number of responsibilities, especially if that life is equine. Here are some points to consider before breeding your horse:

- ✔ **Cost:** Obviously, you'll be feeding and caring for mama before, during, and after breeding, and at least until you wean the baby. (Coauthor Dr. Kate recommends weaning foals at five to six months.) Figure on your mare's regular healthcare and feeding costs, plus that of the baby when he arrives. (Remember that mares need special vet care, so this will cost you more than her normal routine care.)

  Unless you own the stallion, you'll also have to pay a stud fee for breeding services. If you'll be taking your mare to the stallion to be bred, plan on the costs of boarding at the breeding facility, transportation of your mare to the stallion, nonrefundable *chute* fees (the monitoring of your mare during reproductive procedures), and other possible fees.

  If you plan to sell your foal to make up for all these costs, be aware that you may not be able to sell the foal! You may end up having to keep him. As a wise old horseman once told Dr. Kate: "You'd better breed for something that you'd like to keep and ride, in case it doesn't sell."

- ✔ **Time:** Aside from the time it takes to breed your mare, you'll also spend time caring for her while she's pregnant. When she gets close to foaling, you need to monitor her closely. Before the day (or likely night) that she foals, plan to spend many hours watching her — possibly for days or weeks beforehand. (We describe foaling in detail later in this chapter.)

  After the foal is born, you need time to care for the baby, get him started on early training (see Chapter 16), and keep a close watch on him to make sure that he's healthy and getting along okay.

- ✔ **Work:** Foals are a lot of work. Cute as they are, they need attention and training. If you want your baby to grow up to be a good, easy-to-handle horse, you need work with him when he's young. You can't just ignore him until he's ready for a saddle. During his young, impressionable months, he needs to learn all kinds of stuff to prepare him for adulthood. As his first owner, your job is to teach him (or hire someone who can).

Judging the mare

Before breeding your mare, think about why you think she deserves to be a mother. That's right. It sounds cold, but not every mare deserves the right to reproduce. Although you may think that she's a nice horse, she objectively needs to be more than that. She must be healthy, have a good disposition, and be physically well put-together. Why? Because any flaws that she has have a good chance of being passed along to her offspring. You won't be doing the horse world a service bringing another equine into the world who's sickly, difficult to handle, or so badly conformed that the poor horse can't stay sound with normal work.

Conformation is the way that your horse is put together; signs of good conformation include legs with the correct angles and overall balance. Figure 15-3 shows a horse with good conformation.

Dr. Colleen Brady, Purdue University

Figure 15-3: Before breeding your mare, make sure that both she and the stallion have good, balanced conformation.

So look at your mare very critically. Is she healthy? Is she sound? Does she have good conformation? Does she have a pleasant temperament?

If your mare is registered, ask yourself whether she has genetics desirable for your breed. If you aren't sure, get advice on this subject from a good judge for your breed.

Judging the stallion

The mare is only half of the equation when making a foal. The stallion is a big factor as well. You can find stallions by looking at ads in local equine publications, in breed magazines, and on the Internet.

Do a lot of homework before choosing a stallion. Study the stallion's conformation and show record, and ask a lot of questions about his disposition. Try to see as many of his adult progeny as possible in order to discover any genetic predisposition for health problems. Also, check out this horse's offspring because some stallions (and mares) are incredibly prepotent — which means almost all of their progeny look similar no matter the cross!

Next, consider the hypothetical product of your mare with this stallion. Be as objective as possible.

Try if at all possible to visit the stallion in person. You want to select a stud that truly complements and enhances your mare, and compensates for any of her faults. (And, yes, she does have them. All horses do.)

Surveying Different Breeding Methods

There's more than one way to breed a horse! Seriously, you can put horses together for breeding in a number of different ways. The way you ultimately choose depends on your situation, and the stallion owner's situation and preferences. Take a look at each of the three most common types of breeding methods.

Live cover

Live cover is when humans manage the actual breeding process — that is, they carefully control the actions of the stallion and mare (see Figure 15-4). This is how many horses are bred these days. Some breed registries don't register foals who are conceived in any other way. That's because they want witnesses that the stallion did actually impregnate the mare who gave birth to the foal. Live cover is also cheaper than using artificial insemination.

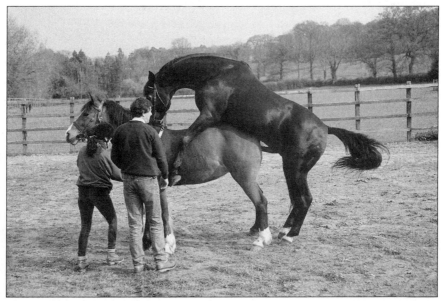

Figure 15-4:
Live cover involves handling of the stallion and mare during breeding.

Bob Langrish

Stallions who participate in live cover breedings are trained to do so. They learn to mount the mare when told to do so. Mares, on the other hand, aren't as well-trained at this task as stallions and often wear hobbles on their back legs to make sure that they don't kick and injure the stallion. They may also be placed in breeding stocks so that they can't move around too much.

Before the breeding can take place, a teaser stallion prepares the mare and helps the handler determine whether the mare is receptive to breeding. This stallion puts the mare in the mood through a barrier so that when the breeding stallion is brought into the shed, she's ready to receive him. Another preparatory step to breeding is the washing of the private parts of both mare and stallion to lessen the chance of infection during the mating process.

Only experienced breeding handlers should be involved in live covers. Both stallions and mares can get out of control during this very exciting time, and people can be seriously injured if they don't know exactly what they're doing. Handling of the breeding is the responsibility of the stallion owner. Make certain that the stallion owner has an experienced person managing the breeding.

Pasture breeding

Probably the simplest and most natural way of putting two horses together is pasture breeding. In this type of breeding, the mare is placed in a pasture with the stallion during her regular reproductive cycle (see Figure 15-5). Here, nature takes its course.

Pros and cons exist to this method. Here are the pros:

- ✔ Pasture breeding is probably the most effective way to get a foal. For many mares who have trouble conceiving with live cover, pasture breeding may do the trick. The reason is probably that some mares have a very quiet estrus cycle and don't exhibit many of the signs of a mare in heat (squatting, urinating frequently). In a pasture setting, a good stallion knows exactly when the mare is receptive to his overtures. He also has more opportunities to breed with her.

- ✔ Pasture breeding can also be helpful to a *maiden mare* (one who has never been bred). Sometimes, maiden mares are afraid of the stallion and resist breeding. In pasture settings, they have time to get to know the stallion, and that seems to make them more receptive to his advances.

The greatest downfall of pasture breeding is an increased chance for injury to both mare and stallion. Some stallions are quite aggressive when they breed and can viciously bite mares during the act of breeding. On the flip side, mares can kick and injure stallions, especially if the stallion tries to mount her when she isn't in the receptive part of her cycle. The risk of infection to both horses is greater with pasture breeding. Owners of very valuable stallions and mares are usually reluctant to go the pasture-breeding route.

If you like the idea of pasture breeding your mare, you need to find a stallion owner who uses this method.

Figure 15-5:
Pasture breeding is the most natural way for horses to mate.

Bob Langrish

Artificial insemination

The most common breeding practice among serious breeders, artificial insemination, allows mares and stallions in different parts of the country to come together to make a foal without ever actually meeting each other.

Artificial insemination requires collection of the stallion's semen. This is done by teasing a trained stallion with a mare who's in estrus and then having him mount a breeding dummy. The ejaculate is collected in an artificial vagina, and the semen is processed so that it can be shipped to one or more mares around the country for insemination (see Figure 15-6). Mares are inseminated during their estrus cycle.

Testing for genetic problems before you breed your horse

Before you put your mare with a stallion, you need to take some precautions to make sure that your foal isn't born with a genetic disease. If the breeding stallion and mare are of certain at-risk breeds, they should both be tested for known genetic problems. Some of these conditions include:

- **Hereditary equine regional dermal asthenia (HERDA):** Other names for this condition include Ehlers-Danlos syndrome and dermatosparaxis. This hideous disease, which has been seen in Quarter Horses and horses of Quarter Horse lineage, occurs due to an inherited connective tissue disorder resulting in defective collagen formation. Horses with this illness have skin that's stretchy and not adequately attached, allowing it to tear easily. These animals suffer from the pain involved, secondary skin infections, and disfiguring scars. Because no cure exists, most animals are euthanized.

- **Hyperkalemic Periodic Paralysis (HYPP):** Also seen in Quarter Horses and those of Quarter Horse lineage, this disorder tends to be found in those horses bred for extreme muscle development. HYPP is a genetic disease that results in unpredictable attacks that may vary from muscle fasciculation or trembling to extreme weakness with collapse and even death. Though some of these animals can be managed with diet and treatment, breeding of such carriers is discouraged and homozygous individuals born in 2007 or later are ineligible for Quarter Horse registration.

- **Overo Lethal White Syndrome:** Usually the result of breeding two Paint horses who are carriers of a particular color gene, this condition results in early death of the foal.

- **Glycogen branching enzyme deficiency (GBED):** Seen in Quarter Horses and Quarter Horse related breeds, this disease results in abortion, stillbirths, and foal deaths.

- **Severe combined immunodeficiency (SCID):** A genetic disease of Arabian horses, SCID causes affected horses to have inadequate immune response against infectious diseases. Foals with this condition rarely live to the age of 6 months.

- **Junctional epidermolysis bullosa (JEB):** This disease is usually manifested by missing patches of skin and mucosa at birth. It shows up in several draft horse breeds, as well as Saddlebreds. This condition is also called Epitheliogenesis Imperfecta, or EI. Foals with this defect are usually euthanized at birth.

By having your horse tested before breeding, you can be sure not to pass these lethal genes along to the next generation of foals. Talk to your veterinarian about having your horse screened.

Figure 15-6:
Artificial insemination has become the most popular method of reproduction for purebred horses.

Bob Langrish

Some stallions have semen that ships very well; others have semen that doesn't. Some breeders process semen for shipping by cooling it by a very strict process. Other breeders may use a freezing process to preserve the semen for breeding. Both processes have advantages and disadvantages. Costs and equipment needs also differ.

Artificial insemination is more costly than live cover because it requires the services of a veterinarian. It also costs money to ship the semen. The advantages are that you can breed your mare to a stallion who's on the other side of the country without having to ship your horse. You also don't have the risk of mare or stallion being injured during the breeding process.

Not all breed registries allow the registration of foals who are the result of artificial insemination. The Jockey Club, which registers Thoroughbreds, doesn't permit this type of breeding at the time of this writing.

If you want to use artificial insemination to breed your mare, talk to your vet to make certain that he or she offers this service. Discuss the timing of the insemination with your vet as well because the semen needs to inseminated when the mare is in estrus.

The Skinny on Horse Pregnancy

On the day you breed your mare, you'll be beside yourself with glee. This feeling may soon be replaced by momentary panic when you realize that you have a baby on the way and all the responsibility that comes with it. But have no fear. You have almost a year to prepare for your new arrival. In the following sections, we explain how to make sure that your horse really is pregnant, describe the stages of equine pregnancy, and give you tips for prenatal care. We also let you know the signs of a possible pregnancy problem.

Verifying that your horse is pregnant

First, you need to make sure your horse really is pregnant. Just because you bred her doesn't mean that she conceived.

To be sure that the breeding took, your vet uses either palpation by hand or a combination of palpation with ultrasound to see whether your mare is pregnant (see Figure 15-7). In most cases, this exam and ultrasound should take place about 14 to 16 days after the breeding. Ultrasound exam at this stage helps to rule in or out the possibility of twins. And the veterinarian can use the ultrasound exam to evaluate the ovaries, embryo, uterus, and cervix. If the vet sees any hint of an abnormality, he or she may recommend additional tests or medications.

Many equine veterinarians also recommend evaluating the pregnancy by ultrasound around day 24. By this time, you can see the heartbeat, which means that the embryo is alive. As a general rule, most mares should also be checked for pregnancy at about day 40. If a mare loses her pregnancy after about day 35, she's unlikely to come into heat again for many months.

After pregnancy is verified, the mare can be released from the breeding facility.

Figure 15-7:
A veterinarian palpates a mare to determine whether she's pregnant.

Bob Langrish

What if your mare is pregnant with twins?

If having one foal is awesome, wouldn't two be double the fun? Actually, no. When it comes to horses, twins aren't a cause to celebrate.

The cold reality is that in 95 percent of the cases, mares carrying twins abort the entire pregnancy before the due date. Healthy twins carried to term are very rare in the horse world.

When a veterinarian checks a mare 14 days into her pregnancy, he or she may discover twins. In most cases, mare owners opt to have one of the twins eliminated to help ensure survival of the second one. This procedure is done by a veterinarian, who ruptures the embryo.

Although eliminating one of the embryos is a sad decision to make, it gives the other a fighting chance to survive. But, sometimes, both embryos can be lost when the attempt is made to eliminate one of them. Where the embryos are positioned in the uterus relative to each other can make this task very difficult or impossible. Sometimes aborting the entire pregnancy and starting over is wiser.

Looking at the stages of pregnancy

At 40 days of pregnancy, the developing embryo is now mature enough to be called a fetus, with limbs and organs. Throughout the coming days, the fetus begins to slowly morph into a horse. Consider the following:

- ✔ At around 90 days, the baby has tiny ears and little hooves, but its size is close to that of a hamster (see Figure 15-8).

- ✔ By 180 days, it looks a lot like a small horse and is the size of a beagle (see Figure 15-9).

- ✔ At 10 months, the baby appears as it will at birth, complete with mane and tail (see Figure 15-10). At this point, its front legs are already starting to move into the birth canal.

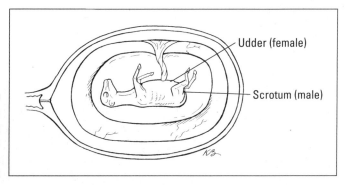

Udder (female)

Scrotum (male)

Figure 15-8: The fetus at three months.

As the foal is developing, the mare's belly grows larger. Pretty soon, she starts to look like she's going to burst. That and the calendar tell you that you're near the end of her pregnancy.

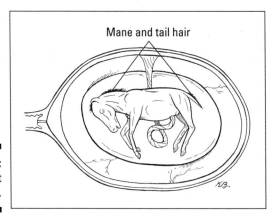

Mane and tail hair

Figure 15-9:
The fetus at
180 days.

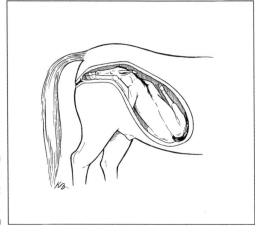

Figure 15-10:
The fetus at
10 months.

Caring for the mom-to-be

As your mare's baby is growing inside her, your job is to help her maintain a healthy pregnancy. Here are some things to keep in mind when caring for your mare:

✔ **Good weight:** Make sure that the mare's body condition is good; don't let her get too fat or thin. If she gets too fat, she's predisposed to metabolic syndrome or laminitis, each of which can cause her to lose her foal. (See Chapter 11 for more information on these conditions.)

Conversely, if your mare becomes too thin, her pregnancy will be compromised because her body may have to make a choice between sustaining her health or that of the foal.

✔ **A smart diet:** Your pregnant mare is eating for two, so take that into account when serving her meals. Discuss her diet with your veterinarian.

During the first two trimesters (the first six months), you don't need to change your mare's ration, assuming that she's in good health and body condition and is neither fat nor thin. (Vitamin/mineral intake or supplementation may be necessary for mares on pasture or forages only.)

In the last few months of pregnancy, the baby makes big demands on mama. Her energy requirements, protein needs, and vitamin/mineral requirements are likely to increase. She should already be eating 90 percent of her food as roughage (mostly hay). Discuss increasing her daily protein intake 8 to 10 percent with your vet, and talk to him or her about increasing calcium, phosphorus, copper, and zinc — these are the building blocks for the foal's healthy bones. (See Chapter 6 for details on high-protein feeds.)

✔ **Preventative care:** Follow the deworming program outlined for your mare by your veterinarian; a worm infestation can threaten your mare's pregnancy (see Chapter 4). And give your mare the recommended rhinopneumonitis vaccines during her pregnancy to prevent an abortion caused by the equine herpes virus (see Chapter 12).

Be sure to use only vaccines provided by your veterinarian because you need to use a special rhinopneumonitis vaccine for pregnant mares.

Also, ask your veterinarian about boostering your mare for immunity to other diseases while she's in late gestation. Vaccines at this time may increase her antibody levels and thus provide greater protection to the foal.

✔ **Low stress:** Keep your mare's stress to a minimum. You can still ride her and give her light exercise to keep her fit, but coauthor Dr. Kate recommends letting her be a happy pasture girl with pregnancy leave from work from the sixth month of gestation until she weans her baby.

✔ **Being careful:** Never give your pregnant mare any medications or supplements without consulting your veterinarian first. A healthy mare on a good diet doesn't need any special supplements or vitamins unless your vet recommends them for a specific reason.

Staying aware of possible pregnancy problems

Unfortunately, things can go wrong during a mare's pregnancy. Signs of a possible problem with the pregnancy include vaginal discharge or dripping milk. If you see either of these symptoms in your mare, call the vet right away. In addition, if your mare becomes ill for any reason, goes off her feed, or acts depressed, call your veterinarian immediately. Abortion is relatively rare, but any time a pregnant mare seems ill, she should be seen by a vet.

Viral and bacterial infections can certainly cause abortion, and so can ingestion of toxic plants, and certain drugs and chemicals. Diseases of the placenta and umbilical torsion can also result in abortion.

Although this all sounds scary, chances are good that your mare will enjoy her pregnancy without any problems at all.

Delivering a Baby Horse

Of course the most exciting moment in the entire breeding and pregnancy process is the moment of birth. When your new little baby horse comes out to meet the world, you'll be moved beyond words.

You need to be ready for that big day and know what to expect; we tell you what you need to know in the following sections. Being prepared helps you stay calm and provide the best care for mama and baby.

Preparing a place for foaling

The place your mare foals depends on your facilities and your personal preferences. She can foal out in a pasture, in a paddock, or in a cozy box stall.

Coauthor Dr. Kate likes to let her mares foal in a clean, grassy pasture by themselves, even though she has 12-x-24-foot foaling stalls at her facility just for this purpose. Her reasoning is that the foaling process can be quite an athletic event, and she doesn't want to risk her mares getting *cast* (stuck against a wall) in the stall during delivery. So she puts her mares in a foaling pasture 30 days before their expected delivery date to give them time to become familiar with their surroundings.

If you prefer to have your mare foal indoors, as many horse owners do, you must provide her with a stall that's at least 14 x 14 feet in size, although bigger is better. The stall must have clean bedding, preferably straw because shavings, sawdust, or sand can cling to the new, wet baby and the mare (see Figure 15-11) and result in umbilical cord infection. You should also keep the stall scrupulously clean at all times.

Figure 15-11: A foaling stall must be at least 14 x 14 feet in size and very roomy.

Bob Langrish

Recognizing the signs of foaling

Toward the end of your mare's pregnancy, she starts to show signs that she's ready to foal. The signs of eminent delivery are variable between mares, but many give the following clues before giving birth:

- ✔ Two to four weeks before foaling, the udders fill up and appear swollen.

- ✔ Four to six days prior, the teats of the udders become distended.

- ✔ One to four days before, a waxy buildup shows on the nipples. Honey-colored colostrum may also drip from the teats.

- ✔ When foaling is imminent, your mare's udders may begin to drip milk. You may also see changes in her behavior. She may start to act restless or uncomfortable, and may even rub her tail on a wall or fence or start to kick at her belly. She may pace or get up or down a lot. At this point, if you're really astute, you may notice that the muscles of your mare's croup soften and flatten and the vulva relax.

  If your mare's restless behavior lasts for more than a couple of hours without producing a foal, call your veterinarian. She may be having a problem.

Taking action just before foaling

Hopefully, before your baby is about to be born, your vet has given you a video to watch that shows the foaling process. If you haven't watched it yet, now is the time!

As foaling time approaches, wash and clean your mare's vulva and hindquarters; you can also wrap her tail carefully with gauze to keep it clean and out of the way as the foal comes out of the birth canal.

Make sure that you have your veterinarian's phone number ready in case you need him or her. (You should need your vet only if your mare starts having problems, described later in this chapter.)

Watching the stages of foaling

As soon as your mare goes into labor, she begins the three stages of foaling. Stay outside your mare's stall or pasture and watch from afar as the miracle unfolds:

- ✔ **Stage one:** Contractions begin in this stage and can last from one to two hours. The mare's uterine contractions push the baby through the cervix and into the correct position in the birth canal. The mare gets up and down several times and may roll during this stage. The fetal membranes, called the *allantoic sac,* may be visible at the mare's vulva. When the sac breaks and fluid goes all over the place, stage one is over.

- ✔ **Stage two:** This is the actual expulsion of the foal. This process happens extremely fast, so if it's taking more than 30 minutes for your mare to deliver her baby, call your vet right away.

  When the foal is in normal delivery position, he looks like a diver going off the high-dive as he comes out of the birth canal (see Figure 15-12).

- ✔ **Stage three:** During this stage, the placenta is expelled. Placentas should be passed one to three hours after delivery.

Offering postpartum care

Your foal will be born with a sac known as the fetal membrane around him. As he struggles after birth, he breaks the sac with his mom's help. (If he doesn't, you should get involved by using a clean towel to clean membranes and secretions off the nose and mouth.) After this breakage happens, check to see whether the foal is breathing. Watch the foal's flanks to see whether they go up and down as he breathes.

Figure 15-12:
When the
foal exits
the birth
canal, he
should be in
the classic
diving
position.

Bob Langrish

The umbilical cord may have broken during delivery, or it may break when the foal stands up. No need for you to cut it. In fact, doing so can be dangerous to the health of the baby. Instead, let it break on its own and then treat the stump with whatever antibacterial solution your vet recommends.

You may feel the urge to get your hands all over the baby right away, but coauthor Dr. Kate recommends letting the mare and foal rest for at least 30 minutes so that they can form a strong bond. (If you want to imprint your foal — a method of early training in newborn horses — see Chapter 16 for details.)

Keeping an eye out for possible problems during and after foaling

Horses have been giving birth without the help of humans for millions of years, so it's likely that everything will go smoothly when your foal is born. However, things can go wrong during the process. If you see any of these problems unfolding, step in and intercede or call your veterinarian right away:

- ✔ **Wrong position:** If you notice the foal coming out in any other position other than front feet first, call your vet right away. Other positions include hind feet first, head but no feet, feet turned upward, or anything other than feet first followed by the head, neck, torso, and hindquarters.

- ✔ **Water doesn't break:** Before the mare can safely deliver the foal, her water must break. If this doesn't happen and you see a balloon of water showing from her vulva, break it yourself with your fingers.

- ✔ **Fetal membrane doesn't break:** If the foal has already been born and the fetal membrane hasn't broken, intercede and break it yourself. Start at the foal's nose to enable him to breathe. Clear his nasal passages of the membrane by using a clean towel.

- ✔ **Umbilical cord won't break:** Letting the cord break on its own is a good idea, but if the placenta has passed and the cord is still attached to the foal 20 minutes later, consult your veterinarian, and follow his or her instructions.

- ✔ **Retained placenta:** If the placenta isn't expelled within 1 to 3 hours, call your vet. Retained placentas can be dangerous and can lead to laminitis and serious uterine infections.

- ✔ **Foal is unresponsive:** If the foal has been born but isn't moving, clear the baby's nostrils by sweeping your hand down the face from the eyes across the nose. Move the baby around to see whether he stirs. If not, call your vet immediately.

- ✔ **Any other concerns:** If something just doesn't seem right to you, don't take a chance with the health of your mare and foal. Call your vet right away. Being on the safe side is better than waiting, because your foal could die if you don't act quickly.

Chapter 16

Caring for the Newborn

. . . .

In This Chapter

▶ Making sure that your foal and mare are healthy after delivery

▶ Caring for and feeding your foal

▶ Training your foal

. . . .

*J*oy of joys, your baby horse is here! And man, is she cute!

If you can stop staring at her long enough to read this chapter, you'll find that we give you a great start in figuring out how to care for your new infant equine. You find out how to make sure that she's healthy, how to keep from panicking as you watch her try to stand up, and how to examine Mom to make sure that everything is hunky-dory. You also discover how to provide healthcare and good nutrition to the baby and how to get that baby started in her basic training.

Monitoring Mom and Baby after Delivery

Out on the open range, mares have their babies in the grass, away from the safety of the herd. Their offspring stand quickly, nurse on their own, and eventually make their way back to the other horses. So why do humans need to get so involved with newborn baby horses? Can't they make it on their own without human intervention?

Well, chances are, they can. But out on the open range, not every foal makes it because no one is there to help in case of a problem. And because you definitely want your foal to survive, you need to get involved to make sure that she has the best chance possible. You also want to keep an eye on Mom to make sure that she's in good shape, too.

Watching the baby

As soon as your baby is born, you need to check her to make sure that she's healthy and doesn't need veterinary intervention. In Chapter 15, we describe several problems that can occur at the moment of birth. Review these conditions to make certain that your foal has made it this far without a problem.

After the baby has been born, she should be bright and alert to her surroundings. She should try to get up within 30 minutes after birth. Seeing your foal trying to get her legs under her for the first time will make you want to laugh and cry at the same time. It can be a big struggle for one so small and weak to get those long, spindly legs in order. But a healthy foal tries to make it happen within only half an hour of birth.

You may feel the urge to jump in and help your baby learn to stand and walk, but try not to intercede. Your foal needs to do this on her own, and as long as she has plenty of room in the stall — and plenty of soft bedding beneath her feet — to stumble and fall over without getting hurt, she'll be fine (see Figure 16-1). Have no fear while you watch — she'll eventually figure it out.

Figure 16-1:
This stall gives the mare and foal plenty of room while the foal is learning to stand.

Bob Langrish

When foals stand to nurse, they're very adept at finding the udder. Again, resist the urge to interfere and help. The mare and foal need to have time to bond and adjust to one another without you being in the middle of it.

If your baby stands, but seems to be completely unable to find the udder after about 10 minutes of searching, you can assist at this point by gently guiding her to the udder location — put your arms around her neck at chest level and around her buttocks as you help her walk in the direction she needs to go, as shown in Figure 16-2. (If she struggles a lot and seems more interested in fighting you than in looking for the teat, back off and let her find it on her own.)

If, despite your efforts to help and a lot of searching, the baby still can't find the udder, she may have a problem. Call your veterinarian.

If your foal doesn't stand and nurse at all within two hours, call your veterinarian. The foal may be weak and need medical attention. Foals need to receive *colostrum* (the mare's first milk, which is high in protective antibodies) within 8 to 12 hours of birth, when their intestines are able to absorb it. Colostrum provides the foal with passive immunity to prevent disease and provide protection until her own immune system develops. If the baby is too weak to nurse, you may have to milk the mare and give the foal milk and colostrum through a stomach tube.

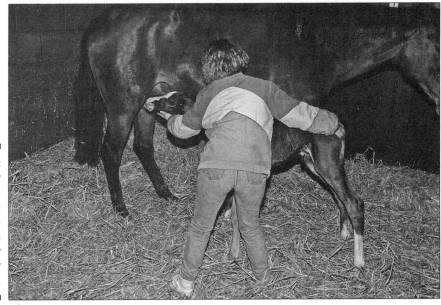

Figure 16-2: If the baby is having a hard time finding the nipple, you can gently guide her to it.

Bob Langrish

Foals should pass a sticky, dark stool called *meconium* — which forms in their intestines before birth — within the first 12 hours, after eating a meal or two. If your foal doesn't pass meconium, she needs an enema. Ask your vet to show you how to do this procedure before your foal is born so that you're ready to perform this task if needed. (If you're uncomfortable with the idea of giving your new baby an enema, be prepared to call your veterinarian to come out and do it for you.)

Examining the mare

Let your mare rest for about an hour after she gives birth. She's tired and needs a break. During this time, she bonds with her foal. (You'll know the two are bonding because the mare will lick the foal and clean her up, nuzzle her, and maybe even nicker to her.)

After your mare rests for an hour, start taking her temperature every eight hours. If her temperature goes much above normal — 101 degrees Fahrenheit — call the vet. (See Chapter 2 for details on how to take a horse's temperature.)

Your mare should be producing milk for her foal. You can probably see the milk dripping from her udders. If not, give them a very gentle squeeze to see whether milk comes out. (Be careful when you do this — most mares are fine with it, but if this is your mare's first foal or if she's touchy about that area, she may kick out. Put a halter on her and have someone hold her while you squeeze the udder.) If no milk comes out, contact your vet immediately. Without milk from her mother, the baby has nothing to eat.

If your mare seems okay within these first 24 hours — that is, she's alert and is eating, drinking, taking care of her foal, and passing urine and manure — she's probably fine. If anything seems amiss, including signs of distress or lethargy, call your vet immediately.

The signs of a good equine mom

You'd expect your mare to be delighted with her new baby, and most mares are. She should be curious but not aggressive toward her baby, and she should begin to nuzzle and lick her. First-time mothers may be frightened of their babies, however, and may even reject them.

If your mare seems to be aggressive toward her foal, put a halter on the mare, remove the baby, and reintroduce the foal with the mare under control. Let her slowly get used to the foal and hope for her maternal instincts to kick in. If after a couple of hours the mare still doesn't accept the foal, call your veterinarian. Your baby needs to nurse and get much-needed colostrums from the mare, and if the mare won't let this happen, you may need to milk the mare and bottle feed the baby. Your veterinarian can help you with this task.

Make an appointment with your veterinarian to perform a thorough exam on mom and baby approximately 24 hours after the birth. The vet will check both for any possible complications (see the next section for details).

When your mare passes her placenta (also known as the afterbirth), save it all in a bucket so that your vet can examine it. Your vet needs to make sure that the mare passed the entire placenta because retained placenta can cause serious infection and laminitis.

Providing Healthcare and Good Nutrition for Mom and Baby

If you managed to get through the birthing process without having to call your vet, congratulations! Your job isn't over, however. In the following sections, we explain how to offer the best healthcare and nutrition to your new equine friend and his mom.

Taking care of the first vet appointment after delivery

When your veterinarian comes 24 hours after the foal's birth to check on the mare and foal, he or she examines the placenta that you saved in a bucket (see the earlier section "Examining the mare") to ensure that the mare passed the entire thing.

Your vet also performs a complete exam of the foal to be certain that everything is progressing as it should. This is the perfect time to ask any additional questions that you may have about foal care, especially if this is your first foaling adventure. Your vet can also check your foal for good antibody protection if you request this test (and we recommend that you do). The foal should have acquired antibodies from the mare's colostrum (see the earlier section "Watching the baby" for details). If not, the vet can administer plasma to the baby if necessary.

The vet then examines your mare to be certain that she isn't having postpartum complications. If she's having trouble letting down her first milk, the vet may give her an injection to encourage it. The vet may also want to deworm your mare at this time to further decrease possible transfer of parasites to the baby, even if you've kept up with a good deworming program all along (as we recommend in Chapter 4).

Nursing and feeding

Your foal was born with the instinct to nurse and makes his way to the mare's udders not too long after standing. Newborn foals suckle an average of four to six times per hour during the first week of life, drinking about 30 percent of their body weight daily. During this time, they grow very fast, gaining one to three pounds of weight each day!

Watch your foal suckle. He should be vigorous, and you should see him swallowing. If you notice that milk comes out of his nose, or if feeding is accompanied by coughing, call your vet right away. These problems indicate a possible blockage in his esophagus.

As the foal ages, his nursing decreases to one to two times per hour. By the time he's about three to four weeks old, he starts to show an interest in solid food. This stage is where managing his diet gets tricky. You don't want your foal to eat too much of certain foods because he can get *developmental orthopedic disease* (DOD), which causes limb deformities. Grain and concentrated feed aren't good for your baby and may make him grow too fast, which brings on DOD. (Some researches also believe feeding too many carbohydrates to a young horse can encourage the habit of cribbing — see Chapter 3 for more information on this vice.)

If your mare is getting these kinds of foods and allowing the baby to share them, find another way to feed the foods to your mare so that your foal doesn't have access to them. If your foal is still growing too fast, limit his access to hay too, particularly alfalfa. Discuss your foal's diet with your veterinarian so that you know you're feeding him right.

Your mare should remain on the same diet she was eating during the latter stages of her pregnancy. She can stay on this diet while she's nursing her baby. Talk to your vet to make sure that the mare is getting the diet she needs.

Baby's eating what?

Be prepared for this one: Your cute little foal is probably going to horrify you by eating some of his dam's manure. Although that sounds yucky, it's actually normal and necessary behavior. Called *coprophagy,* this eating of stool allows the baby to get necessary bacteria into his gut and acquire other nutrients.

Keep your foaling stall clean, especially of urine, but allow some normal feces from the mare to remain. Foals eat feces several times daily for the first week of life, and usually cease altogether by two to three months of age.

Recognizing and treating foal-specific health problems

In the days after birth, foals can sometimes develop problems. Some of these include:

- ✔ **Infection:** Foals can sometimes develop bacterial or viral infections requiring immediate veterinary care.

- ✔ **Parasites:** Intestinal worms can make a foal sick.

- ✔ **Gastroduodenal ulcers:** Foals sometimes develop ulcers in their intestines. Symptoms include grinding teeth, pain after eating, and excessive salivation.

- ✔ **Pneumonia:** The cause of pneumonia can be bacterial, fungal, or viral. Foals may develop pneumonia from accidentally breathing in milk while nursing (if the baby was born with a cleft palate), or when nursing from a bucket or bottle. Lack of cleanliness of the stall can also cause this condition.

- ✔ **Polyarticular septic arthritis:** A septic arthritis and joint infection usually affects multiple joints. Foals with this condition have swollen and painful joints, depression, poor appetite, and fever. This condition is usually the result of a failure of passive antibody protection, uterine infection from the mare, or poor hygiene during foaling, allowing infectious agents to enter the foal's body via the navel. This condition can have serious consequences and can lead to chronic lameness and death if not treated. Vets use aggressive supportive veterinary care and appropriate systemic antibiotics to treat septic arthritis.

When a young foal becomes sick, it's serious business. Seriously ill foals usually require IV fluid therapy, plasma transfusion, and antibiotics. If a foal is having great difficulty breathing, the baby may need bronchodilators to open up his air passages, as well as oxygen therapy. The foal may also need tube feeding to keep his energy and protein intake at high levels.

When an older foal — anywhere from three to six months — gets sick, the young horse is more likely to exhibit the kinds of respiratory symptoms seen in adult horses, including coughing, raspy breathing, depression, fever, and loss of appetite. This is the time in the foal's life when maternal antibodies are waning and the foal's immune system is developing. During this period, limit a foal's exposure to strange horses who have been at shows or in other places where large numbers of horses congregate. If you handle any horses like this yourself, wash your hands well before handling your foal.

Keep a close eye on your foal so that you can monitor his health. Don't hesitate to call the vet if something isn't right. If you see the following symptoms in your foal, the time to act is now!

- Lethargy
- Diarrhea
- Coughing
- Difficulty breathing
- Elevated temperature
- Refusal to nurse (check the mare's udder; if you notice distention, it may mean that the foal isn't nursing)
- Struggle to defecate
- Inability to urinate

Training Your Baby Horse Early On

It'll be years before you (or someone else) start riding your new horse. But that doesn't mean that you should wait several years before you start her training. Teaching your young horse should begin early in her life. Setting a strong foundation now makes your horse easier to train as she gets older.

Imprinting

Imprinting is a term used to describe a method of early training developed by Robert Miller, DVM. The principle behind imprinting is that you teach the foal that humans are part of her herd and that she's subordinate to them. By imprinting the foal and making this strong first impression, the foal becomes easier to train in the future.

Imprinting has become a controversial subject in the horse world. Some people believe that imprinting creates a pushy horse who doesn't respect humans. Others believe that it's too invasive and interferes with the bond between a mare and her foal.

Other people find that, if done right, imprinting creates a calm, malleable horse who's easy to train and handle. According to Dr. Miller, the key to successful imprinting is to do it right. Badly done imprinting is worse than none at all.

If you choose to imprint your foal, study this method carefully long before your baby even hits the ground. Videotapes — available from equine catalogs and Web sites — give you detailed step-by-step advice on how to perform this training method.

Before you begin imprinting, allow the mare and foal to bond. After you get the sense that the two have made that connection, you can proceed with the imprinting. Bonding usually reveals itself by the baby and mother interacting with each other.

You should imprint over three separate sessions. Conduct each session as follows:

- ✔ **Session one:** Performed immediately after the foal is born, this step consists of placing a halter on the foal; bending the foal's head and holding it to teach yielding; rubbing the foal all over with a towel; handling the foal's legs and tapping the hooves; placing a finger in the foal's ears, nostrils, mouth, and anus; and rubbing the foal with different objects, such as clippers, a white plastic bag, and a newspaper. These steps help to teach the foal to submit to human handling.

During the session, the foal may struggle in an effort to get away from the stimuli. The key to successful imprinting is to continue the stimuli until the foal relaxes. This crucial point is where many handlers go wrong. If you stop the stimuli while the foal is struggling, you teach her to resist you.

- ✔ **Session two:** This session takes place after the foal is standing and has nursed for the first time, and it lasts about 15 minutes. The objective is to desensitize the foal's back where the saddle will sit, as well as the girth area. The foal also learns to be sensitized in certain areas of her body, like the flanks, and to back up in response to chest pressure, to move forward in response to butt pressure, and to turn on the forehand and hindquarters with pressure. The session also consists of follow-up desensitization of areas covered in the first session.

- ✔ **Session three:** Designed to further sensitize the foal in certain areas of her body, you perform this session when the foal is 12 to 36 hours old, depending on the foal. (The baby needs to be strong on her feet and well-coordinated for this session.) First, halter the foal and repeat all the desensitizing steps from sessions one and two. Then add a leading lesson (see the section "Lead training" for more information).

Now that you know the basics of imprinting, we want you to know that you can overdo imprinting and take it to the extreme. Coauthor Dr. Kate believes that mare and foal must have time alone together early on in order to form a strong bond. This period is especially critical for a maiden mare and her first baby, when foal rejection is a possibility. Don't let imprinting interfere with your mare's ability to bond with her foal. Keep sessions short and don't keep your mare away from her baby.

Mom and baby: A real team

Mother horses are among the most protective and doting of all domestic animal species. And baby horses are among the most devoted offspring. The two are deeply bonded. Keep this fact in mind when you're handling them, and check out these pointers for dealing with mom and baby as a team:

✔ If you want the baby to move, you have to move mama first. The foal takes her cues from mom, and if mom isn't going in that direction, neither is baby.

✔ Mom won't leave her baby, no matter what. She can be the best-trained horse in the world, but if the baby isn't coming along, mom isn't going either. (And no human is big or strong enough to make it happen.)

✔ Mom has only one thing on her mind: Protecting and staying close to her baby. She has no qualms about risking her own life to save her foal. Remember this before doing anything with the baby that mom may perceive as threatening. If the baby acts scared or upset, mom may very well jump in to protect her.

✔ Baby will always go to mom for comfort. In fact, if the baby gets scared or nervous, she runs to mom's udder and puts her nose near it. The smell of the udder means safety and security to the baby. (You can help the baby feel more comfortable with you by adding this smell to your hands by handling your mare's udders.)

Additional handling

Whether you choose to imprint your foal or not, it's a good idea to continue to handle her a lot during her young weeks and months. Dr. Kate uses a specific method that works well for her foals.

At about a month of age, Dr. Kate brings her mares and foals in from pasture and puts them in stalls for four or five days so that the babies can get a refresher course on handling. The babies get lots of pats and scratches from people and get their feet picked up, their ears played with, and both sides of their bodies rubbed.

Dr. Kate starts putting halters on her babies at this stage, but she doesn't leave them on for safety reasons. (The halter could get caught on something out in the pasture, including another foal; see the next section for more about halter training.)

Because Dr. Kate's broodmares come to the edge of the pasture daily to get petted (they love attention), the babies come with them and get additional handling, too. They get their feet handled and their bodies and faces touched. At this point, she also starts teaching the babies how to give when light pressure is applied to their bodies — an important lesson for them to learn now so that they're easier to train when they get older. Dr. Kate asks them to back up by putting pressure on the chest. She also asks them to *sidepass* (move sideways) by applying light pressure to their sides.

Dr. Kate follows all early training with immediate praise. Soon, she has a very responsive, respectful, and eager group of babies.

Halter training

Foals get used to wearing a halter pretty quickly. At first they may react like a giant fly has landed on their faces. But in short order, they come to ignore the halter.

Breeders and trainers use different methods for teaching babies how to wear a halter. Some people put a special foal-sized web halter on the baby after she's only a couple of hours old. Others wait a month or more to introduce this piece of equipment.

Coauthor Dr. Kate waits to halter break her babies until they're weaned, which is at about five to six months of age. (We discuss weaning in more detail later in this chapter.) Working with the foals in a small pen, she puts a halter that's loose enough to be comfortable but snug enough to prevent getting a foot caught in the webbing on each horse. She attaches a soft cotton lead rope long enough to trail on the ground for about 1½ feet. (When the baby steps on the rope, she learns how to stop and give to pressure — an important lesson when you're teaching her to accept a rider.)

Dr. Kate takes her babies into a pen several times each day and works with them. This exercise is where the foals' early training with handling comes in. Because the babies aren't afraid of pressure on their heads, she can gently restrain them with the lead rope. While she has the foal restrained, she picks up the foal's feet, gives her injections, and deworms her. This lesson requires time, patience, and repetition.

You can begin halter training your foal at birth by putting a halter on her right after she's born, or you can wait until the foal is anywhere from one week to four weeks old to get started. The sooner your start with your baby, the sooner your foal will know how to wear a halter.

If you're new to horses and don't have a lot of experience handling adult horses, get a trainer or experienced horse person to help you teach your foal her early lessons.

Lead training

Training a foal to lead is trickier than teaching her to wear a halter. The best age to start is when the baby is a couple of weeks old, after she's already learned to wear a halter.

People use different methods to teach foals to lead. One of the more popular methods is using a butt rope and halter (see Figure 16-3). The butt rope attaches to the halter and goes around the baby's rump, behind the back legs. This method works because it teaches the baby to give to the pressure of the rope instead of resisting it, as she would if you just pulled on her head.

The details on training a foal to lead are beyond the scope of this book, so we suggest that you check out the appendix for some of the books we suggest on foal training to get you started.

Figure 16-3:
A butt rope works well when teaching a foal to lead.

Bob Langrish

Weaning

Mares and their foals stay together at all times until the weaning process begins. A lot of different ideas exist as to when to wean a foal (in other words, when to permanently remove her from her mother). In nature, foals wean themselves at around five or six months of age. In domestic situations, they sometimes wean as early as three months. Some people believe that it's easier on the mare to have the baby removed early. Others believe that it's better to leave the foal with the mare until the baby is more mature.

Both of your authors believe that it's better to wean a foal in its fifth or sixth month. By this time, the foal has become much more independent of her mom and is eating well on her own. The mare's milk production begins to decrease gradually at about the third month, which encourages the baby to eat more solid food.

A number of different weaning methods exist. Some handlers wean foals gradually, slowly separating them at a farther and farther distance from their moms. On the other hand, some handlers take foals away cold turkey.

Although your individual situation determines what works best for you, the most important factor in your plan should be to minimize as much stress as possible for both mare and foal, to prevent injury to both, and to maintain adequate nutrition for the growth of the foal. See the appendix for resources that you can use to wean your foal.

Coauthor Dr. Kate's method of weaning starts with putting the broodmares and foals all together in a group so that the babies make friends with each other. (This togetherness is also helpful because it teaches the babies how to behave properly around other horses.) At weaning time, the mares move into a pasture next door with a safe 5-foot no-climb woven fence between them. Although the mares and weanlings hang out at the fence for several days to be near each other, Dr. Kate doesn't hear much whinnying or see signs of stress. The moms and babies can all see one another, but the babies can't nurse. The mares' milk quickly dries up, and the babies have friends to play with.

Chapter 17

Helping Your Horse Age Gracefully

Senior horses are absolutely wonderful. They have a wisdom about them that you just don't see in a young horse. They're also much more sensible, less easy to spook, and often a real joy to be around.

In this chapter, we tell you how to keep your senior looking and feeling good well into old age. You discover some of the common health problems seen in older horses, and we give you pointers on feeding and exercising your old faithful. We also give you pointers on how to know when it's time for your buddy to retire.

Knowing How Old Is Old

It used to be that horses didn't live much into their 20s. But these days, it's not uncommon to see a horse in his early- to mid-30s still doing light work and enjoying life despite a few aches and pains.

Just as with people, every horse is an individual, and some age better than others. Technically, a horse is considered a senior when he hits about the age of 15. Many horses work well past this age, and for some horses, 15 finds them in their prime.

The way a horse is cared for early in his life does seem to play a significant role in how well he navigates his senior years. So take the advice in the rest of this book to heart!

Handling Common Health Issues in Your Senior Horse

When horses age, their bodies begin to slowly give out. They start developing problems much like senior humans do. That doesn't mean that they still can't be productive, however. You just need to understand the difficulties that come with equine old age so that you can help manage them.

Vision problems

As horses age, their eyes undergo changes. Your senior horse may not see as well as she did in her younger days.

As the lenses of your horse's eyes age, the tissue fibers become more densely compacted, leading to something called nuclear sclerosis. Most people know this condition as cataracts (see Chapter 11 for details). The retina also undergoes aging, and between the two issues, your horse's vision declines.

One of the first changes that you'll probably notice about your horse's eyesight is her loss of night vision. Light can't get through the cloudy lens to get to her aging retina. Some loss of peripheral vision is common too.

The result of this vision loss is that your horse may be much more prone to spook at stuff she didn't spook at before. For this reason, some older horses suddenly act as though they're 2 years old even though they're going on 20! (Chapter 3 has more information about spooking.)

You can continue to ride your senior horse with these vision changes. Just be aware that she may not see that well, especially at night. (Have your vet examine your horse's eyes if she acts particularly spooky at night.) Let your horse know when you're near her by talking to her as you approach.

Even if your senior horse's vision seems normal, keep a close watch on her eyes. As her immunity weakens with age, she's more susceptible to eye disease. If you see any kind of change in your horse's eyes, such as opacity, inflammation, squinting, or increased tearing, contact your veterinarian.

If you have a horse with serious vision loss, and your veterinarian has addressed all treatable causes, don't make sudden changes to your horse's environment. Horses who are sight impaired develop almost a sense of "radar" and do very well in familiar surroundings.

Tooth problems

Old horses can be plagued by tooth problems. That's because they can literally wear down their teeth with years of chewing fibrous material.

Dental care is hugely important as your horse ages. Some horses live long enough to outlive their teeth!

One problem more common in older horses than younger ones is periodontal disease. Infection in the gum progresses until the tooth is lost or must be extracted. This isn't good because your senior horse needs all the teeth she can get. Tooth loss can compromise chewing and affect the wear of remaining teeth. (Figure 17-1 shows the worn teeth of a 20-year-old horse.)

Watch your horse for signs of tooth trouble. These include:

- ✔ Dropping food while eating
- ✔ Salivating excessively while eating
- ✔ Bouts of colic (see Chapter 11)
- ✔ Eating very slowly
- ✔ Unexplained weight loss
- ✔ Coarse-looking manure (Chapter 2 describes the appearance of normal manure)
- ✔ Fussing while wearing a bit
- ✔ Reluctance to have face or muzzle touched

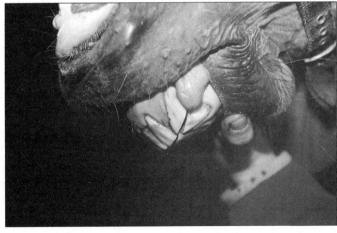

Figure 17-1:
Worn teeth are common in older horses.

Bob Langrish

If you see any of these symptoms in your horse, call your veterinarian right away. If the vet confirms a tooth problem that can't be corrected with dental care, be sure to adjust your senior's diet, as we explain later in this chapter.

Arthritis

Finding a senior horse who doesn't have some level of arthritis is hard to do. After a while, the joints start to give out and stiffen.

Although some horses have very bad arthritis — so bad that they can barely walk — others have just a mild case. If your older horse seems stiff when you first take her out of her stall in the morning, and then she loosens up after a bit of exercise, she probably has arthritis. Or, if she has persistent lameness on one or more legs and your vet has ruled out laminitis and navicular or another type of lameness, arthritis is the likely cause.

Here are some steps that you can take to manage your horse's arthritis:

- ✔ **Give her room.** The more space an arthritic horse has to live in, the better her arthritis will be. A pasture is the best environment for an arthritic horse because she's more likely to move around. (See Chapter 4 for more about pastures.)

- ✔ **Provide daily exercise.** If your horse lives in a stall, it's imperative that you take her for at least a 30-minute daily walk around the barn to get her joints moving. Talk to your vet about how much and what kind of riding you should be doing with your horse; hard riding will make her arthritis worse. (We discuss exercising a senior in detail later in this chapter; flip to Chapter 5 for general exercise information.)

- ✔ **Warm up slowly.** When you exercise your arthritic horse, start slowly. She'll be stiff at first and will need more time to loosen up than she did when she was younger. Allow at least 10 minutes of warm-up time before a workout.

- ✔ **Give joint supplements.** Talk to your veterinarian about putting your horse on daily joint supplements containing glucosamine, chondroitin, and MSM. (Chapter 8 has the full scoop on supplements.)

If your horse's arthritis gets worse despite these guidelines, consult with your vet about putting your horse on medication to help her feel more comfortable. We discuss arthritis and other soundness issues in more detail in Chapter 11.

An inability to keep weight on

Senior horses sometimes get pretty thin in their old age. Sometimes, they can't digest their food as well as they did in their younger days, resulting in getting less nutrition and less weight on their bones. Or their thinness could be the result of another problem. Whatever the cause, you can take steps to manage the weight loss.

If your older horse is losing weight, follow these steps to help her:

- ✔ **Contact your veterinarian.** First, you need to make sure that your horse isn't suffering from a serious illness or condition. Have your vet examine her.

- ✔ **Check her teeth.** Older horses are more susceptible to tooth problems, which can keep them from properly chewing their food. Poorly chewed food doesn't digest well, leaving your horse with a void in her nutrition. (We talk about tooth problems earlier in this chapter.)

- ✔ **Change her diet.** If your older horse is eating grass hay and can't seem to keep weight on, you may need to add a legume hay to her diet, or perhaps a concentrated senior feed. (See the later section "Feeding Your Senior Horse" for more information.)

A loss of muscle

As horses age, their muscles start to lose some elasticity and tone, especially if they aren't being worked very much. Coauthor Audrey first got her horse, Red Playboy, when he was 18. This senior horse had a bad case of being out of shape, and his loss of muscle had caused his back to sag and his belly muscles to hang down, causing him to develop back pain. (Figure 17-2 shows a horse with a loss of muscle.) Audrey got him back into shape by providing him with regular exercise every day; she gradually increased his exercise over a period of time to lessen the stress on his body.

The best way to keep an older horse from losing muscle is to keep her busy. Even a light workload goes a long way toward keeping those muscles in shape. Walking up hills is good for your horse, as is backing up and trotting in a straight line. (Avoid trotting in circles because it can put undo stress on her legs.) See the later section "Making Sure Your Senior Horse Stays Active" for more information.

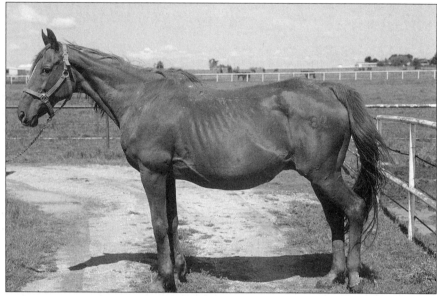

Figure 17-2:
Senior
horses often
experience
muscle loss
because of
inactivity.

Bob Langrish

Feeding Your Senior Horse

Older horses often need to be on a special diet, for a number of different reasons. These include:

- ✔ **Worn teeth.** Old horses sometimes have teeth that are so worn that they have trouble chewing (see the earlier section "Tooth problems" for information). These horses should be on feed that's easy for them to swallow without having to chew much. These can include some types of complete senior feeds, or hay cubes or pellets that have been soaked in water.

- ✔ **Protein intolerance.** Senior horses can't metabolize protein as well as their younger counterparts. Diets high in protein (such as all alfalfa diets) result in excessive urination and very wet stalls. Switching to a mostly grass hay diet can help with this issue.

- ✔ **Weight issues.** Some senior horses have trouble maintaining their weight (as we explain earlier in this chapter). These horses should be fed hay cubes or a complete senior diet in addition to hay to help them keep some meat on their bones.

Before you make any changes to your senior horse's diet, talk to your veterinarian. He or she can guide you toward the best food for your horse in his golden years. Flip to Chapter 7 for the skinny on feeding fundamentals.

Making Sure Your Senior Horse Stays Active

Some people make the mistake of thinking that an older horse should be left alone to spend her remaining days in peace and quiet. This couldn't be further from the truth. Older horses — especially those who have worked throughout their lives — often do poorly when put out to pasture to live a quiet life of retirement.

Just like people, horses need to feel needed, and having a regular job to do — even if it's for just half an hour a day — gives an old horse a reason to keep living. Plus, the exercise is good for those old joints, tendons, and muscles, as long as it isn't too strenuous.

You can give your senior horse exercise in a few different ways, as we explain in the following sections. (We start with the most strenuous activity first.) Chapter 5 has general information on exercising your horse.

Riding

If your senior horse is relatively sound, you can keep riding her for as long as your veterinarian says it's okay. Many horses well into their teens and 20s are ridden frequently, taken out on the trail (see Figure 17-3), or even shown and competed. (In fact, coauthor Audrey's senior gelding, Red, entered his first parade at the age of 19.) As long as your senior horse is healthy, you can keep riding her.

That said, remember that older horses take longer to warm up than young horses, so they need time to limber up. Give your horse at least 10 minutes of walking before you start to trot or canter.

When riding a senior horse on the trail, be aware that a lot of hill work may not be good for her legs. Going up and down a lot of hills can be tough on the joints, tendons, and muscles, and may shorten the amount of time that your horse stays sound into her senior years. Working in small circles isn't great for old horses either. Lots of walking straight on flat ground is the best exercise for seniors.

Figure 17-3:
Healthy, older horses can still be used for light trail riding.

Hand-walking

Some older horses can no longer be ridden, but that doesn't mean that they need to spend the rest of their lives stuck in a pasture or stall. Hand-walking a senior horse can do wonders for her body and her mind.

Even half an hour a day of hand-walking helps your senior feel like she has a job to do. It provides her with much needed attention and helps solidify your bond. It also loosens her joints, muscles, and tendons and gives her something to look forward to each day.

Before you hand-walk your old buddy, be sure to clean out her feet and groom her (see Chapter 4 for details). Senior horses thrive on attention, and some people believe that horses live longer when they're regularly fussed over by their favorite human.

Turning out

Healthy, sound senior horses benefit from regular turnout. If your senior is kept in a stall or small paddock, she needs to be turned out regularly so that she can stretch her legs. Because of her age, however, you need to handle her turnout carefully.

Hand-walk your horse for 10 minutes before turning her out to make sure that her joints, tendons, and muscles are loose. You don't want her tearing around the turnout without a warm-up because she may hurt herself. Don't chase her around the turnout, either. Let her do what she feels like doing in there. Even if it's just standing in a corner looking at the scenery, give her the option of doing what she feels up to.

Retiring Your Senior Horse

As we explain earlier in this chapter, senior horses can work well into their 20s, and sometimes into their 30s. Coauthor Audrey once knew a lesson horse who carried little kids around until he was 32 years old. He was working the day before he passed away from natural causes.

Don't be too quick to retire your senior horse just because he's up there in age. Before you do it, take a close look at him to make sure that he's really in need of retirement.

Judging your horse's condition

The most important aspect to determining whether your senior needs to be retired is his condition. Ask yourself the following questions:

- ✔ Is my horse serviceably sound?
- ✔ Can my horse still be ridden?
- ✔ If he has a health issue, can it be managed so that he can still work?
- ✔ What is his attitude about work? Is he still willing to perform when asked?

If you answer yes to these questions, retirement may be premature for your senior horse.

If you aren't sure whether your senior horse needs to quit working altogether, ask your veterinarian for advice. He or she can evaluate your horse and give you an expert opinion on the subject.

Tapering off work

If your older horse definitely needs to be retired — and you verified this with your veterinarian — it's important that you slowly taper off your horse's work instead of just stopping it cold turkey. A sudden, complete halting of work will be a shock to your horse, both mentally and physically. If he's physically fit and you suddenly cease all exercise, he will become pent up and unhappy. He will also miss his daily routine and may ultimately become depressed and lethargic.

Instead, slow your horse's workload gradually. If you were riding him for an hour a day, cut down to riding an hour a day just a few days a week. Then, eventually ride him only 30 minutes for those few days a week. Get down to one day until you eventually stop riding him altogether, and replace the riding with hand-walking (which we discuss earlier in this chapter). Do this over a period of several weeks to help him get used to his new life of leisure.

Putting your horse out to pasture

If your horse is definitely in need of retirement, and you have the means to put him out to pasture for the remainder of his days, remember that you still need to take care of your horse. You can't just put him out in a field and forget about him. He still needs daily care.

Your older horse needs company too. Don't put him in a pasture by himself. Get him a buddy so that he's not lonely. (But keep an eye out to make sure that the buddy isn't bullying him, or vice versa!) You can provide him with a buddy by boarding him at a pasture with other horses, boarding a friend's horse in your pasture, or getting another horse (senior or otherwise) as a companion.

Before you place your horse in a pasture, make certain that the pasture is safe and can provide for your horse's nutritional needs (see Chapters 7 and 9 for details on this). Your horse may need additional forage, instead of just living on pasture grass alone. Talk to your veterinarian for advice on what to feed him.

Although your senior horse is out in a pasture and not working, don't forget his feet! Horses in the wild don't need their feet trimmed because they travel for so many hours a day on such rough terrain that they wear their feet down naturally. A horse in a pasture is a whole different situation.

Your retired horse requires the same foot care as he did before. As an older horse, his feet may grow more slowly, but they're also more prone to cracking and brittleness. Talk to your veterinarian about pulling your horse's shoes (if his feet are shod), and consider having his feet trimmed regularly by an experienced barefoot trimmer. (See Chapter 4 for the basics of hoof care.)

Keep a close watch on his feet, too. Clean them daily, especially if the pasture becomes muddy, because this is when a fungal infection of the frog called thrush can rear its ugly head. (Chapter 11 has general information on fungal infections.)

Observe your pasture pet every day, too, and watch how he walks. Note any pain or changes in his gait, and call your vet if something doesn't look right.

Keep an eye on other aspects of your senior horse's health, as well. For example:

- ✔ Give him treats every day, and watch how he chews to make sure that he's not experiencing difficulty. (See the earlier section "Tooth problems" for details.)
- ✔ Take him out of the pasture and groom him. Give him the once-over while you brush him, and apply insect repellant during bug season.

With regular attention, your retired horse will learn to love being out to pasture and enjoying his golden years.

Chapter 18

Reaching the End of Your Horse's Life

*I*n the old days, horses were just commodities, easily bought and sold and often worked into the ground. People didn't spend much time thinking about what would happen when the horse became old and couldn't work anymore.

These days, many horses are more like members of the family than just tools to get a job done. Caring horse owners make provisions for their senior horses so that they can retire (see Chapter 17 for details), and for horses who are ill and can't be cured. These people often choose to give these horses a dignified end as a thank-you for years of service and companionship.

When a horse is too old or too ill to be able to go on without horrific suffering, the kindest thing a caring owner can do is help that horse have a swift, pain-free end to her life. This is done with euthanasia, administered by a veterinarian. Although giving the order to put a horse down is always a difficult one, it's a selfless act when done with the horse's best interest at heart.

In this chapter, we take a look at euthanasia, and we give you guidance on when to choose this option for your horse. We also provide information on what to do with your horse's remains and how to cope with grief from losing your equine friend.

Facing the Process of Euthanasia

The technical term for putting a horse "to sleep" is *euthanasia*. Although other methods of ending a horse's life are still used in certain parts of the country — like shooting a horse in the head or sending it off to slaughter — we maintain that euthanasia administered by a qualified veterinarian is the most humane way to put a horse down. In the following sections, we give you a few guidelines for deciding when euthanasia is the right option for your horse, and we look at the basic process.

Sometimes owners choose to be present during the euthanasia to be with their horse during her transition to the "other side." We don't know how much this helps the horse during the process, but being present can help some owners deal with their grief by saying goodbye. For other owners, it's a traumatic experience. When euthanasia is administered to a horse who's standing, the horse falls over or collapses during the process. This can be upsetting to some owners, who may opt not to be present during the euthanasia.

Deciding when it's time to put down your horse

Knowing when it's time to put a horse down can be tricky. Most people are reluctant to give the go-ahead to a veterinarian to give a horse the necessary injection. People feel like they're "playing God," and are loath to make this decision. No doubt about it, this is one of the hardest decisions you'll ever make. Fortunately, your veterinarian can help you figure out when the time is right. Veterinarians are trained in euthanasia in vet school and, unfortunately, have plenty of opportunity to practice it in their day-to-day work. Although the vast majority of equine veterinarians would rather do anything else than put a horse down, it's part of their job and one that they understand very well.

Keeping the following elements in mind while discussing the situation with your vet can help you make this very difficult decision:

- ✔ **Quality of life.** Think about the horse's quality of life. Is the horse suffering? Is her life filled with pain? Does she have more bad or marginal days than good days? Will her disease continue to worsen as time goes on? Having your horse euthanized is more humane than letting her suffer if the condition is painful and incurable.

- ✔ **Pain.** Consider how much pain the horse is experiencing. Does walking cause the horse pain? Is the horse's pain so bad that medication can no longer control it?

✔ **Mobility.** Horses are very mobile creatures. Walking, trotting, and galloping are all essentials to equine happiness. Old horses can get so stiff and sore that doing anything other than walking can be difficult. But can the horse do at least that? Is even a slow walk painful for the horse?

✔ **Ability to stand.** Because they're prey animals, horses are meant to stand most of the time so that they can make a quick getaway if danger presents itself. When a horse gets to the point in life where she can no longer stand, she's suffering not only mentally but also physically. A horse who's forced to lie down because she's unable to stand is a horse who's ready to be euthanized.

✔ **Your finances.** It may be difficult to consider, but is keeping the horse alive costing more than your pocketbook can stand? Does the horse stand little chance of recovering, and just keeping her alive is costing more than you can spare? One of the most painful aspects of deciding on euthanasia comes with having to consider the cost of continued vet care. However, if your horse is very old or if her condition is incurable, and throwing more money at the situation isn't going to help her but will undoubtedly hurt you, don't feel guilty about making finances a part of your decision.

Human beings have a hard time letting go of what they love. Sometimes, because of this, owners hold on too long to their horses. Coauthor Dr. Kate has seen this time and again — owners who let horses suffer too long before making the decision to give them a peaceful rest with dignity. She says:

> I will say that I personally have never heard an owner say, "I put him to sleep too soon," but all too often owners lament, "I should never have let her suffer this long . . . I should have done this sooner." I will always speak for those who cannot speak because this is my job and honors the oath I took — that I will alleviate suffering. I'm sure that I practice more euthanasias than most veterinarians because of my ER experience and my alternative practice. Often, owners come to me when all other avenues of treatment have been exhausted, so whether Traditional Chinese Veterinary Medicine (TCVM) can help their horse or not, I'm the last veterinarian they experience. It's a huge and humbling responsibility.

Having memories of your horse feeling good at the end is best. Don't let the last memory you have of her be one of pain or suffering, if at all possible. Trust your veterinarian to help you understand that some problems won't get better, and that everything ages and dies. What a blessing that you can help your horses and give them the gift of euthanasia when it's time.

Understanding how euthanasia works

When a veterinarian administers euthanasia to a horse, he or she uses a barbiturate drug. Euthanasia drugs are injected in large quantities into a horse's bloodstream, stopping brain function almost instantly. The horse doesn't feel any pain during this process; essentially, she feels as if she's just going to sleep. She loses consciousness (similar to being anesthetized for surgery) and then stops breathing. Soon afterward, the heartbeat ceases. The entire process takes only a few minutes.

In many cases, veterinarians may administer a sedative to the horse before administering the euthanasia drug to help make an excited horse more relaxed. A relaxed horse may accept the euthanasia drug more easily and is less likely to fight the sensation that comes with the final injection. Sedation prior to the final injection also may allow your veterinarian to help the horse lie down safely and quietly, which is much less stressful for both owner and horse. Ask your veterinarian whether sedation can help to ensure that your horse isn't distressed during the process.

Taking Care of Your Horse's Remains

Because horses are such large animals, disposing of their remains can be rather tricky. Unlike a cat or a dog, even transporting the body requires considerable work and planning. Local laws can also determine what you're allowed to do with your horse after he passes. You have a few options for your horse's remains after euthanasia, as you find out in the following sections.

Plan ahead and decide what you want to do before your horse is put down. Emotions can be raw right after the horse's passing, and making a decision may be difficult at that time. In addition, coauthor Dr. Kate strongly recommends to her clients that they not be present when their horse's remains are removed. Ask a friend to securely cover the horse with a blanket or tarp and let him or her handle the removal.

Burial

If you're fortunate enough to have your own expanse of land and live in a county where it's legal to bury a horse on your own property, your first option for your horse's remains may be burial.

In order to bury your horse on your own land, you need to rent a backhoe (if you don't have one yourself). A backhoe can not only dig a grave deep enough for your horse's remains (the hole must be six feet deep or more depending on the legal requirements in your area), but can also transport your horse's body from where it lies elsewhere on your property. The backhoe can also fill the grave with dirt, covering the body thoroughly.

If your horse will be buried on your property, let someone else put him in the grave and cover his body with dirt. Watching the process of moving such a large body can be unpleasant, and as a grieving owner, you don't need to see it.

If you don't have your own property and don't know anyone who will permit you to bury your horse on their land, consider having your horse buried at a pet cemetery. Keep in mind that this option costs a few thousand dollars, including the money that you pay to have your horse's body taken to the cemetery. The plus side is that you always have a place where you can go to visit your horse. Most pet cemeteries are bucolic places, and many owners find great solace in knowing that their beloved equine is buried in such a place.

Cremation

If you don't have your own land, a less expensive alternative to burial at a pet cemetery is cremation. More and more pet cemeteries are starting to offer cremation services for horses. Although this method of disposing of your horse's remains is still costly (usually between $1,000 and $2,000), it's cheaper than burial.

If you have your horse cremated, you can keep his ashes with you at your home, or scatter them on your property. If you choose to keep them, you can purchase an urn or memorial box for the ashes. You can purchase urns and boxes on the Internet, or through the pet cemetery that does the cremation.

If you want to scatter your horse's ashes, be sure to inform the pet cemetery of this before you have your horse cremated. The crematorium handles your horse's remains differently if the ashes are to be scattered than if they'll remain in an urn or box.

Rendering

The least expensive way to handle your horse's body is to have it rendered. For a relatively small fee of usually just a few hundred dollars, a livestock remains transport company or the rendering company comes to pick up your horse's body and takes it to a rendering plant.

For most horse owners — especially those who don't have their own property for burial and have limited funds — this is the best option. The horse's body will be used to make fertilizer or other organic materials.

Not all counties have rendering plants that accept horse carcasses. Discuss disposal of your horse's body with your veterinarian when the time comes. He or she can tell you whether rendering is an option where you live.

Grieving for Your Horse

Losing a horse you love is one of the most painful things you'll ever endure. Both of your coauthors have gone through this loss and speak with experience.

In order to get past the pain and anguish of losing your horse, you must experience grief. Some people think that grief is appropriate only when you lose a beloved human. But if you love your horse, you're entitled to grieve as if you had lost a human in your life. In fact, you need to grieve in order to heal.

Surveying the stages of grief

Psychologists have discovered that grief has various aspects to it. These aspects are sometimes called "stages of grief," but they don't always come in any particular order, and in fact can come and go alternatively.

The following emotions are normal and part of the process of grieving the loss of your horse. Allow yourself to feel them, and try not to judge yourself. You may feel at times like you're losing your mind, but in reality, you're experiencing what all people experience when they lose someone they care about. Here are the different aspects of grief:

- **Denial.** You have trouble believing that your horse is dying or has died. The situation feels unreal.
- **Anger.** You feel enraged that this has happened to you and your horse.
- **Guilt.** You irrationally feel like your horse's death is somehow your fault.
- **Depression.** You have trouble caring about things you normally enjoy.
- **Numbness.** You have moments when you can't feel anything at all.
- **Anguish.** You have waves of intense emotional pain, and sometimes you can't stop crying.
- **Acceptance.** You start to feel a sense of acceptance about your loss.

Be aware that you may even experience some of these aspects to grief before your horse dies, if you know that the end is coming.

The amount of time that it takes to finally reach acceptance — and stay there — varies from person to person. If you find that you're unable to accept what's happened, or if you just need support as you grieve your horse, contact one of the support group hotlines listed in this book's appendix. For additional information about grieving, check out *Grieving For Dummies,* by Greg Harvey, PhD (Wiley).

Remembering and honoring your horse

After your horse has passed, you may want to do something to acknowledge her passing. Although holding a funeral for a horse is rare, people do other things that help them find closure. Here are some ideas that may help:

- Lay flowers in your horse's stall.
- If your horse has been buried, lay a marker on her grave.
- If your horse has been cremated, scatter her ashes in a place that means something to you — perhaps a favorite place she liked to trail ride, or in her pasture.
- Write a letter to your horse telling her how you feel about her.
- Create an album of photos and keepsakes.
- Donate to a charitable cause in your horse's name, plant a tree or flowers, or help another animal in need.

When coauthor Audrey's blind Appaloosa mare Rosie died, Audrey donated the board she was about to pay that month to a horse rescue, in Rosie's name. The rescue put a plaque with Rosie's name in its memorial garden.

Friends may like making donations for you, too. Receiving a note in the mail from a charitable organization saying that a donation has been made in your horse's honor is touching. After Rosie died, one of Audrey's friends donated money to help find a cure for the disease that caused Rosie to lose her eyesight.

Coauthor Dr. Kate was fortunate enough to be able to bury her sweet old mare, Glo, in a pasture on her Texas farm, beneath a grove of trees in Glo's favorite spot. Dr. Kate planted daffodils there that will naturalize and spread every year (horses and deer won't eat daffodils). The flowers remind Dr. Kate of how Glo brought so much joy into her life. Dr. Kate further honors Glo by always wearing at shows the first buckle she ever won in cutting, on Glo, even though Dr. Kate has won lots of fancier, more impressive buckles since.

The bottom line is that you should do whatever works best for you to help you remember and honor your horse. Acts such as these help you grieve and enable you to accept what's happened to your horse. In time, you'll find that you're able to open your heart to love another horse.

Part V
The Part of Tens

The 5th Wave   By Rich Tennant

"Sitting in the tub relaxes his muscles."

In this part . . .

The Part of Tens is a mixture of important information regarding your horse's health. In these chapters, we provide you with ten signs that your horse is under the weather, as well as ten pointers on how to keep him healthy.

Chapter 19

Ten Signs of Horse Illness

In This Chapter

▶ Recognizing signs of equine distress

▶ Discovering the causes of bad behavior

Good horse owners get to know their horses very well. They see them every day and come to understand all their behavioral nuances: how they eat, how often they lie down, how they behave under saddle. Good horse owners figure out how their horses act when they're feeling fine — and how they act when they aren't.

In this chapter, we alert you to behaviors or conditions that you may notice in your horse if he's under the weather. Your horse can't talk, so all he can do is demonstrate his discomfort in the following ways. Pay close attention. Your horse is depending on you.

A Fever

When a horse is feeling well, his temperature is usually between 99 and 101.4 degrees Fahrenheit. If he's battling an infection, whether bacterial or viral, his temperature is either below or above that range.

When a horse has a fever, he may exhibit some or all of the following behaviors:

✔ Lack of appetite

✔ Lethargy or depression

✔ Heavy breathing

A horse with a fever may have other symptoms as well, depending on what's plaguing him. The fever may be accompanied by nasal discharge, coughing, or diarrhea. Or, it may be completely void of symptoms other than those previously listed.

If you suspect that your horse has a fever, take his temperature by using the directions we give in Chapter 2. If the fever is below 97 or above 102, call your veterinarian immediately. If it falls between 97 and 99, or between 101.4 and 102, wait a few hours and take the temperature again to make sure that this was just a normal variation and that it hasn't gone up or down in range.

Diarrhea

The equine digestive system is an efficient tool that's good at processing difficult-to-digest plant material. Bacteria located in the horse's gut are instrumental in breaking down cellulous plant fiber and turning it into a nutritional element.

When the delicate bacterial population in the horse's gut becomes imbalanced, she can develop diarrhea. Other issues can also cause diarrhea, and may include:

- Salmonella
- Potomac Horse Fever
- Clostridium colitis (irritation of the colon caused by the Clostridium bacteria)
- Cryptosporidia (a protozoan parasite that affects the digestive system)
- Blister beetle poisoning
- Drug toxicity
- Sand impaction
- Intestinal parasites
- Oak and acorn poisoning

If your horse develops diarrhea — very loose stool that's watery — possibly accompanied by lack of appetite, call your vet right away. Diarrhea can rob your horse of valuable nutrients and minerals, and cause severe dehydration and malnutrition in a very short amount of time. (See Chapter 2 to find out what normal manure looks like.)

An Inability to Pass Manure

One of the most dangerous conditions for any horse is an intestinal impaction, which can cause an inability to pass manure. A horse with an untreated impaction won't live long.

You can tell that your horse is having trouble passing manure if you see one or more of the following signs:

✔ Lack of normal amount of manure in his stall or pasture

✔ Signs of colic, including stretching out, biting at sides, pawing, or rolling (see Chapter 11 for more about colic)

✔ Difficult passage of hard, dry balls of manure (Chapter 2 explains what normal manure looks like)

If you see any of these symptoms, call your vet right away. He or she can treat your horse with medications that provide a laxative effect and can get the manure passing through as it should.

Always keep a source of clean, fresh water available to your horse. One of the leading causes of intestinal impaction is lack of water intake.

Heavy or Noisy Breathing

Horses are athletic by nature and have large lungs and substantial airways. So if you hear your horse breathing noisily, or if you see her breathing hard even though she hasn't been exercising, something is amiss.

Noisy breathing during exertion can be a sign of chronic obstructive pulmonary disease (COPD), also called heaves. This can be similar to asthma in humans, and is often allergy related. Horses with this condition can be treated with medication and environmental changes to help them breathe better. (See Chapter 11 for more about COPD.)

Heavy breathing without exertion can be a sign of a high fever. It can also be an expression of pain and stress.

If your horse's breathing changes from its normal pattern to something faster or noisier, call your veterinarian so that he or she can figure out what's going on.

Weight Loss or Gain

If your horse's diet has been consistent but you notice a dramatic weight loss or gain, something is going on with his health. (Chapter 2 can help you determine a normal weight for your horse.)

Weight loss can be caused by any number of health problems, including tooth problems, digestive troubles, kidney or liver disease, Cushing's disease (a metabolic disorder), parasite infestation, or cancer. Only your vet will be able to help ascertain the cause of the problem, so you need to get him or her in the loop.

Weight gain can be the result of a lack of exercise and too much feed. If your horse's food and exercise routine has remained the same and your horse is putting on weight, he may be suffering from a metabolic or endocrine disease. If you have a mare who you recently acquired, she may be pregnant. Again, only your vet can help you figure out why your horse is putting on weight.

Limping

If your horse is limping, she's considered lame. This diagnosis means that she's sore on one or more of her feet or legs, and isn't carrying her weight evenly on all four legs. Lameness can be apparent at the walk, trot, or canter.

Lameness can be caused by something as minor as a rock lodged in the bottom of a hoof, or something as serious as a bone fracture. Other causes of lameness can include:

- ✔ Hoof abscess
- ✔ Laminitis (a condition where the coffin bone rotates inside the hoof)
- ✔ Muscle soreness
- ✔ Navicular disease (a condition affecting the navicular bone inside the hoof)
- ✔ Arthritis
- ✔ Osteochondritis dissecans (OCD) (a disorder affecting joint cartilage)
- ✔ Tendonitis (a damaged or injured tendon)

Lameness can be very obvious or almost imperceptible to all but a very trained eye. But if you learn to really know your horse, you'll be able to spot even minor problems before they become serious.

When your horse is doing well, feel her legs to determine what's normal so that you can spot any subtleties in heat, tenderness, and swelling early on. Start at the top of each leg and run your hands down to the hoof. Notice the temperature of your horse's legs and hooves, and the look and feel of all the nuances of her normal bone structure.

If your horse acts lame when you're riding her, stop and get off. Check her hooves for signs of a foreign object. If you see something minor like a stone in her hoof, remove it and see whether that solves the problem. If you find something that's gone deep into her foot, or if you find no visible problem at all, put your horse back in her stall, and call your veterinarian.

Many horse owners are tempted to just let a lame horse rest in her stall for a few days in hope that the lameness will disappear on its own. But without a vet's involvement, you have no way of knowing the cause of the lameness. Your veterinarian can provide treatment as well as recommendations for rehabilitation. Remember that untreated lameness can often worsen and become even more serious.

Lethargy or Depression

Horses are generally cheerful creatures, acting alert when new stimuli are added to their environment and enthusiastically accepting good training. When a horse acts lethargic or depressed, something is bothering him. In some cases, the trouble is physical. Pain and physical discomfort can prompt a horse to act depressed and void of energy. If your horse starts acting depressed, suspect a physical malady.

Psychological issues can also cause a horse to act depressed. Unlike humans, who have complicated psychological problems, horses usually have simple issues. They're lonely, bored, or unhappy about the way they're being handled. They don't like their living conditions or they don't get along with their herd mates. Any of these things can cause a horse to become depressed.

A veterinary behaviorist is your horse's best friend if something like this is bothering him. Have your horse checked out for a physical problem first. If your vet gives him a clean bill of health, contact a behaviorist through the Animal Behavior Society. (See the appendix for contact information, and check out Chapter 3 for details on the connection between a horse's mind and health.)

Aggression

A horse who's born nasty is rare. Horses become mean when they're unhappy. Often this unhappiness can be traced to pain somewhere in the body.

Some horses are nasty because they have dominant personalities and have never been trained to treat humans with respect, but these horses have shown this behavior for a very long time. Normally nice horses who start acting mean are letting you know that something is wrong with them.

Horses who aren't getting enough to eat can become nasty, trying to bite their handlers and other horses with the least provocation. Horses who suffer pain from a poorly fitting saddle can get aggressive when they're being taken from their stalls.

If your horse suddenly becomes mean and aggressive toward you or any other human, ask your vet to examine her to see whether she's experiencing pain or discomfort somewhere on her body.

Misbehavior under Saddle

Imagine having to carry weight on your back while it's being pinched. That's what a horse with a poorly fitting saddle has to go through. It's not long before many horses in this situation start to rebel.

Misbehavior under saddle is often a clue that something is amiss with a horse's body. Bucking may be a sign of back pain when being ridden, as is refusing to go forward. Refusing to hold the head in a normal position may indicate mouth pain. Neck, shoulder, and croup pain can be demonstrated in any number of ways.

Some horses are nonspecific in their protest, behaving in an uncooperative manner the entire time they're being ridden because they're uncomfortable. If your horse starts to misbehave when being ridden, have your veterinarian give him a complete checkup. Before you call in a trainer for help with bad behavior, be certain that it's not the result of pain or discomfort. (See Chapter 3 for more information about equine misbehaviors.)

Additional Signs of Pain

Horses tend to be stoic creatures. In the wild, the animal who acted sick was the one most targeted by predators. So pretending not to be in pain was a boon to your horse's ancestors.

If you get to know your horse well, you'll be able to recognize whether she's in pain. The signs of pain depend on where the pain is coming from. Here are some guidelines to help you determine whether your horse is feeling pain in a particular part of her body:

- ✔ **Leg:** Limping, holding it up, not bearing full weight on a limb (we talk about limping in more detail earlier in this chapter)
- ✔ **Eye:** Squinting, tearing, holding it closed
- ✔ **Ear:** Holding to the side, shaking head
- ✔ **Mouth:** Dropping food when eating, resistance to having bit inserted
- ✔ **Head:** Tilting while chewing, shaking while being ridden
- ✔ **Abdomen:** Rolling, pawing, kicking, and biting at belly, pacing
- ✔ **Back:** Flinching when pressure is applied, pinning ears or threatening to bite when girth is tightened, misbehaving when ridden

Some horses are hard to figure out because they don't show you where it hurts by doing the things in this list. Instead, they're just lethargic or irritable (we discuss both conditions earlier in this chapter). In these cases, you need a vet to help you figure out where the pain is coming from.

Avoid the temptation to give your horse any painkilling drugs (like phenylbutazone or Banamine flunixin meglumine) before a veterinarian examines her. These drugs can mask the signs of pain and make it harder for the vet to make a diagnosis.

Chapter 20

Ten Ways to Keep Your Horse Healthy

*E*ven if you do everything right, your horse may someday get sick. But the better you treat her on a daily basis, the less likely that is to happen.

In this chapter, we give you the top ten things that you need to do to keep your horse happy and in good health. Follow these guidelines and you reduce your chances of having to deal with equine illness.

Minimize Stress

Horses are watchful creatures, and some are downright nervous. It's understandable if you look at their history: horses evolved as prey animals over eons. The habit of looking over their shoulders is genetically ingrained in them.

Consequently, horses are more prone to stress than a lot of other creatures. Many horses get worked up when they're placed in new situations. Most get upset when they're taken away from other horses. Some become overwrought when they're asked to ride in a trailer. Others get stressed when they're taken to shows and competitions.

Stress is bad for horses, just like it is for people. Too much stress can cause the following problems in your horse:

- ✔ Diarrhea
- ✔ Digestive tract ulcers
- ✔ Compromised immune system
- ✔ Bad behavior
- ✔ Depression

Keeping stress completely out of your horse's life is almost impossible. The activities that owners ask their horses to partake in do put some pressure on them. But you can certainly keep stress to a minimum. Here are a few pointers to keep your horse relaxed and happy:

- ✔ Take care of her health by following all the advice in this chapter (and in this book, for that matter!).

- ✔ Don't ask her to live without another horse as a companion; if you can't afford more than one horse, consider boarding a friend's horse on your property, or keeping your horse at a boarding stable or friend's house.

- ✔ Be patient when you're riding or training her, and seek professional help if necessary.

- ✔ Try to see the world from her perspective (such as understanding that horses are prey and herd animals).

- ✔ Prepare her for new experiences by slowly introducing her to them.

- ✔ Let her be a horse. Give her time to unwind and just hang out, doing what horses like to do: grazing, being around other horses, rolling, and running loose in a big paddock or pasture.

Be aware that horses stress easily. Even if yours doesn't show it outwardly, she may be internalizing her stress. Keep her mental health in mind at all times, and you'll be sure to keep her stress to a minimum. See Chapter 3 for more information about the connection between your horse's mind and health.

Schedule an Annual Vet Exam

When money is tight, the first thing that horse owners often give up is having a well-horse exam every year. After all, if your horse is feeling fine, why have the vet come out?

Just like humans need to see their doctor every year for an annual checkup, horses need to see the vet every year. Although your horse may seem healthy, your vet can determine whether or not a problem is lurking undetected.

When you call your vet out for an annual exam, one of the first things that he or she checks is your horse's teeth (we talk about teeth in more detail later in this chapter). He or she will also listen to your horse's lungs and heart.

The vet will also ask you questions about your horse's appetite and manure, his performance when asked to work, and other basic questions. This is the time to let the vet know if you're seeing anything unusual, or if you have any concerns about your horse. If something seems amiss, your vet can follow up with whatever tests are deemed necessary to help get to the bottom of your horse's condition. You can also use this time to discuss your horse's vaccination and deworming program (which we discuss later in this chapter), and have shots given if they're due. (In fact, many owners schedule their horse's annual exam around the time vaccinations are needed so that the vet can give these at the same time that he or she conducts the exam.)

You may also want to consider having your vet draw blood and run a full blood count on your horse. This test allows your vet to see how well your horse's organs are functioning, whether he has any issues with white or red blood cell count, and a host of other things.

By having your horse checked out once a year, you're sure to stay on top of his healthcare. You also build a rapport with your veterinarian, who will be there to help you and will already know your horse in the event of an emergency.

Have Your Horse Vaccinated Annually

Horses are susceptible to a whole host of infectious diseases, many of which can kill them. Fortunately, veterinary medicine has developed vaccines for many of these diseases, making it easy for horse owners to protect their equine companions.

The vaccines regularly given by veterinarians may include the following:

- Equine encephalomyelitis
- Influenza/rhinopneumonitis
- Tetanus
- West Nile virus

In addition to these vaccines, your veterinarian may recommend others specific to your area of the country and your horse's circumstances.

The veterinary community is currently revising some of its long-standing vaccination protocols. Many vets are recommending vaccination less often than in the past. Nevertheless, having your horse inoculated against common horse diseases every year is still important. Discuss a vaccination protocol with your veterinarian and stick to it. Your horse's life depends on it. Check out Chapter 4 for more information on vaccinations.

File Your Horse's Teeth Regularly

Horses have amazing jaws and teeth. They're strong enough to grind down the most fibrous of plant materials in a short amount of time. The catch is that, in domestic life, a horse's teeth need special care.

In the wild, horses manage to wear down their teeth evenly as they chew, probably because of the varied plant life they ingest. When living with humans and eating the same type of feed over and over, however, their teeth develop problems. Molars in the back of the horse's jaw wear unevenly, leaving points on the outside and inside of the teeth that can cut into the horses' cheeks and tongue when she chews. Hooks can also form on the molars.

All this causes the horse to chew her food improperly and predisposes her to infections in the mouth, as well as the development of more complicated dental/oral problems. These situations may lead to problems such as weight loss or poor overall body condition, colic (see Chapter 11 for details on colic), choking, or sinus infections, as well as misbehavior when a bit is in her mouth.

The best way to remedy the situation of unevenly worn teeth is to have the points filed down as often as your veterinarian recommends it. The best person for this job is an equine veterinarian. Vets are trained to file teeth correctly and to also examine the horse's mouth for other issues, such as an abscessed or loose tooth.

Take Good Care of Your Horse's Hooves

If you watch horses play or run, you get a good sense of how important their feet and legs are to them. Nature built them to stand almost all the time, and to move swiftly in a moment's notice. Without healthy hooves and legs, a horse isn't all he should be. In fact, without healthy hooves and legs, your horse may end up unable to be ridden or even function as a pasture ornament. Horses need to be able to stand and move in order to survive.

As a horse owner, you have an obligation to keep those hooves and legs in good condition. You do this by providing quality hoof care on a regular basis. As with feed, this isn't an area to skimp on. Find a good farrier and stick to the hoof-care schedule that he or she gives you. (For details on how to best care for your horse's hooves, see Chapter 4.)

Deworm Regularly

Internal parasites can wreak havoc with a horse's internal organs. The sight of a domestic horse who hasn't been dewormed for much of her life is a sad one indeed. Horses who are infested with internal parasites have a shortened lifespan; these parasites literally suck the life out of them.

Deworming is easy to do thanks to many different deworming products now available to horse owners. These dewormers aren't expensive and they're easy to administer to your horse. You can buy them at your local tack and feed store, through mail order catalogs specializing in equine products, or through the Internet.

Your veterinarian is your best friend when you're developing a good deworming program. The frequency of deworming and the type of dewormer that you use is dependent on your horse's age, how she's kept, and the area of the country where you live. Ask your vet to provide you with a good deworming program, and stick to it. Your horse will be all the better for it. For more details on internal parasites and deworming, see Chapter 4.

Exercise Daily

Horses were designed to move all day long, taking little steps as they graze. When kept in stalls or paddocks, horses tend to stand around a lot. This puts pressure on their joints, tendons, and ligaments because it's unnatural. It also reduces the motility of the horse's digestive system.

By getting your horse out of his stall or paddock every day and getting him to move around, you're providing his legs with the movement that they need to stay healthy. You're also helping your horse's circulation, and stimulating his digestive system. All this adds up to a horse who has a healthier body that will stay in good working order for a longer period of time.

Daily exercise also does wonders for a horse's attitude. Horses who are cooped up in stalls or paddocks become bored. Some get depressed. Others develop stable vices (see Chapter 3 for a description of these unfortunate behaviors). Just about any horse who is regularly cooped up in a stall and doesn't get out much will be unmanageable or difficult to ride on the rare times he does get to come out. In fact, lack of exercise is one of the leading causes of training and behavioral issues in horses used for recreational riding. Getting your horse out once a day for some exercise and mental stimulation helps him stay sane.

Chapter 5 has the scoop on exercising your horse to keep him healthy.

Feed Quality Food

You are what you eat, even if you're a horse. Feed your horse quality food and you have a healthier horse. It's very simple.

Horses need roughage to stay healthy, and that means hay or pasture. It can be frustrating to spend your money on hay or to slave over your pasture and see it vanish so quickly, coming out the other end as loads of poop.

Because of this, one of the toughest aspects of horse ownership is resisting the urge to buy cheap hay, graze on not-so-good pasture, or purchase low-end grain or commercial feed. Horses are expensive, and horse owners often look for any way they can to save money.

But saving money on your horse's feed is pennywise and pound foolish. Your horse won't stay healthy if you don't provide her with good nutrition. Not only will her general condition suffer, but she may also become ill from eating hay or grain that's moldy, or pasture that's contaminated with toxic weeds.

Always buy the best hay or grain that you can afford and that's appropriate for your individual horse's needs, and work hard to keep your pasture producing quality grass. For details on how to judge the quality of feed, see Chapter 7.

Keep Your Horse at an Optimum Weight

Nothing is sadder than seeing a horse who's grossly underweight. Seeing such a noble creature with all his bones protruding is incredibly depressing. But just as depressing to those who know horses is seeing a horse who's grossly overweight. Fat horses have owners who mean well, giving them as much food as they'll eat in the hopes of keeping them happy. The result is an animal whose joints and ligaments are being unnecessarily stressed, and who's at risk for laminitis. (See Chapter 11 for details on this disease.)

Use the guidelines in Chapter 7 to determine how much your horse should eat every day. Keep a close eye on his weight, and if he's getting too thin, ask your veterinarian about the best way to increase his dietary intake. After a physical exam to help rule out medical causes, your veterinarian can recommend changing the amount of food that you give your horse or possibly a change in type of food. If he's getting too fat, reduce his grain intake and/or increase his exercise. If you aren't sure whether your horse is too fat or too thin (or if you see changes in body condition despite food and exercise being the same as before), check out Chapter 2 and consult with your veterinarian. Keeping your horse at the optimum body weight increases his chances of staying healthy throughout his life.

Use Joint Nutraceuticals

Although it hasn't been proven beyond a shadow of a doubt in clinical studies, anecdotal evidence has shown that joint nutraceuticals containing glucosamine, chondroitin sulfate, and methylsulfonylmethane (MSM) may help a horse's joints stay healthy.

You can find a vast array of products containing these ingredients in tack stores, in equine product catalogs, and online. Selecting the best one can be tricky because no real guidelines exist on how to pick these products. Ask your veterinarian for guidance. He or she may have experience with some of the products that are out there, and will most likely have an opinion on which one you should use for the best results.

For more information on joint nutraceuticals, see Chapter 14.

Resources for Horse Care

*T*hese resources will help you take better care of your horse's health and nutrition.

Veterinary Teaching Hospitals

When you're talking about state-of-the-art vet care, nothing compares to veterinary teaching hospitals. These working hospitals are located within veterinary schools, and you can find them around the country. They're the source of the latest in research on issues affecting equine care, and they employ specialists who are up-to-date on all the latest treatments for horses. You can rely on these hospitals for detailed information on just about any disease or condition affecting horses. Your veterinarian may refer you to one of these hospitals if you live within driving distance to one, or he or she may consult over the phone with a specialist at one of these facilities.

Alabama

Auburn University College of Veterinary Medicine
www.vetmed.auburn.edu

Tuskegee University School of Veterinary Medicine
tuskegee.edu

California

University of California-Davis School of Veterinary Medicines
www.vetmed.ucdavis.edu

Western University of Health Sciences College of Veterinary Medicine
www.westernu.edu/cvm.html

Colorado

Colorado State University College of Veterinary Medicine and Biomedical Sciences
www.cvmbs.colostate.edu

Florida

University of Florida College of Veterinary Medicine
www.vetmed.ufl.edu

Georgia

University of Georgia College of Veterinary Medicine
www.vet.uga.edu

Illinois

University of Illinois College of Veterinary Medicine
www.cvm.uiuc.edu

Indiana

Purdue University School of Veterinary Medicine
www.vet.purdue.edu

Iowa

Iowa State University College of Veterinary Medicine
www.vetmed.iastate.edu

Kansas

Kansas State University College of Veterinary Medicine
www.vet.ksu.edu

Louisiana

Louisiana State University School of Veterinary Medicine
www.vetmed.lsu.edu

Massachusetts

Tufts University School of Veterinary Medicine
www.tufts.edu/vet

Michigan

Michigan State University College of Veterinary Medicine
cvm.msu.edu

Minnesota

University of Minnesota College of Veterinary Medicine
www.cvm.umn.edu

Mississippi

Mississippi State University College of Veterinary Medicine
www.cvm.msstate.edu

Missouri

University of Missouri-Columbia College of Veterinary Medicine
www.cvm.missouri.edu

New York

Cornell University College of Veterinary Medicine
www.vet.cornell.edu

North Carolina

North Carolina State University College of Veterinary Medicine
www.cvm.ncsu.edu

Ohio

The Ohio State University College of Veterinary Medicine
www.vet.ohio-state.edu

Oklahoma

Oklahoma State University College of Veterinary Medicine
www.cvm.okstate.edu

Oregon

Oregon State University College of Veterinary Medicine
oregonstate.edu/vetmed

Pennsylvania

University of Pennsylvania School of Veterinary Medicine
www.vet.upenn.edu

Tennessee

University of Tennessee College of Veterinary Medicine
www.vet.utk.edu

Texas

Texas A&M University College of Veterinary Medicine & Biomedical Sciences
www.cvm.tamu.edu

Virginia-Maryland

Virginia Tech Virginia-Maryland Regional College of Veterinary Medicine
www.vetmed.vt.edu

Washington

Washington State University College of Veterinary Medicine
www.vetmed.wsu.edu

Wisconsin

University of Wisconsin-Madison School of Veterinary Medicine
www.vetmed.wisc.edu

Horse Care Magazines

Equus
656 Quince Orchard Rd., Suite 600
Gaithersburg, MD 20878
301-977-3900
www.equisearch.com/equus

The Horse
3101 Beaumont Centre Circle
Lexington, KY 40513
800-582-5604
www.thehorse.com

Horse Illustrated
2008 Mercer Rd.
Lexington, KY 40511
949-855-8822
www.horseillustrated.com

Natural Horse Magazine
P.O. Box 758
Leesport, PA 19533
800-660-8923
www.naturalhorse.com

Horse and Rider
2000 S. Stemmons Freeway, Suite 101
Lake Dallas, TX 75065
www.equisearch.com/horseandrider

Practical Horseman
656 Quince Orchard Rd., Suite 600
Gaithersburg, MD 20878
www.equisearch.com/practicalhorseman

Western Horseman
3850 N. Nevada Ave.
Colorado Springs, CO 80907-5339
www.westernhorseman.com

Horse Books

101 Longeing and Longlining Exercises, by Cherry Hill (Howell Book House)

Centered Riding, by Sally Swift (Trafalgar Square)

Complementary Therapies for Horse & Rider, by Susan Mc Bane & Caroline Davis (Charles & David)

Complete Book of Foaling, by Karen E. N. Hayes, DVM (Howell Book House)

Emergency! The Active Horseman's Book of Emergency Care, by Karen E. N. Hayes, DVM (Half Halt Press)

The Foal is the Goal, by Tena Bastian (Trafalgar Square)

The Foaling Primer: A Month-by-Month Guide to Raising a Healthy Foal, by Cynthia McFarland (Storey Publishing)

Hands-On Senior Horse Care, by Karen E. N. Hayes, DVM, MS and Sue Copeland (Primedia)

Horse Conformation, by Equine Research and Sherrie Engler (Lyons Press)

Horses For Dummies, 2nd Edition, by Audrey Pavia with Janice Posnikoff, DVM (Wiley)

Horseback Riding For Dummies, by Audrey Pavia with Shannon Sand (Wiley)

Horsekeeping on a Small Acreage, by Cherry Hill (Storey Publishing)

Imprint Training of the Newborn Foal, by Robert M. Miller (Western Horseman)

Mindful Horsemanship, by Cheryl Kimball (Carriage Horse Publishing)

The Natural Horse, by Jaime Jackson (Northland Publishing)

Physical Therapy and Massage for the Horse, by Jean-Marie Denoix and Jean-Pierre Pailloux (Trafalgar Square Publishing)

Think Harmony with Horses, by Ray Hunt (Ag Access Corporation)

True Unity: Willing Communication Between Horse and Human, by Tom Dorrance (Word Dancer Press)

Understanding Equine Nutrition, by Karen Briggs (Eclipse Press)

Health and Nutrition Web Resources

American Association of Equine Practitioners
www.aaep.org

Animal Behavior Society
www.animalbehavior.org

Cybersteed
www.cybersteed.com/veterinary/index.html

The Equine Connection National AAEP Locator Service
800-443-0177
www.bayerdvm.com/GetADVM

TheHorse.com: Your Guide to Equine Health Care
www.thehorse.com

United States Department of Agriculture Cooperative Extension System Offices (listings)
www.csrees.usda.gov/Extension/index.html

Horse Health Stores Online

Horse Health U.S.A.
www.horsehealthusa.com

United Vet Equine
www.unitedvetequine.com

Valley Vet
www.valleyvet.com

Hoof Care Resources

American Farriers Association
www.americanfarriers.org

Hoof Care
www.hoofcare.com

The Horse's Hoof
www.thehorseshoof.com

Hoof Rehab
www.hoofrehab.com

Resources for Alternative and Complementary Therapies

Academy of Veterinary Homeopathy
P.O. Box 9280
Wilmington, DE 19809
866-652-1590
www.theavh.org

The American Academy of Veterinary Acupuncture
100 Roscommon Dr., Suite 320
Middletown, CT 06457
860-632-9911
www.aava.org

American Veterinary Chiropractic Association
442154 E. 140 Rd.
Bluejacket, OK 74333
918-784-2231
www.animalchiropractic.org

Horse Breed Resources

American Miniature Horse Association
5601 S. Interstate 35 W.
Alvarado, TX 76009
817-783-5600
www.amha.com

American Morgan Horse Association
122 Bostwick Rd.
Shelburne, VT 05482-4417
802-985-4944
www.morganhorse.com

American Paint Horse Association
P.O. Box 961023
Fort Worth, TX 76161-0023
817-834-2742
www.apha.com

American Quarter Horse Association
P.O. Box 200
Amarillo, TX 79168
806-376-4811
www.aqha.com

American Saddlebred Horse Association
4083 Iron Works Pkwy.
Lexington, KY 40511-8434
859-259-2742
www.saddlebred.com

Appaloosa Horse Club
2720 W. Pullman Rd.
Moscow, ID 83843-0903
208-882-5578
www.appaloosa.com

Arabian Horse Association
10805 E. Bethany Dr.
Aurora, Colorado 80014
303-696-4500
www.arabianhorses.org

Horse of the Americas (Colonial Spanish Horse)
19005 S. 580 Rd.
Stilwell, OK 74960
www.horseoftheamericas.com

International Colored Appaloosa Association
P.O. Box 99
Shipshewana, IN 46565
219-825-3331
www.icaainc.com

The Jockey Club (Thoroughbreds)
821 Corporate Dr.
Lexington, KY 40503-2794
859-224-2700
www.jockeyclub.com

Missouri Fox Trotting Horse Breed Association
P.O. Box 1027
Ava, MO 65608
417-683-2468
www.mfthba.com

North American Peruvian Horse Association
3095 Burleson Retta Rd., Suite B
Burleson, TX 76028
817-447-7574
www.pphrna.org

Paso Fino Horse Association
101 N. Collins
Plant City, FL 33563-3311
813-719-7777
www.pfha.org

Racking Horse Breeders' Association of America
67 Horse Center Rd.
Decatur, AL 35603
256-353-7225
www.rackinghorse.com

Rocky Mountain Horse Association
P.O. Box 129
Mt. Olivet, KY 41064
606-724-2354
www.rmhorse.com

Spanish Mustang Registry
323 County Road 419
Chilton, TX 76632
www.spanishmustang.org

Tennessee Walking Horse Breeders & Exhibitors Association
P. O. Box 286
Lewisburg, TN 37091
931-359-1574
www.twhbea.com

United States Icelandic Horse Congress
6800 East 99th Avenue
Anchorage, AK 99507
907-346-2223
www.icelandics.org

United States Trotting Association (Standardbreds)
750 Michigan Ave.
Columbus, OH 43215
614-224-2291
www.ustrotting.com

Pet Loss Hotlines

University of California, Davis
800-565-1526

Michigan State University College of Veterinary Medicine
517-432-2696

Tufts University School of Veterinary Medicine (Massachusetts)
508-839-7966

Virginia-Maryland Regional College of Veterinary Medicine
540-231-8038

Washington State University College of Veterinary Medicine
509-335-5704

Index

• C •

• U •

BUSINESS, CAREERS & PERSONAL FINANCE

Fundraising FOR DUMMIES
0-7645-9847-3

Investing FOR DUMMIES
0-7645-2431-3

Also available:
- Business Plans Kit For Dummies
  0-7645-9794-9
- Economics For Dummies
  0-7645-5726-2
- Grant Writing For Dummies
  0-7645-8416-2
- Home Buying For Dummies
  0-7645-5331-3
- Managing For Dummies
  0-7645-1771-6
- Marketing For Dummies
  0-7645-5600-2

- Personal Finance For Dummies
  0-7645-2590-5*
- Resumes For Dummies
  0-7645-5471-9
- Selling For Dummies
  0-7645-5363-1
- Six Sigma For Dummies
  0-7645-6798-5
- Small Business Kit For Dummies
  0-7645-5984-2
- Starting an eBay Business For Dummies
  0-7645-6924-4
- Your Dream Career For Dummies
  0-7645-9795-7

HOME & BUSINESS COMPUTER BASICS

Laptops FOR DUMMIES
0-470-05432-8

Windows Vista FOR DUMMIES
0-471-75421-8

Also available:
- Cleaning Windows Vista For Dummies
  0-471-78293-9
- Excel 2007 For Dummies
  0-470-03737-7
- Mac OS X Tiger For Dummies
  0-7645-7675-5
- MacBook For Dummies
  0-470-04859-X
- Macs For Dummies
  0-470-04849-2
- Office 2007 For Dummies
  0-470-00923-3

- Outlook 2007 For Dummies
  0-470-03830-6
- PCs For Dummies
  0-7645-8958-X
- Salesforce.com For Dummies
  0-470-04893-X
- Upgrading & Fixing Laptops For Dummies
  0-7645-8959-8
- Word 2007 For Dummies
  0-470-03658-3
- Quicken 2007 For Dummies
  0-470-04600-7

FOOD, HOME, GARDEN, HOBBIES, MUSIC & PETS

Chess FOR DUMMIES
0-7645-8404-9

Guitar FOR DUMMIES
0-7645-9904-6

Also available:
- Candy Making For Dummies
  0-7645-9734-5
- Card Games For Dummies
  0-7645-9910-0
- Crocheting For Dummies
  0-7645-4151-X
- Dog Training For Dummies
  0-7645-8418-9
- Healthy Carb Cookbook For Dummies
  0-7645-8476-6
- Home Maintenance For Dummies
  0-7645-5215-5

- Horses For Dummies
  0-7645-9797-3
- Jewelry Making & Beading For Dummies
  0-7645-2571-9
- Orchids For Dummies
  0-7645-6759-4
- Puppies For Dummies
  0-7645-5255-4
- Rock Guitar For Dummies
  0-7645-5356-9
- Sewing For Dummies
  0-7645-6847-7
- Singing For Dummies
  0-7645-2475-5

INTERNET & DIGITAL MEDIA

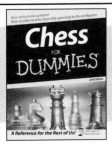

eBay FOR DUMMIES
0-470-04529-9

iPod & iTunes FOR DUMMIES
0-470-04894-8

Also available:
- Blogging For Dummies
  0-471-77084-1
- Digital Photography For Dummies
  0-7645-9802-3
- Digital Photography All-in-One Desk Reference For Dummies
  0-470-03743-1
- Digital SLR Cameras and Photography For Dummies
  0-7645-9803-1
- eBay Business All-in-One Desk Reference For Dummies
  0-7645-8438-3
- HDTV For Dummies
  0-470-09673-X

- Home Entertainment PCs For Dummies
  0-470-05523-5
- MySpace For Dummies
  0-470-09529-6
- Search Engine Optimization For Dummies
  0-471-97998-8
- Skype For Dummies
  0-470-04891-3
- The Internet For Dummies
  0-7645-8996-2
- Wiring Your Digital Home For Dummies
  0-471-91830-X

* Separate Canadian edition also available
† Separate U.K. edition also available

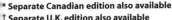

Available wherever books are sold. For more information or to order direct: U.S. customers visit www.dummies.com or call 1-877-762-2974.
U.K. customers visit www.wileyeurope.com or call 0800 243407. Canadian customers visit www.wiley.ca or call 1-800-567-4797.

SPORTS, FITNESS, PARENTING, RELIGION & SPIRITUALITY

0-471-76871-5

0-7645-7841-3

Also available:
- Catholicism For Dummies
  0-7645-5391-7
- Exercise Balls For Dummies
  0-7645-5623-1
- Fitness For Dummies
  0-7645-7851-0
- Football For Dummies
  0-7645-3936-1
- Judaism For Dummies
  0-7645-5299-6
- Potty Training For Dummies
  0-7645-5417-4
- Buddhism For Dummies
  0-7645-5359-3
- Pregnancy For Dummies
  0-7645-4483-7 †
- Ten Minute Tone-Ups For Dummies
  0-7645-7207-5
- NASCAR For Dummies
  0-7645-7681-X
- Religion For Dummies
  0-7645-5264-3
- Soccer For Dummies
  0-7645-5229-5
- Women in the Bible For Dummies
  0-7645-8475-8

TRAVEL

0-7645-7749-2

0-7645-6945-7

Also available:
- Alaska For Dummies
  0-7645-7746-8
- Cruise Vacations For Dummies
  0-7645-6941-4
- England For Dummies
  0-7645-4276-1
- Europe For Dummies
  0-7645-7529-5
- Germany For Dummies
  0-7645-7823-5
- Hawaii For Dummies
  0-7645-7402-7
- Italy For Dummies
  0-7645-7386-1
- Las Vegas For Dummies
  0-7645-7382-9
- London For Dummies
  0-7645-4277-X
- Paris For Dummies
  0-7645-7630-5
- RV Vacations For Dummies
  0-7645-4442-X
- Walt Disney World & Orlando
  For Dummies
  0-7645-9660-8

GRAPHICS, DESIGN & WEB DEVELOPMENT

0-7645-8815-X

0-7645-9571-7

Also available:
- 3D Game Animation For Dummies
  0-7645-8789-7
- AutoCAD 2006 For Dummies
  0-7645-8925-3
- Building a Web Site For Dummies
  0-7645-7144-3
- Creating Web Pages For Dummies
  0-470-08030-2
- Creating Web Pages All-in-One Desk
  Reference For Dummies
  0-7645-4345-8
- Dreamweaver 8 For Dummies
  0-7645-9649-7
- InDesign CS2 For Dummies
  0-7645-9572-5
- Macromedia Flash 8 For Dummies
  0-7645-9691-8
- Photoshop CS2 and Digital
  Photography For Dummies
  0-7645-9580-6
- Photoshop Elements 4 For Dummies
  0-471-77483-9
- Syndicating Web Sites with RSS Feeds
  For Dummies
  0-7645-8848-6
- Yahoo! SiteBuilder For Dummies
  0-7645-9800-7

NETWORKING, SECURITY, PROGRAMMING & DATABASES

0-7645-7728-X

0-471-74940-0

Also available:
- Access 2007 For Dummies
  0-470-04612-0
- ASP.NET 2 For Dummies
  0-7645-7907-X
- C# 2005 For Dummies
  0-7645-9704-3
- Hacking For Dummies
  0-470-05235-X
- Hacking Wireless Networks
  For Dummies
  0-7645-9730-2
- Java For Dummies
  0-470-08716-1
- Microsoft SQL Server 2005 For Dummies
  0-7645-7755-7
- Networking All-in-One Desk Reference
  For Dummies
  0-7645-9939-9
- Preventing Identity Theft For Dummies
  0-7645-7336-5
- Telecom For Dummies
  0-471-77085-X
- Visual Studio 2005 All-in-One Desk
  Reference For Dummies
  0-7645-9775-2
- XML For Dummies
  0-7645-8845-1

HEALTH & SELF-HELP

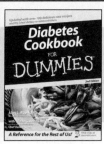

0-7645-8450-2

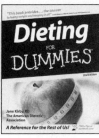

0-7645-4149-8

Also available:
- Bipolar Disorder For Dummies
  0-7645-8451-0
- Chemotherapy and Radiation
  For Dummies
  0-7645-7832-4
- Controlling Cholesterol For Dummies
  0-7645-5440-9
- Diabetes For Dummies
  0-7645-6820-5* †
- Divorce For Dummies
  0-7645-8417-0 †

- Fibromyalgia For Dummies
  0-7645-5441-7
- Low-Calorie Dieting For Dummies
  0-7645-9905-4
- Meditation For Dummies
  0-471-77774-9
- Osteoporosis For Dummies
  0-7645-7621-6
- Overcoming Anxiety For Dummies
  0-7645-5447-6
- Reiki For Dummies
  0-7645-9907-0
- Stress Management For Dummies
  0-7645-5144-2

EDUCATION, HISTORY, REFERENCE & TEST PREPARATION

0-7645-8381-6

0-7645-9554-7

Also available:
- The ACT For Dummies
  0-7645-9652-7
- Algebra For Dummies
  0-7645-5325-9
- Algebra Workbook For Dummies
  0-7645-8467-7
- Astronomy For Dummies
  0-7645-8465-0
- Calculus For Dummies
  0-7645-2498-4
- Chemistry For Dummies
  0-7645-5430-1
- Forensics For Dummies
  0-7645-5580-4

- Freemasons For Dummies
  0-7645-9796-5
- French For Dummies
  0-7645-5193-0
- Geometry For Dummies
  0-7645-5324-0
- Organic Chemistry I For Dummies
  0-7645-6902-3
- The SAT I For Dummies
  0-7645-7193-1
- Spanish For Dummies
  0-7645-5194-9
- Statistics For Dummies
  0-7645-5423-9

Get smart @ dummies.com®

- **Find a full list of Dummies titles**
- **Look into loads of FREE on-site articles**
- **Sign up for FREE eTips e-mailed to you weekly**
- **See what other products carry the Dummies name**
- **Shop directly from the Dummies bookstore**
- **Enter to win new prizes every month!**

* Separate Canadian edition also available
† Separate U.K. edition also available

Available wherever books are sold. For more information or to order direct: U.S. customers visit www.dummies.com or call 1-877-762-2974.
U.K. customers visit www.wileyeurope.com or call 0800 243407. Canadian customers visit www.wiley.ca or call 1-800-567-4797.